# FACE VALUE

## FROM WORKING THE POLE TO BARING MY SOUL

A MEMOIR

CHRISTINE MACDONALD

# FACE VALUE

## FROM WORKING THE POLE TO BARING MY SOUL

### A MEMOIR

**Face Value: From Working the Pole to baring My Soul**

ISBN: 978-1-946274-91-5 Paperback
ISBN: 978-1-946274-92-2 e-Book

Library of Congress Control Number: 2022916736
First Edition Wordeee

Published in the United States 2022 by Wordeee, Beacon, New York

Photography: Sascha Knopf
Makeup artist: Kevianno Guerrero

Cover design: Okomota
Book Layout: Amit Dey

Website: www.wordeee.com
Twitter: wordeeeupdates
Facebook: facebook.com/wordeee/
e-mail: contact@wordeee.com

Printed in the USA

# Advance Praise
## For *Christine Macdonald and Face Value*

"Christine Macdonald looks back on rough roads traveled with intimate emotion, clear-eyed distance, and, above all, a strong, open, and hilarious heart. Hers is a page-turning story you will never forget."

—Piper Kerman, author of *The New York Times* bestseller, *Orange is the New Black*

"Christine Macdonald's writing is raw, pure, moving, self-deprecating & thought-provoking. Magical yet relatable. I dare anyone who reads Macdonald's stories not to get goosebumps."

—Kristen Johnston, Emmy-winning star of 3rd Rock from the Sun, *New York Times* bestselling author of the memoir, *Guts: The Endless Follies and Tiny Triumphs of a Giant Disaster*

"Christine is a brave, honest writer, and a beautiful woman who is just beginning to know it."

—Joyce Maynard, *New York Times* bestselling author of *At Home in the World, Labor Day, To Die For,* and *Count the Ways*

"Christine Macdonald's story is everything personal essays want to be and rarely are. Her writing gets inside your soul and sticks closely to your bones."

—Larry Smith, Editor and Founder, *SMITH Magazine*, and Creator of The Six-Word Memoir Project

"Christine Macdonald is both a chronicler of the underworld and a beacon of hope. What never fails to inspire me is her deeply held, hard-won belief that a girl with a dark past can have a bright future."

—Lily Burana, author of *Strip City, Try,* and the memoir, *I Love A Man In Uniform* and Founder of Operation Bombshell, the world's only burlesque school for military wives.

# DEDICATION

To the trolls behind their avatars: I feel your pain and send you love.
To the little girl on the beach: This is for you.
For my mom: We sure have come a long way, and I love you.
For my stage-sorority sisters, for whom I am a brash and unwavering voice: I hold you close and feel your stories.

For those loves on the other side (too many of you, and way too soon): You are never forgotten, and I cherish the time we shared. You are as much a part of these pages as I am.

And lastly, for anyone wanting to terminate their pain by ending their life, I'm so happy that didn't work out. And look at us. We're still here. Let's keep turning our pages. We never know where our next chapters will take us.

# TABLE OF CONTENTS

Author's Note . . . . . . . . . . . . . . . . . . . . . . xiii

Preface . . . . . . . . . . . . . . . . . . . . . . . . .xvi

**SECTION ONE: GROWING UP IN PARADISE** . . . . **xx**

1. Hawaiian Grown. . . . . . . . . . . . . . . . . . 1

2. Unsupervised. . . . . . . . . . . . . . . . . . .13

3. 'Are You Sure We're Not Hawaiian?' . . . . . . . . . .18

4. Shitfaced . . . . . . . . . . . . . . . . . . . . .23

5. No Trespassing . . . . . . . . . . . . . . . . . .34

6. I'm What? . . . . . . . . . . . . . . . . . . . .38

7. Down the Rabbit Hole, I Go. . . . . . . . . . . . .45

8. Under the Influence . . . . . . . . . . . . . . . .53

**SECTION TWO: IT'S SHOWTIME!** . . . . . . . . . . **61**

9. Rockin' Robert . . . . . . . . . . . . . . . . . .62

10. The Other Woman . . . . . . . . . . . . . . . .71

11. Peas in a Party Pod . . . . . . . . . . . . . . . .79

12. Maid of Dishonor . . . . . . . . . . . . . . . .88

13. Ignorance is This . . . . . . . . . . . . . . . .93

**SECTION THREE: FOR MATURE AUDIENCES ONLY . 96**

14. Sixty Seconds . . . . . . . . . . . . . . . .97

15. Peaches and Cream . . . . . . . . . . . . . . . 104

16. Don't I Know You? . . . . . . . . . . . . . . . 112

17. Breast Intentions . . . . . . . . . . . . . . . 117

18. The Invitation . . . . . . . . . . . . . . . 125

19. The Customer is Always Trite . . . . . . . . . . . 130

20. Sisterhood . . . . . . . . . . . . . . . . 136

21. The Other Sunset Strip . . . . . . . . . . . . . 158

**SECTION FOUR: SHIT'S GETTING REAL . . . . . 164**

22. I'm with the (Hair) Band . . . . . . . . . . . . 165

23. That Shit'll Kill You . . . . . . . . . . . . . . 172

24. Marley . . . . . . . . . . . . . . . . . . . 176

25. Denial, Anger, Bargaining, Ki . . . . . . . . . . . 183

26. Me and Madonna's Backup Dancer . . . . . . . . 188

27. Losing Control . . . . . . . . . . . . . . . 193

28. Voluntary Termination . . . . . . . . . . . . . 198

29. Gay Pride, Straight Sex, and Bloody Marys . . . . . 201

30. A New Life . . . . . . . . . . . . . . . . . 210

31. Xanapalooza . . . . . . . . . . . . . . . . . 213

32. Living with Depression . . . . . . . . . . . . . . . 224

33. Poetry in Emotion . . . . . . . . . . . . . . . . . . 235

34. Fascination Street: A Dream Journal Entry. . . . . . 242

35. 'Your Skin is Like an Orange' . . . . . . . . . . . 252

36. Valentina. . . . . . . . . . . . . . . . . . . . . . . 257

37. A Safe Kind of High . . . . . . . . . . . . . . . . . 265

38. Falling Up . . . . . . . . . . . . . . . . . . . . . . 269

39. Eyes Wide Open . . . . . . . . . . . . . . . . . . . 273

**SECTION FIVE: LET'S TRY THIS AGAIN. . . . . . . 281**

40. Healing . . . . . . . . . . . . . . . . . . . . . . . 282

41. Does Your Mother Know? . . . . . . . . . . . . . 287

42. Fan Male. . . . . . . . . . . . . . . . . . . . . . . 292

43. It Gets Better. . . . . . . . . . . . . . . . . . . . . 297

For the curious - Why We Strip (It's Not What You Think) 304

Your Top Five Stripper Questions, Answered. . . . . . . 308

Glossary of songs: The Soundtrack of my Story . . . . . 310

Acknowledgments . . . . . . . . . . . . . . . . . . . 313

"It's so hard to forget pain, but it's even harder
to remember sweetness.
We have no scar to show for happiness. We learn
so little from peace."

—Chuck Palahniuk

# AUTHOR'S NOTE

What a long and wild road writing this book has been. From the moment I decided to chronicle my often painful, and sometimes hilarious experiences, starting at age 19. Taking notes on cocktail napkins in various dressing rooms so I wouldn't forget, I knew even back then that I was living a unique life. Though not typical, my story has the universal theme of finding one's self-esteem and strength in the face of adversity.

What I didn't know at the time was that my desire to write Face Value would be overshadowed by nearly twenty years of self-sabotage and doubt. Never knowing a world where you feel normal, even if you're born that way, can be cruel. It doesn't matter what ailments or flaws come in the deck of cards we're dealt, if you're different, it can be all-consuming.

But the darkness passed for me.

The events in this book are portrayed to the best of my memory. While every story in *FACE VALUE* is true, some identifying details and scenarios and names have been changed to protect people's privacy. This in no way diminishes the weight of each word on these pages. Unvarnished, this is my story.

Many of us can probably tell a story of survival and circumstance, perceived or real. As you read this story, I hope you connect with your own story and find empathy both within yourself and for those whose lives are different from your own.

Where there is doubt in your heart, may you find courage. If you feel shame about your choices, may you learn self-forgiveness. And if thinking about letting go of your pain leaves you feeling lost without it, may you trust that a healthier life awaits.

Unconditional love and inner peace may not be familiar to some of us. But this doesn't mean we aren't deserving of it.

What I learned from writing this book is that many of us spend lifetimes seeking validation, but it is something we will never receive until we find it within ourselves. When we stop worrying about others' perception, what remains is left to thrive—and therein lie the universal attraction. In other words, stop giving a fuck what people think.

After nearly ten years on the pole, I finally got it. The money wasn't about me; it didn't define my beauty or strength of character. But it did hold me hostage with promises of forever. Once I learned that living a 'lush' life was an illusion and that freedom and true wealth comes from within, I was able to walk away.

You don't need to have been a stripper or an abuse survivor or a drug addict to relate to my story. Everyone has a past, and we're all in recovery from something.

The process of writing this book has been long and arduous. There were many times when I didn't think I would ever finish. But as I navigate my way through these pages, the reasons for my passion to tell my story are clear: I'm finally giving that little girl a voice and a purpose to her pain. Thank you for listening.

*       *       *

You will notice throughout this book unique spellings of some of the Hawaiian words, like "Oʻahu," "Hawaiʻi," and "Kūhiō." These are diacritical markings in the Hawaiian language and are comprised of two symbols: the glottal stop (ʻokina) and the macron (Kūhiō), which lengthens and adds stress to the marked vowel. To honor the Hawaiian language properly, I chose to use the above-mentioned spellings. Most publications choose to omit the authentic spelling partly because search engine optimizations like Google can't easily locate the words when spelled this way. Also, some computer operating systems and installed fonts cannot display the marks properly. In these pages, I am honoring my homeland's culture and history.

# PREFACE

There was once a young girl who was so lost, she feared she would never be found. Her voice—muffled by feelings of never being enough—searched for its place through empty corridors of circumstance and fate.

But it was lost.

Every action she took was a reaction to survive in a world she struggled to understand. Her heart was a patchwork quilt of hope that served as her only safety net, pumping reliably and steadily despite her wish that it would stop beating forever.

Through countless landmines of self-sabotage and self-doubt, she fell into a world that validated her beauty and purpose, only to have them stripped away inside the very life she sought solace. It was a plot from the universe designed to teach her lessons she would need to learn again and again. And again.

Pain without purpose is agony. After decades of trying to make sense of my suffering I'm here to share its purpose through this book.

I started working on this book as a vanity project, exploiting my personal history to retain the novelty of having lived a unique life that at times was a great deal of fun.

What began as bragging rights that I was once a stripper in my hometown of Waikiki on Oʻahu in the late Eighties became a soul-searching labor of love of a young woman, so lost, she didn't know she needed to be found.

DICTIONARY OF MY HEART
Read these pages
As if you were reading my eyes
I hold no secrets secret,
I cover no lies.
With all its imperfections —
These pages,
Simplified.
Writing how I feel —
Every syllable too real.
Through mine words.
I Illistrate
The Dictionary of my heart.

From my personal diary, written at age 16.

"I just wanna let them know that they didn't break me."

– Andie
(*Pretty in Pink*, written by John Hughes)

# SECTION ONE

# GROWING
# UP IN PARADISE

# CHAPTER ONE

# HAWAIIAN GROWN

Burlingame, CA, just outside of San Francisco. That's where I was born. I almost grew up in Canada, but instead, I was raised in Paradise. Sometimes, I wonder if life would've turned out differently had I been from The Great White North. Would a stiff upper lip, or the result of bearing the harsh elements of Canadian winters versus the year-round tropics of the Hawaiian Islands, have built my confidence to withstand suffering? Would strict British morals and principles have changed my outlook or influenced my life choices?

Or was destiny afoot?

It's certainly possible that seventies-era Ottawa, decidedly British with its grand architecture and unbelievable cleanliness, streets and otherwise, might have steered me in a direction that altered a destiny I would have happily bypassed.

Then again, if my fate was to run with the tropical island breeze and play in the Waikiki surf growing up, who was I to complain? The only caution I would have about running with the wind (even tropical) is that it's not always at your back. It can hurl you great distances forcing you to find ways to survive its wrath. I suppose if the rare and disfiguring part of my DNA had not spun me into the vortex of chaos and self-sabotage, my childhood would've been different, no matter where I was raised. But when an adolescent is hit with debilitating insecurity and a skin deformity that makes them feel like a monster, destruction can invariably follow. In my case, my visible battle scars were daily reminders of the fight I waged to simply feel normal.

O'ahu, Hawai'i, with its tropical weather and hula girls welcoming tourists all year round, was my childhood home. It was also the most sought-after destination for people who served in every branch of the U.S. military, so many ex-pats were transferred there, though my family didn't fall into this group. In the seventies, Hawai'i was well known as a tropical, novelty playground and celebrity destination that enticed the rest of the country, thousands of miles away from the mainland. Elvis had worked his hips for bikini babes donning grass skirts and plumeria leis in *Blue Hawaii*, while Don Ho's "Tiny Bubbles" was a well-known hit on the radio. Back then, the Hawaiian Islands were also important agricultural hubs for the U.S., with vast sugarcane fields and Dole Pineapple plants being two of the largest sources of commerce. Not to mention Kona Coffee (introduced by King Kamehameha in 1813). The first coffee tree was planted in Kona on the Big Island of Hawai'i by a missionary, and to this day, this unique blend of java is one of the most popular flavors among caffeinated aficionados.

But like everywhere else, the magical islands have much more than delicious treats, coconuts, and palm trees. For one thing, its history of monarchy-turned-stolen-land-turned-statehood is ugly. And its secret, modern underbelly was equally disturbing, but that's where I spent my formative years—coveting its darkness—where I felt comfortable and at home.

For nearly twenty years, I've been writing my story, but parts of my past were permanently closed due to poor management of my mental health. As a result, there were months when I didn't write a single word. I did manage to start a blog a decade ago, tinkering with some fun tales and was even published in some anthologies, but I couldn't muster the courage to do the emotional heavy lifting. Enter a global pandemic. It's January of 2022, and after self-isolating due to COVID lockdown for a year, I had too much time on my hands. Being alone with my thoughts is usually dangerous. Nothing shakes you up like spending your days in isolation ruminating on your life. How you got to where you are? Wondering what the world will be like once it gets back to normal, if that is even possible.

After months of Netflix binges and way too many online food delivery orders, I turned a corner. With a mixed brew of boredom and bravery, something inside me flipped a switch, and I decided to pay attention to my feelings instead of pretending they didn't exist. When a global pandemic enters the scene, somehow life gets a little more fragile, and the storyteller in me didn't have any more time to waste. So, I wiped the cobwebs off my fear and dug deep into the well of my memories. With my headphones firmly clamped over my ears and laptop open, I tore through my mental block and opened the vault to my past. But it didn't come easy. To help my memories flow, I YouTube'd some of the Hawaiian songs I grew up with and allowed myself to free fall into my childhood.

After breathing through a significant panic attack out of fear of what I might remember, I pulled myself together and started typing. Sitting on my couch as Olomana, a local Hawaiian band that was huge in the seventies, sang to me, I was instantly transported. It had been decades since I'd heard these songs. Forgotten memories resurfaced as I silently sang along to "Ku'u Home O Kahalu'u," impressed that I still knew the lyrics. Tears welled in my eyes, but I felt safe in my COVID cocoon and kept writing, knowing I had nothing but time. My reaction was immediate and visceral—and I felt what is known in Hawai'i as 'chicken skin'—all over my body. Most people not from the islands would call these goosebumps.

The music continued as I breathed through my feelings. Shifting in my seat, I let out a heavy sigh and scoffed at the irony of being raised in paradise without ever feeling at peace. The thought wasn't even a little funny. The reality of my circumstance splashed over my body much like the water used to when I played in the Waikiki surf, wearing swim fins, and riding my Boogie Board until sunset. Except now, the only saltwater on my skin emanated from traces of tears I'd long given up trying to stop.

Attempting to reassemble memories from an abusive childhood is like trying to explain an attacker's features to a crime sketch artist. It's even harder when there is zero memory of chunks of time—years—that, for whatever reason, I've been spared from knowing.

"Maybe it's a blessing that you don't know."

This is a familiar sentence I've heard again and again—both on and off the therapy couch.

"I know. Of course, you're right," has been my token answer. "But something in me still wants to know," I'd proffer.

Maybe it's masochistic to harbor illusions of unveiling joy and serenity somewhere in my troubled childhood. It certainly feels romantic: a young girl searching for her memories, believing them to be the missing pieces of her Happiness Puzzle. At least, that's the fantasy. Still, this strikes me as an extraordinary and worthwhile exercise to nurture my younger self. Singing my own lullaby has been my way of creating magic and curing pain, and, far too often, I was out of tune.

In reality, no one owns self-delusion better than I. It's sometimes best to do nothing when you don't belong, but I so needed to belong. For many, working double-time to keep deep scars at bay is a full-time job in denial. But I did not, and will not accept that. Rejecting the notion of giving up on myself might have been part of my saving grace. There was a kernel of hope deep inside that said I am worth it, and though I'd come undone, I've done and will continue to do everything in my power to reclaim the life I want to live…one of happiness, peace, and love. One where the past no longer has power over me.

The first solid memory I have in my life was getting arrested at the age of nine. Period, hard stop. For years, I've dug deep into the annals of my brain's history files to recollect anything from before that unfortunate day. I always come up empty—unable to see even one birthday candle or Christmas present before third grade. So, yeah. Getting arrested as a kid. Good times. At least it jumpstarted my memory. Unfortunately, one that portended all the sorrow that was to come. But in my few short years of "carefree happiness," my imaginary friend and I remember moments of joy. Joy in my Schwinn banana seat yellow bicycle with its tassels that I named Pie after the horse in the movie, *International Velvet*. On Pie, I pretended to be riding a thoroughbred horse, and instead of going over speed bumps in the road, I was gliding over equestrian obstacles on the racecourse, my steed in rare form. Or singing with my trusted boom box that I would take out into our very large backyard that became my Sound system. I once performed a one-woman show to Queen's "Bohemian Rhapsody" in my backyard while the beautiful palm trees dotting the perimeter of our house acted as a hedge between us and our neighbor's home swayed to the breeze. To me, the palms were magically transformed into my audience as I performed along with my boom box…life felt in harmony. It seemed even back then that I was born a creative soul, a little porous, a little sensitive and in need of an audience. My sister Laurie would often get embarrassed as we walked along, and I'd be singing at the top of my voice.

So rarely had I even been touched as a child that I'll never forget the feeling of that touch of the security guard's hand on my shoulder just as my feet met the exit of the grocery store. I was feeling free, basking in the rush of having gotten away with stealing a Barbie doll and Snickers candy bar.

"Come with me, young lady." His voice was stern. I could see the disappointed look in his eyes, so shame trumped any fear I may have had. That was until I saw the police walking toward me. It all happened so fast, yet everything felt like it was moving in slow motion.

Receiving a phone call from the grocery store manager, my mother instructed him to call the police on her adorable nine-year-old felon for its shock effect. It was her own Scared Straight parenting tactic, thinking that once I felt the handcuffs pinching my tiny wrists and experienced the view from the backseat of the cop car and subsequent holding cell downtown, I'd be officially cured of whatever caused me to go on a stealing spree in the first place. It would have the opposite effect. My first walk of shame.

A few hours and many tears later, mom came to collect me— her third grader-gone-wild child—at the police station. The entire experience felt like I was thrust into a school play, and I rationalized sitting in the cold, concrete room as part of the set.

I was so tiny compared to the grown-ups surrounding me. Every adult set of eyes that towered over my body seemed to say how disappointed they were with my behavior. My first memory, and already, I'm a disappointment.

Yet even that didn't feel real—until I heard mom. Nothing breaks you out of your make-believe world like hearing your mother's voice talking to the cops before springing you from the joint.

"What makes you think stealing is, okay?" Her cigarette hand was shaking on the steering wheel as we crept along Interstate H-1, heading home. The Hawaiian sky, neon pink, was morphing into purple wisps of air before my eyes.

"What? Did you even put the things you tried to steal in, your purse?" Mom asked incredulously as menthol ashes fell to her lap, us breathing in minty cigarette smoke in the green Chevy Vega Wagon with its windows rolled up.

"I don't know," I mumbled, unable to look her in the eye. My gaze was locked on the rows of palm trees swishing by with the backdrop of our little island paradise. "I'm sorry," I said remorsefully. I was. Even more so, I was sorry that I got caught. That was never part of the plan.

"Yeah, I bet you are!" my mother replied. "That's it. Give me your purse!" There was a level of authority and excitement in her voice that I hadn't heard before. Like she found the cure for cancer, and it was hiding in my brown suede crossbody purse with fringe on the bottom and yellow stitching of a sunflower on one side.

All the while, I'm sitting there wracking my brain for reasons for my careless behavior. Why was I shoplifting? Did I see a scene in a movie I wasn't supposed to be watching on HBO while the house was asleep and thought it was cool? Was it the thrill of getting caught? Getting noticed? I'm sure hordes of psychological textbooks would say it was a combination of these things, doubling down on simply wanting to be seen. Children, not valued, not recognized unless they have a reservoir of internal strength, will act out, hoping someone will hear their cry. Much like I don't remember my childhood, I don't remember the touch or support of my mother. I now know this to be a direct relation to her childhood. Although mom was duty-bound and provided for Laurie and me, she was not an emotive person. I suppose one can't give what they never had. So, though she would religiously drive my childhood friend and me to the beach where we stayed the entire day and pick us up on the way home during the summer, I could count on one hand, maybe one finger, any emotional attention to my needs, including when I got my first period at The Elks Club when I was twelve. After dragging my sister Laurie to the bathroom to break my news, she told me to tell mom; all mom said was, "Just go in the water…we'll deal with it later!" Laurie, my sister, pretty much echoed the same thing. I was used to going it alone. Mom or Laurie never came to my volleyball games, even when I won trophies and medals in track and field. I even broke the long jump record in 1978 when I was ten. Mom did cut out clippings from the newspaper which featured my scores. I also danced hula in the Polynesian Music Club in high school, but none of my family came to our shows.

My mother was a woman wrapped up in her own chaos. Filled with booze and verbal abuse from her boyfriend Dick (short for Richard, but, come on), she could barely deal with reality herself. Mom and Dick, a thirty-something Vietnam vet, met in the early seventies, a couple of years after my biological father left us (mom, my three-year-old sister Laurie, and me, twenty-one months her junior).

Dick was a loudmouthed, newly divorced charmer with three children who lived with his ex on the windward side of O'ahu. Originally from Michigan, his family had transferred with the U.S. Air Force to the island of O'ahu following his stint in Vietnam. In hindsight, I'm sure he suffered from PTSD piled onto being one of the unloved himself. Dick, who was relocating to our side of town, worked in transportation for the civilian division of Hickam Air Force Base at Pearl Harbor. One afternoon, Dick, with his sandy-blonde wavy locks, green eyes, golden tan, and dimples, wandered off the Waikiki streets into mom's real estate office, searching for a new bachelor pad. Within weeks, they were dating. On the heels of his messy divorce, the charismatic Dick was just the heartthrob my co-dependent mother would find attractive, and Dick was immediately attracted to mom's natural, raven-haired beauty and kind heart, not to mention her professional tenacity. He deeply admired that mom did whatever it took to earn money to raise her two babies on her own.

After her divorce was final and an aborted trip to Canada, mom worked her ass off in real estate school and landed a job managing condo rentals at high-end resort hotel with a small inventory of privately owned condos on the north side of Waikiki, where Dick had wandered. A man like Dick, trained to suss out weaknesses, would not have missed mom's vulnerability. Being abandoned by her cheating husband, mom became fragile and codependent, a perfect match for Dick's narcissism veiled as charm. Shiny and new in a Robert Redford from, *The Way We Were* sort of way; proverbial white military hat in hand and devilish look on his face, he possessed everything my single-with-two-toddlers mother was looking for after her divorce: looks, personality, humor, and perhaps a dad for her daughters. And boy, did Dick know how to woo my sister Laurie and me after one of their screaming matches. They were so bad that when she was in sixth grade, Laurie decided to record their argument on her boom box with a blank cassette tape and took it to school to play for her teacher, just to see if the chaos was normal.

Even at a mere four years old in 1972, I had a feeling Dick was trouble. A younger version of Archie Bunker, he'd turned into our tormenter. By the time I was ten, the ever tanned and darker Archie Bunker had taught me well how to be his personal bartender: Beefeater Gin on the rocks, two drops of vermouth, and three olives. By the time I was in sixth grade, Bartender Chrissy could mix a killer dry martini, making me a huge hit at their cocktail parties.

"That's great, Chrissy," Dick would praise, raising his glass. I'd beam with pride, quickly running to his side in the living room to offer refills whenever I heard ice cubes clinking inside his empty glass, like a servant's bell.

"Make me another, would ya, Shorty? Just like this."

I'd run behind the bar giggling while he shouted at the television, "Bunch of Japs! You don't know the first thing!"

The local Honolulu anchormen were somehow always at fault for whatever they reported that Dick didn't like. I couldn't understand his opinion of Asians or anyone who wasn't white, but his frustration was amusing as he was the minority on the Island. With each drink, his words became louder, like he was Yosemite Sam, and I was Bugs Bunny behind the bar.

"Richard!" Mom would admonish before turning to me. "Oh, Chrissy, he's just teasing," she'd reassure with a nervous laugh from the kitchen while refilling her plastic tumbler of Almaden Chablis and ice. Laurie, meanwhile, would be playing records in her room upstairs, away from the madding crowd. I often wondered why I didn't follow her.

I was eight years old in 1976 when mom and Dick bought a house together on Poipu Drive near Portlock, a swankier part of Hawai'i Kai that stretched along the shoreline and served up spectacular ocean views. As far as everyone was concerned, we were just another stepfamily of divorced grown-ups and two little girls, but no one knew that Dick would rant and rave and call us worthless whenever we didn't toe the line. Lines teenagers often are only too happy to test for boundaries. So, when teenage hormones infiltrated the house in 1982, Dick proposed an arrangement to lessen the chance that he wouldn't strangle my sister and me. The three of us were to live elsewhere during the week and on weekends, Mom would live with him in the Poipu house, leaving Laurie and me to fend for ourselves.

Mom knew all along that Dick was loud and angry, and following his tantrums and meltdowns, she was always apologizing on his behalf with a wet mop soaked in dirty excuses. Still, she couldn't find the strength to leave him and was not about to object to his idea. These unsupervised teenage freedom weekends went on until I graduated high school in 1986.

There wasn't much I liked about Dick, but this idea was something I could get behind. Freedom from the normal chaos of our home and at least a couple of days without his drunken verbal abuse was definitely a plus. As for mom, I'd learned through the years to be less angry and more sympathetic with her frailties as she had no healthy template to mirror when it came to motherhood. Add to that her husband's abandonment, abusive drinking, and Dick's volatile temper, and there you have it—disfunction junction.

Through my more adult lens, it was clear that Mom had her own story. Raised by my grandmother, a bipolar, alcoholic (I'm assuming from stories and experience) from her Mother Country, England, really Scotland, who'd beat her husband openly and threw herself down the stairs to self-abort her never-to-be second child in front of my six-year-old mom while pointing and screaming at her, "This is ALL YOUR FAULT!" must have been life-altering. Her two sisters didn't fare too well either, as both met with unfortunate lives in Montreal. I can't begin to fathom their experiences as children or if they had been marred by madness inherited from my Great Grandpa. A child prodigy, Scotsman and musical genius, Robert "Bobby" McCleod was a musical composer and painter of note who wrote scores for the *Abbott and Costello Show* when it came to Scotland. He was rumored to be quite the dandy, and apparently, he was a real partier and ladies' man. Who knows what my grandmother might have suffered at his hand as a neglected daughter? Whatever the root cause, none of the children fared well, grandma being the sanest of them all.

Mom had long been desensitized with abuse, so Dick was just another abusive person in her life. Apart from a six-month hiatus when Dick had an affair when I was in middle school before he charmed his way back into our lives with flowers and gifts, he and mom were together nearly forty years. As toxic as their pairing was, he was the only father figure in my life. Verbally abusive, "Ah, you kids are worthless! Why even bother trying out for the play? You'll never get the part." Never shying away from his sunset cocktails while reading the newspaper after work, he'd long morphed from Redford to Bunker where all hell broke loose. They had never married all those years until they were in their senior years and wanting to secure my mother's financial future with his vet benefits, Dick finally proposed. After thirty-nine years, it seemed they genuinely loved each other.

CHAPTER TWO

# UNSUPERVISED

I used to wish the way I was raised were different, but now I know it's like wanting my blue eyes to be brown. The East Honolulu suburbs of Hawaiʻi Kai were upper-middle-class neighborhoods with many college-educated people, and our home there was pretty sweet. We had the white picket fences, but ours were made from lava rock and built by Samoan laborers who taught me the word *kefe* (fuck) after pressing them for answers. They said it a lot when carrying heavy loads.

Every weekend, from the late seventies to my freshman year in high school in 1982, our family hung out at the private Elks Lodge (The Elks). Overlooking the Pacific at the South end of Waikiki, I didn't think anything special of the club at the time other than it was a place where the grown-ups drank all day, and we kids got to swim in the pool, or better yet, go boogie boarding in the waves that splashed against the *lanai* (patio).

There was another members-only beach club that bordered The Elks called the Outrigger Canoe Club. The OCC was considered more upper crust than our club, which I was reminded of when talking about my weekends in middle school. I wasn't bragging. I mainly discussed my love of playing in the ocean and how the local surfers would watch our backs the way big brothers do. I loved boogie boarding or body surfing because it gave me a real sense of control, and the older surfers looked after us making us feel safe, like surfer-babysitters. Still, we had a lot of time on our hands, so Laurie and I would entertain ourselves in other ways.

The stories I told in school were just the fat of my Elks Club years. I could never share the real meat on the bone. Outside of a couple of sunburned, freshly showered nights together watching *The Wonderful World of Disney* on Sundays, our family weekends at The Elks were void of typical childhood stories. While mom and Dick were drinking Bloody Marys and playing backgammon with their friends, Laurie and I were left to our own devices and would sometimes grow bored from swimming and surfing. So, we would go on adventures.

"Just stay away from the bongo players," Mom would warn whenever we said we were heading out for a walk. Laurie never disobeyed mom's rules, but of course, I had to know the why of everything. Why stay away? Bongo drummers played music. I loved music. Even fantasized about being a dancer on Broadway.

One day while Laurie and I were playing our usual elevator game, riding the elevators of random hotels in Waikiki, pressing every button, laughing at the faces of frustrated tourists getting on, I separated from my big sister because I needed to hear music. I walked toward the banyan tree across the street from the Honolulu Zoo and next to the Waikiki Aquarium, the hangout spot where we always heard bongos as we drove by on the way to The Elks.

The closer I got to the tree, the louder the music and the stronger the smell of *pakalōlō* (pot). I knew what it was but thought nothing of it. Every time I smelled *pakalōlō*, I figured people partaking were just happy. Besides, where there was weed, there was usually music. And next to catching a four-foot barrel at warp speed into the sand, music was my everything.

As I approached the giant banyan tree, I hid behind its trunk and proceeded to climb the thick roots that stretched into the grass leading to a walkway that framed the crashing waves. I felt like a little spy in my Hang Ten terrycloth romper and flip-flops "slippahs." I couldn't help but start to dance to the beat of the musicians' bongos and ukulele jams. Dance. The beauty of dance...the fulfillment of dance. Dance needed no wind. It flowed by itself, and to me, it's the music of the body. The waves crashing against the edge of the park overlooking the ocean, lit up the blue sky like fireworks, an added gift of the day.

"What are you doing here?" Laurie asked furiously upon finding me. "Let's go!" She grabbed my wrist and walked me away from the tree and my new favorite band.

"But...I was just dancing!" My reply was honest. I couldn't understand the danger of a young girl shaking her bum to the beat of stoners' tunes in the middle of the day. I would continue to harbor a dream of dancing and, indeed, dancing would find me. My dream was to somehow find my way off the island and head to New York City to be the next *Solid Gold* dancer. I was pretty sure the show was filmed in Hollywood, which speaks of how little I knew about life on the mainland at the time. I wanted to "dance like those ladies on TV" (my words to mom when watching Marilyn McCoo and her dancers on the small screen, to which she'd reply offhandedly, "Yes, dear.") The truth is, I was a great dancer and singer and even tried out for school plays, which, if I didn't get the part, became another taunt from Dick.

Whenever I thought about professional dancing, I marinated in all things Bob Fosse. Fosse was New York to me, and New York was my Oz. It was a foreign land so far away from O'ahu, it would take three plane rides and six meals to reach at the time. But if there was anything the movie *All That Jazz* taught me when I was eleven, was that all the dancing, revelry, bright lights, and stargazing were on Broadway. In New York. I was desperate to be a part of that world, performing on stage like a Fosse Girl.

Though we were with Mom and Dick at the club, they didn't pay much attention to Laurie or me. Period. Dinners at The Elks usually consisted of whatever was placed in the tiny Koa wooden bowls at the bar, generally Pepperidge Farm Goldfish crackers, miniature pretzels, and Chex Mix. When mom's friend Shelly was there, she'd come over to keep me company at the bar while I ate. Mom and Dick were well into round "I've lost count," so I welcomed her company.

"What are you doing here?" Mom asked Shelly while stumbling by after visiting the restroom. She needed her female drinking buddy to come back to the table to even out their squad outside on the lanai.

"I'm watching your kid!" Shelly replied. A fiery strawberry blonde with sun-damaged lines on her chest, Shelly always smelled of Camel smokes, coconut tanning oil and Bacardi.

"Oh. Hi Chrissy, where's your sister?" Mom slurred.

"I dunno," I admitted. I didn't want to know. She was becoming a drag and preferred to be off playing with her friends.

"C'mon, let the boys do their thing. Whattdya have?" Shelly asked, offering mom a drink as I crunched on my dinner.

"Oh shit. Okay, gimme a beer, would ya?" Mom answered while falling into the barstool.

"What are you drinking?" Mom asked me. I was sipping on a Coke with three cherries out of a real glass, feeling very grown-up.

"A Coke," I whispered, embarrassed by the volume of her voice.

As soon as I spoke, Shelly called the bartender over while mom was talking to someone on the other side of her stool. She pointed to my glass, gave him a $5 bill, and nodded. He took the cash and very quickly poured something into my coke. I took a sip at Shelly's command and almost threw up. But I loved how whatever was happening made her laugh, so I pretended to enjoy it.

After a couple more sips, I did.

A few minutes later, after Shelly ordered me a refill, mom caught on, and she and Shelly cackled.

"Hey! Sip slowly," she warned, "and no more after that!" Even as she said it, she was laughing. I'd found something to make me laugh also.

"I'm gonna go see what the boys are up to," Mom said, needing help to get up. "C'mon, Chrissy."

But I stayed at the bar with Shelly, whom I'm pretty sure was having an affair with the bartender, a young Filipino guy with a thin mustache and loud tiki shirt who had become my new best friend.

I had no desire to go see "the boys" (Dick and his buddies, German ex-pats who owned auto mechanic shops for high-end German cars). Besides, I never liked how overly friendly they were, always patting me on the ass while they tried to touch my privates outside of my bathing suit. So, I got drunk at the bar instead.

From that day forward, I no longer pretended to fall asleep in the car on the way home from The Elks club, hoping mom would carry me in her arms to the bed. She never did. She would leave me in the car, knowing I was "faking it for attention." This new comfort was far better. I became a drinker. And I learned to laugh.

# CHAPTER THREE

# 'ARE YOU SURE WE'RE
# NOT HAWAIIAN?'

In May of 1977, I was excited to finish the fourth grade. Instead of daydreaming of riding the exhilarating water coasters on my boogie board in Waikiki, my immediate focus was how to convince my mom to let me skip the inevitably terrifying last day of school. Differences cause problems the world over, and I was particularly sensitive to what amounted to a Hawaiʻi ritual. They even had a name for it:  Kill Haʻole Day. I am not sure why I was scared, but I was.

Kill Haʻole Day was a cult phenomenon among the local Polynesian and Asian kids in Hawaiʻi that encouraged bullying of the white students on this day. Kill Haʻole Day. Haʻole (how-lee) is a Hawaiian word meaning white (and not of the land), and was used to describe anyone who wasn't a *kamaʻāina* (calm-ah-eye-nah)—full-blooded Polynesian which translates to "of the land." The irony is, anyone raised on the island is a *kamaʻāina*, except white folks who were still called *haʻoles*."

Kill Haʻole Day was eerily ceremonious in the same way an after-school rumble behind the bleachers was in the movies, only without the musical numbers and choreography. I was never witness to any real scuffles, but the folklore surrounding this childhood island tradition was enough to serve my nine-year-old soul with some hardcore anxiety.

It was my first taste of direct racism, people being treated differently because of the color of their skin. I didn't understand why it was happening and desperately searched for loopholes.

"Are you sure we're not Chinese?" I cried to mom in the kitchen as she stirred a pan of Hamburger Helper with one hand, holding her Benson & Hedges Menthol 100s in the other.

"What?" she asked, throwing me a look of sheer amusement. "Why on earth?" She shook her head, took a drag of her smoke, and continued stirring.

"What about Japanese? Or Hawaiian…maybe a little Filipino?" I pushed.

"Chrissy. What on earth are you going on about?"

"Kill Haʻole Day, Mom."

Mom rolled her eyes. She saw Kill Haʻole Day as a harmless prank, but what did she know? She wasn't the blue-eyed freckle-face on the front lines.

Mom poured our dinner into her favorite Corning Ware dish and refilled her plastic tumbler with her usual Chablis and ice. "You'll be fine, sweetheart," she assured me. "Miss Kunishima won't let anything happen to you. Now go set the table and call your sister for dinner."

My sister. She, too, thought I was overreacting. But Kill Haʻole Day was just one more anxiety to add to my fast-plummeting self-esteem from constant neglect and verbal abuse. Did it contribute to tipping my scale? How? Why didn't it seem to bother Laurie?

Our house was located at the end of a cul-de-sac in a neighborhood just ten miles from Waikiki. Laurie was outside roller skating with the neighborhood kids and didn't share in my white-girl panic. Even though she was nearly two years older than me, her courage was light-years tougher.

All Laurie cared about, and couldn't wait for, was the last day of fifth grade because it meant, the following year, she'd be part of the leaders—the sixth graders, rulers of us minions in grades 1 through 5. Kill Ha'ole Day didn't faze her in the slightest, and I secretly envied her balls, wondering if she knew something I didn't.

Our heavenly metropolis was small, but every branch of the service was within about a fifty-mile radius, so the number of mainland transplants was vast. Of the small group of white kids in school, children of families stationed on the island from the mainland, Laurie and I were part of an even smaller assembly who weren't among military offspring. We were in Hawai'i in the first place due to our father's career with a major international airline. Shortly after my birth, we relocated from the San Francisco area to O'ahu, not the largest of the eight Hawaiian Islands, but the main hub for businesses and tourists alike and housed the state capital, Honolulu, and the historic Pearl Harbor. Plus, the jewel of paradise, Waikiki, was my nearby playground instead of cold, cold Ottawa.

Mom and dad had met on a Montréal train en route to a hockey game in the early sixties. Really, what's more Canadian than beer and hockey while meeting up on a train? If Google existed back in the day, a photo of my parents would show up in the top search results after typing, "Cheesiest Canadian love story." But love morphed into disloyalty after the taste of freedom became too tempting for a new father working with random stewardesses flying on and off the islands. One night after work in the early seventies, my dad came home to confess his love for his stewardess du jour. Mom was in her early thirties, with two toddlers, and as it turns out, Pan Am stewardesses were more exciting. After a couple of years, fleeing the country to avoid pesky child support payments was in vogue in the eyes of my father and he left the island. Mom probably didn't know how lucky she was 'cause I later heard dad had remarried four or five more times and had done some pretty horrendous things. But when dad left, mom was still licking her wounds from his affair and was, I imagined, completely distraught.

Both mom and dad were from the Great White North. When they split, mom thought it a good idea to move back home, so she packed us up and carted us off to live with her parents in Ottawa. Not long after we arrived at Winnie and Eddie's, mom decided that the bone-crushing cold and the insanity of her (alleged) bipolar mother beating the shit out of her prince of a father was too much, and she immediately had a change of heart. I don't know if mom had been waiting on her Prince Charming to come to his senses, but that never happened because mom and dad never got back together. Mom decided if she were going to be miserable and lonely raising two little girls on her own, she would do it in paradise. So, we packed up and moved back to Hawai'i.

Mind you, it never felt like paradise to me. And while living there, the more I learned about the place I called home, the more I knew it was anything but. Living in paradise and visiting paradise as a tourist are worlds apart. A dream vacation destination for people all over the world, Corporations are only too happy to bolster its economy with tourism dollars. But living there brought into clear view the two sides of some of the *kamaʻāinas.* The more I learned about this Paradise, the angrier I became. Why were Polynesian *kamaʻāinaʻs* who worked in Hospitality nice to the white people on vacation, but the *Haʻole kamaʻāinaʻs* were treated as pieces of shit? Didn't anyone know about Kill Haʻole Day?

Somewhere between eighth grade and high school, the racist bullying threats stopped. I have no idea why, but whatever the reason, I was happy to be on more level ground with the rest of the kids. By the end of ninth grade, I couldn't have predicted how much I would miss the relative innocence of Kill Haʻole Day. It would prove nothing compared to what I was about to face. Turns out, all dad left me was his faulty DNA which caused so much more pain than his leaving.

# CHAPTER FOUR

# SHITFACED

I couldn't seem to catch a break in my short life so far. At thirteen years old, out of nowhere, my skin erupted. It was a sight to behold. I was so frightened and scared because I didn't know what was happening to me. Day by day, it got worse, and it became the bane of my existence.

"Whoa! Did somebody hit you?"

My swollen face was covered in black and blue blood-filled cysts. The one near my right eye was large enough to affect my peripheral vision, and I looked like Rocky Balboa after the third round.

My schoolmate, Bruce, known for his juvenile commentary, had mistaken my skin deformity with abuse and asked about what he thought were physical bruises in front of our entire 9th grade gym class. I was embarrassed but relieved. Bruce didn't see my freak show of a face like a Halloween mask I couldn't peel off; he saw me as a punching bag—which I honestly preferred. I'd take abused over ugly any day.

I played off his question, hoping to garner sympathy from the rest of the class. "Is it noticeable?" I crouched, hiding behind my overly teased hair. I blew a tiny bubble with my stale, grape-flavored Blow Pop gum, trying to conceal my shame as we all began to run laps around the basketball court.

Unfortunately, most of the kids in school didn't follow Bruce's assumptions. Relentless and taunting, they'd yell out, "Who ordered pizza?" when they saw me. Whenever I walked into a classroom, laughter and high-fives soon filled the room, making me feel like a pariah. Every class was the same, and the taunts were unyielding. Any attempts to shield the world from my face, using my Trapper Keeper binder as a forcefield, were feeble at best. Still, I tried. Puberty was shaping up to be torture, and I, a recluse, left to figure out what was going on.

I didn't know what was happening to me. It hadn't happened to Laurie. Day by day, I got more troubled. The never-ending taunts. The emotional abuse began seeping into my veins, and though I tried not to show it outward, it was eating me up on the inside. I was truly in pain from the heckling and badly wanted any relief from the ugly invasion attacking my face.

I talked with mom about what was happening, looking to her for any advice and a way out of the pain…from the ugliness.

"It's just normal teenage acne, hon," she assured, hugging me while inhaling a puff from her Marlboro Menthol, dismissing me from the kitchen. "It'll clear up soon."

Sitting on the green shag carpet too close to the television, I thought about my mother's reasoning over an episode of *The Love Boat*. I noticed Vicki, Captain Stubing's daughter didn't have acne, so I angrily turned off the TV, convinced life was unfair. I appreciated Mom's attempt to normalize my skin, but *Love Boat* child actors aside, I knew in my bones that I was a freak. Alcohol, no stranger to our house, I began drinking in earnest, and alcohol began to work its magic. It gave me liquid strength to continue to be nonchalant about my deformity, but it also opened me up to physical abuse that would change the course of my childhood.

I'd find a seat in the back of the room in the class and sink my head into my chest, wishing I could disappear. Other kids in school had pimples, but something else was happening with me. Mine turned into golf ball-sized lumps that covered most of my face. They sprouted as bright red pustules but morphed into bruise-colored boulders filled with blood. It hurt to lay my head on the pillow at night. My skin felt like it was being pulled from the inside, and with any facial expression I made, it became tighter and grew more painful. If I stretched my head to the left, the cysts on the right side of my jawline and neck would tear open, leaking blood. The oozing liquid was so dark it was purple, almost black, and carried a distinct odor of rusted decay and horror.

"This is not normal," I muttered, wiping my neck with toilet paper as I stood in front of the bathroom mirror. The wastebasket was always filled with blood-stained pieces of toilet paper. I would've given anything to feel normal.

After waking up with blood-stained pillows every morning, I started sleeping with a beach towel over my pillowcase. One Saturday, I noticed something new on my sheets. After running to the bathroom mirror, I discovered a new nightmare.

"Mom!" I cried out in fear.

She ran upstairs and saw me sobbing with my mouth wide open in disbelief.

"Oh my God!" she said with panic in her voice. We couldn't believe what we were seeing. My cysts had spread to my chest, back and inner thighs. "Okay, hon, first thing Monday morning, I'll make an appointment with a doctor."

I kept crying. Before my very eyes, I was morphing into a monster, but I was happy mom finally agreed this wasn't normal. She reached for a hand towel on the rod, but I resisted.

"It's okay, Mom, I've got it," I said, motioning her out of the bathroom. I shut the door in front of her, took off my pajamas, and turned on the bathtub faucet. Soaking my body didn't erase my disgust but lying in the comfort of warm water and placing a hot washcloth over my face always calmed my nerves and softened my skin, so the pain relented, if only for a little while.

Dr. Izumi was a kind and gentle middle-aged man who wore black horn-rimmed glasses like Elvis Costello. His tall, robust frame reminded me of a life-sized Asian Pillsbury Doughboy, and I liked him immediately. I grew to love his touch on my skin and imagined him as a trusted family member (if only I had one) because I knew he was there to help me—even if he did use a syringe.

Weekly visits to Dr. Izumi served up flavors of rubbing alcohol and cortisone shots directly injected into each newly formed cyst. The shots were followed by finger-like rolling pins of dry ice, which he slowly rotated over my face, chest, and neck with the precision of a pastry chef. It stung with each touch but was a welcome treat after the needles.

There was also a method to the doctor's madness. The cortisone injections were designed to halt any new growth and hopefully dissipate the harder cysts before they filled with blood, stretching so thin they'd break open. The dry ice was applied to de-puff the inflammation of my "Freddy Krueger" face, the lovely new nickname my schoolmates saddled me with and of which I was mortified.

Dr. Izumi's treatment helped calm the breakouts a little, and I looked forward to our time together. He was a trained professional who didn't call me names or make me feel like a monster, so our connection gave me comfort. Unfortunately, the damage had already been done, and outside our safe haven, I was ruthlessly teased, woefully insecure and struggling to keep it together.

I guess my skin disease was so rare that one week, I became a case study for Dr. Izumi's students. "If you don't mind, I've invited some students to audit our visit today," Dr. Izumi said. He smiled and tilted his head with a look of "I'm on your side, and we will figure this out." I trusted him but still glanced over at mom, standing in the corner next to a poster of an epidermis drawing explaining hair follicles and pores.

"It's okay, sweetie," she assured.

"Okay," I mumbled, shrugging my shoulders, and forcing a grin. Well, it's official, I thought. I am a freak.

Shortly after our conversation, a class of postgrads walked in, ready to audit my torture. There was no longer any question that my face was a freak show. Dr. Izumi escorted the group to where I was lying on the table. They seemed fascinated as eye after eye landed on me. I closed mine while struggling to ignore the weight of their attention, rendering me a circus act. Ladies and gentlemen, step right up!

Dr. Izumi explained to the class my condition, which turned out to be an extremely rare but serious form of cystic acne called Stage IV Acne Vulgaris, which later morphed into an even more serious condition called Acne Conglobata. I kept my eyes shut, trying to find my breath.

Dr. Izumi finally reached for the syringe, saying. "Well, let's get started."

After the needles and ice, I opened my eyes and noticed the facial expressions of the crowd in the room. They were concerned but captivated. I was raw yet indifferent.

As my mom collected parking validation stickers from the receptionist, I scanned the waiting room. There were a couple of elderly patients. The rest of them were teenagers like me. But none of them had a face that looked like mine.

Regular visits with Dr. Izumi continued for what seemed like forever. Then on one of our visits, he said, "I'd like you to try a new drug that seems very promising and ideal for your case," glancing over at mom and then smiling at me with that look. His smile always warmed my heart, but this one was different. I wrapped myself in his word "promising" like it was a fresh blanket straight from the dryer. Mom and I looked at each other, our eyebrows raised with optimistic intrigue.

"Oh?" Mom asked.

"It's called Accutane."

That day I froze in time, allowing myself the possibility of believing that a little pill could be a way out of my hell instead of trying to ease the pain of my skin every week with needles and dry ice and rubbing alcohol. I had to remember to breathe when hearing his words.

"It's basically an extremely potent dose of Vitamin A." Dr. Promising continued. "In fact, it's so potent that if we agree to have you try this medication, I'll need to have pregnancy test results from you every two weeks in the form of blood samples I will draw."

Mom and I looked at each other in awkward silence. I tried to hide the fact that his darling patient was, indeed, sexually active and that these wouldn't be the first pregnancy tests I'd take, so no biggie, Doc. It was 1984, and I was fifteen, so why ruin the energy of assumption? I kept it cool and then surprised myself with my words: "Even if I'm not having sex?"

My question hit the air like glitter from The Bullshit Factory after an explosion.

Mom nodded in concert with my lies.

"Yes," Dr. Izumi continued. "Females on Accutane after puberty need to be tested because of how potent the side effects are. Part of this is related to the fetus, so we need to continually confirm our patients aren't pregnant for insurance purposes."

"I see," Mom answered in agreement.

After learning about the amazing results with the few other severe Acne Vulgaris patients across the country (I was Izumi's only case), I decided to go for it, and mom agreed.

Within an hour, we were on our way home after picking up my first prescription from Long's Pharmacy in Kahala Mall. I couldn't wait to take this magical pill. Just the thought of waking up with my face pain-free and not bleeding felt like a dream. I was scared to allow myself permission to imagine it. But I couldn't help it.

Fast forward a few months, and holy cow. The phrase "When you're right, you're right" was made for these moments. Dr. Izumi was right about Accutane. In less than a year, my skin cleared up. No more purple bumps so large they affected my vision and posed as bruises. No more leaky blood down my throat and hot baths to ease the pain or bed pillows covered in towels. I started to feel like less of a freak show in public, even allowing myself to exhale when riding the jam-packed bus to Waikiki or standing in a crowded elevator. But unfortunately, the nightmare wasn't quite over. When my skin began to heal, I was faced with a new and permanent reality.

My facial volcanoes had dissolved, but they left crater-like scars in their wake. As much as I appreciated my new cyst-free face, I was mortified by how deep the moon-like fissures were and how many of them I saw—covering over eighty percent of my face; I was a new kind of freak. Crater Face.

As kids, my sister and I were greeted with compliments and talked about affectionately how much we looked like twins. Laurie was nearly two years older than me, but our features were damn near identical. It didn't help that mom dressed us in matching polyester get-ups, straight from the McCall's patterns she cranked out on her trusty sewing machine. Being considered my sister's twin in the fourth grade was a compliment. She was smart, pretty, and popular. Who wouldn't hitch their wagon to that star? But Laurie had her own set of friends, and they were not mine, so my hitch didn't take. In fact, it seemed we were developing into polar opposites.

Puberty had kicked my ass badly. Laurie had been spared this inherited trait passed on by our absentee father. I didn't understand why I was the only one affected and whined about it. Laurie was not sympathetic to my angst, and like everything else, she brushed it off. She was not the supportive older sister I had hoped for who'd have helped me cope and weather the storm of my traumatized childhood. Laurie was just lucky, I guess, and I was not. When high school rolled around, our differences became massive and were quickly revealed. I was the awkward, insecure, crater-faced teenager, while Laurie, with a normal complexion, effortlessly found her clique of popular friends. She was the free-flowing water to my clingy, goopy oil.

At fourteen, my nickname in school was Freddy Krueger, while Laurie was nominated for the homecoming court. I believe this is called getting the short end of the sibling stick. My self-esteem, which had started to plummet at age thirteen, took a steep nosedive. I might have survived any singular irregularities in my childhood, but compounded, they buried me under a mountain of fear, loneliness, and a lack of self-worth. The harder I tried to fit in, the worse it became, and believe me, I tried so hard to fit in. With every new fringe fad, I was ready to try it, anything to fit in.

My goth semester was where I styled my hair with egg whites, used heavy eyeliner above and below my eye (take a match to light the pencil and make an even darker line), and dressed only in black. A smart move for living in the tropics, no?

Then came the grueling cheerleading tryouts, where I was taunted just for showing up during the jump split as part of my audition routine (alone in front of a bleacher full of kids).

I forced my way into countless social events where I wasn't invited: parties, bonfires on the beach, and sleepovers, all with the hope of feeling normal. All of that was hell, but one of the worst experiences that still affects me to this day is my fear of not being included. Seriously, I'd unfriend people I loved on social media because I'd freak out every time I saw photos of them posted without inviting me to whatever they were doing.

On one occasion, I was invited to a house party sometime during my junior year. There were at least five of us in a Volkswagen Beetle, and after everyone piled out, they all laughed and jumped back in the car, driving off, leaving me alone standing at the home of some stranger who obviously wasn't throwing a party. Even today, I struggle to believe people could be so cruel. A prank at my expense. I was hurt, angry and petrified. Tears welled in my eyes, but I refused to let them fall. That day changed me, and there was no looking back. Just one moment in time and my elasticity snapped...but I was a survivor and would show those "friends" a thing or two. In the end, I would win. That's what I thought. I moved one step at a time down the road in full armor.

There were no cellphones back in the eighties, and I was in the middle of suburbia, so I took off my shoes and walked the three miles home, too embarrassed to knock on a stranger's door and ask if I could use the phone to call my mom to come and get me. She was with Dick at the Poipu house anyway, so I knew she wasn't legally able to drive. One martini, two martinis, three martinis, floor.

At that moment, I envied my sister. While my desperation served as a social repellant, her effortless sense of self drew people closer to her. Each of my failed attempts to fit in was another ingredient in my self-induced pity pot, where I marinated in a recipe of anguish and uncertainty.

"Your sister is so pretty. What happened to you?" shouted one of my classmates from the hallway as I was walking to class one day after my horrific incident of being abandoned. An audience of her friends chanted with laughter, "Kruuueger! Kruuueger! Kruuueger!" They were merciless. And Laurie did nothing. In fact, Laurie would side with her friends and once even publicly disowned me, calling me a slut in front of the school. I stopped trying to hitch my wagon to my sister's after that, and by now, I had stopped relying on my mother. In her own alcohol-induced world, all I would get was the smile of a broken woman herself and, "Don't worry dear; everything will be fine."

By my junior year, I had unraveled completely. I would have a stack of fake excuses for skipping school I'd written, and I'd pick the right time to ask my mother to sign them ...on her way out the door. I would then add to the original excuse whatever I wanted. I started skipping school and began drinking alone at home. Erica Kane (*All My Children*) was my faithful companion, and thanks to heavily played reruns, so were June Cleaver from *Leave It to Beaver* and Hazel from *Hazel*. They kept me and my tumbler of apple juice and mom's Chablis company while I zoned out all day in front of the television.

Accutane had been a big help in controlling my skin disease, but the damage had already been done emotionally, psychologically, and physically. I had to find a way to keep living…I amped up my drinking, and soon drugs entered my life. I was now floating on an alcohol and drug-induced cloud.

## CHAPTER FIVE

# NO TRESPASSING

Before and after Accutane, I needed validation of my beauty in any way. By the time I was thirteen, I was a complete wreck, thanks to puberty. Doing whatever I could to bolster my self-esteem came in the form of liquid courage and progressed in new and seemingly exciting ways to stay in denial. My denial that I was sexually active when Dr. Izumi decided to put me on the miracle pill, was so far from the truth. Two years earlier, I had been deflowered.

Before my alarm went off, I opened my eyes and rushed to the bathroom mirror.

This wasn't a dream.

The hickeys on my neck were even darker and more pronounced than the previous day.

I ignored my mother's voice coming from downstairs and stayed with my thirteen-year-old reflection. Standing frozen as a witness to the aftermath, I stepped outside myself in awe. Getting ready for school would have to wait.

"Okay!" I shouted from behind the closed door, turning on the shower to appease my mom. But I couldn't move.

Seconds morphed into minutes, and all I could do was stare. Raising my chin, I slowly traced each marking, gently probing them with the tips of my fingers while avoiding my blood-filled cysts as if to prove these love bites were real. Lost in the blurry maze of my memory, I struggled. Where was I when this happened? How could I not remember someone sucking on my neck? My ten-year-old self drinking coke and whatever the bartender had added to it at Shelly's instructions to stave off boredom had morphed into a thirteen-year-old who drank daily to cope with every day that dawned.

Just one day earlier, our high school canoe paddling team, "Punahele O'Kaika," which I was part of, was on an overnight camping trip on the island's north shore. With a couple of liquid malt liquors under my belt, I walked over to Laurie's best friend's boyfriend, standing with Tony, a guy I was crushing on. I had thrown my arms over their shoulders in camaraderie to have a chat. Realizing I was wasted, the guys walked me further away from the campfire and started to get handsy. The next thing I knew, I'd woken up on the beach to the sight of Tony walking away from the tent we'd shared toward the rest of our canoe-paddling team's campsite. My bathing suit was rolled up in a ball on the sand and stained with blood. It was two weeks after my thirteenth birthday.

Confused and hungover, I sat up on the sandy grass, trying to piece the night together while listening to his friends laugh and praise him for his conquest. Tony was the high school varsity quarterback, and I would work extra hard at cheerleading when he was around, even though I never made the squad. Unbeknownst to me, my soon-to-be rapist's name was always shouted out in concert by the football boys as they'd watch me try out for cheerleading. "That's for Tony," the boys would say as I did a jump split. I thought Tony had liked me back. The last thing I remember was kissing him, my head spinning full of Mickey's Fine Malt Liquor. Floating on alcohol, knowing I was wanted even with my freak-show of a face assuaged my feelings of validation.

I should have been mortified at the hickeys, but I wasn't. Walking through the halls in school with them exposed, I'd felt proud—beautiful, even. The only people I knew of who had these markings on their necks were gorgeous girlfriends of popular football players. Varsity cheerleaders and homecoming queens got hickeys, not an awkward freshman nick-named Freddy Krueger because of a skin disease on her face.

Naïve and hopeful, I'd really thought he was into me and was just shy, and certainly, after our night together, I was his girlfriend. It didn't bother me that the entire school knew we had slept together; I thought this meant I was pretty and popular. Yes, of course, it must mean I'm pretty.

I couldn't have been more mistaken. At sixteen years old, Tony had raging hormones, and he had no intention of being my boyfriend. He went so far as to go in the opposite direction whenever he saw me, and no matter how I stalked him, he never responded. I'd put myself in harm's way, and my innocence was gone forever. At age thirteen, my dignity, whatever there was left of it, was shattered by that defilement, and in my need to survive got ahead of myself. I was still bothered by what had happened, but there was no one to talk with but the priest in confession. Raised Catholic, though we only went to church on Easter and Christmas, I knew what had happened in the eyes of the Catholic church was a sin, so I confessed and did my penance of Hail

Marys and then proceeded to flaunt my sexuality as my calling card. I never went back to church after that day.

It would take years for me to comprehend I was raped. Even longer to believe it wasn't my fault. It was easy to blame myself. I was drunk. We were kissing. The list goes on and on. But when does being unconscious and unaware of such an invasive act as losing your virginity become something a young girl asks for? I wrestled with this question for years, continuing to mask the reality of what happened with drugs and alcohol.

There is a pivotal moment when a single choice can snowball and lead down to the insidious and dark rabbit hole. As a subconscious act of protection, I made it work for me from the moment I was abused. Ever since the day I'd woken up on the beach without my bikini bottoms, I got ahead of sex…I gave it to all who came calling. They didn't even have to call…they could just pick up the receiver. I defined myself through my sexuality and gave it away to whoever I could, to anyone who would have me. In giving them what they wanted, there was nothing left to take.

The truth is denial or not; deep down, my mind knew exactly what I was doing. In the dark of night, in a moment of clarity, the terror and shame pull you even further into the rabbit hole…the never-ending black hole of excess and shame. I was beginning to need more than alcohol to cope. The revolving door of boys never stopped long enough, thank God, to land me in the land of feelings. So, as I became known as the school's slut with a crater face, I went further and further down into the black hole.

# CHAPTER SIX

# I'M WHAT?

Kaiser High School was full of preppy people. Founded in 1971 by the son of a German immigrant credited with developing the detective series, *Hawaiian Eye*, it seems all eyes were on me at the confounded school because of my disfigurement. I had long found a way to tame my anxiety so I could keep moving forward. I was invincible with alcohol, drugs, and my promiscuity, and in a school full of puberty and hormones, it got me more attention than I ever needed.

It was a Wednesday morning in 1985, and I was sitting in second-period English class, hypnotized by a piece of plastic. It's discreetly in the palm of my hand, resting on my lap. My knees are grazing the underbelly of the wobbly desk attached to a metal chair. The discomfort seems fitting.

The plastic looks like a lone chopstick but with one critical difference: a display window near the base that can tell your future.

Three days before, it told me that I was officially, surprisingly— and most unwillingly—pregnant.

I am sixteen.

I can't bring myself to toss this stick in the garbage because that's too cruel a tease, pretending I could throw away my predicament so easily. There was no "away" when throwing an unwanted positive pregnancy test results in the trash. So, I kept my secret hidden, tucked inside the lining of my Pee Chee folder, but slipped it out privately as often as possible. I did this to remind myself of the complete fuckery that was my life—and that I needed to make a decision.

When I turned sixteen, my mother, in another of her brilliant life lessons, sat down with me and together, we drank vodka and orange juice until I was drunk and sick. It was a lesson (that I learned was passed down from Winnie on mom's 16th birthday) she said in learning my limit as I was now a teenager and would be more social. If only she knew how social I was already! The faded pee-marked +/- sign continually glaring at me, mocking me, haunting me, was proof I'd not learned the lesson intended. Instead, it said everything I didn't want to believe as I sat thinking, looking for answers I was not prepared to provide.

Between the ticking of an egg timer in my head and being overly exhausted from too much partying and worry, I was also nauseous. Sara Lee finally threw me under the bus by way of a chocolate cake commercial on the living room television. Unable to make it upstairs, I tossed my cookies in the bathroom downstairs next to the dining room. When I came back to the couch to watch *Mork & Mindy*, my mother asked after hearing me retch, "What, are you pregnant?" She was smoking a cigarette, as usual, and cradling her second tumbler of Chablis for the night. The sweat beads from the plastic dripped onto our green shag carpet, and I panicked. I was a teenage cliché.

"Ha!" I replied, looking for the remote-control volume. "Um, you'd have to actually have sex to get pregnant, Mom." Eye-rolling teenage gold.

I stayed on the couch, hiding in the fantasy that my being with child would be resolved painlessly, somehow. The following morning, I decided to skip school. I tried to lose myself in my mom's Chablis, making my own tumbler with ice. Reruns of *My Three Sons* and *Hazel* were on TV, but the distraction wasn't working. I started walking around the house, caressing my flat stomach. I placed a small pillow under my "Frankie Says Relax" t-shirt and imagined being ready to pop a tiny human being out of my body. Romanticizing the idea of motherhood. But what would I have to offer a child? Would something be wrong with the child with all the drinking I was doing? Those thoughts needed to belong to someone else.

It wasn't me. I was Sigourney Weaver's Ellen Ripley with an alien in her tummy. If only this were a movie. I would love to know that after 117 minutes, I could walk out of this mess knowing everything was make-believe, but it was real. How did I get here? I knew the answer to that much, but it all happened so fast.

I was with a group of kids from school, and we wound up at someone's house, their parents being away. Kimo was the only sophomore and baby of the bunch. We bonded instantly after several shots of Jägermeister and a bottle of Colt 45. Laughing turned into flirting, which led to being naked in the laundry room.

Kimo was about to enter me when he asked if I was on the pill. I wanted him to like me, so I lied. I knew guys didn't like using condoms because I'd heard sex wasn't as pleasurable with them on. I wasn't thinking about the new AIDS virus all over the news or even getting pregnant. But this was not my first-time having sex, nor even my first time with consent. I'd been doing that for three years and should have known better. I was too busy floating on a cloud of alcohol, and the delusion I was wanted in such an intimate way meant I was beautiful.

"Yeah, I'm on…," I breathed in his ear. He exploded inside of me before I finished my sentence.

The next day at school, Kimo acted like he didn't know me.

"What's up?" he inquired, confused why I called him weeks after our tryst.

"Um. I just wanted you to know that you're a daddy." I paused for his reply. There was none.

"But I'm going to take care of it," I added quickly and awkwardly, "so don't worry, I just thought you should know." Sixteen, and I'm a straight-A scholar in passive-aggressive drama.

"What? But you said…." His voice was cracking as all boys do at fifteen.

"I know what I said, but you know, they're not 100% foolproof all the time."

And the Oscar goes to….

"I, I mean…," he stammered. "I, I feel bad." I could barely hear him on the other side of the landline.

"It's okay," I assured him. "I just thought you should know I am going to take care of it, and I'll let you know after it's done."

He thanked me as if he'd asked a question. After we hung up, I thought of calling my BFF Isabelle but knew she was with her beau. So, I ran to my neighbor and other good friend Jenny whose house was up the street and shared my secret.

We were in the doctor's office the following day. Jenny had ditched school with me, and we took the bus downtown to a doctor she'd heard about through her older cousin.

The two of us sat together in the waiting room, thumbing through old versions of Cosmopolitan and Harper's Bazaar. I tried to ignore the parenting magazines, judging me from the corner magazine rack.

After a little while, the receptionist handed me a clipboard, and Jenny took it from me.

"It's okay. We'll go through this together," she said, reassuring me. Jenny read the questions, I answered, and she checked the boxes.

Soon after, my name was called.

"Can she come with me?" I begged the nurse.

"I'm sorry, dear." Her reply was heartbreaking but kind. I'm sure she was used to saying those three words.

Jenny stood up and gave me a supportive squeeze.

"You've got this," she whispered. "I'll be right here when you come out."

"Thanks," I said, exhaling.

My eyes welled with tears, and my voice quivered. And then everything went blank. The mental tick-tick-tick of the egg timer was gone, soon replaced with an actual sound that was far worse than anything I could imagine. My eyes were closed, and I tried to hum over the loud machine vacuuming my insides. I wondered why the nurse didn't provide me with a Walkman and cassette tape to drown out the unforgettable, trauma-inducing noise.

After it was over, I felt instant relief mixed with pangs of guilt. My eyes began to fill up with tears as they trickled down the sides of my cheeks. I couldn't bring myself to sit upright. The doctor was gone, and the nurse gave me all the time I needed to collect myself, but I was paralyzed.

I was no longer an expectant mother, which, deep down, was what I wanted. Someone I could love unconditionally and who would love me right back without judgment. I couldn't stop questioning if I was a murderer.

"You're going to be okay," Jenny assured me after I finally walked out of the office and back to the waiting room. I used her Blondie t-shirt as tissue.

"This sucks," I wept.

"They said this is part of it," Jenny said. "You did the right thing. You did this right away. You're going to be okay."

I loved Jenny so much more now after she held me and tried her hardest to comfort me and alleviate my guilt. But the Catholic-raised side of me was in peril. After Jenny picked up my pain meds and escorted me home, I grabbed one of mom's unopened bottles of wine and locked myself in my bedroom. I blared The Smiths and sat on the floor next to my record player. The Demerol and Chablis started working, and I was self-anesthetized enough to feel a little better.

Then mom knocked on the door.

"Honey?" She sounded concerned. "Why is your door locked?"

"I'm just having a bad day," I replied. "I'm okay, though. Can you just leave me alone?"

I was sobbing.

About an hour passed, and this time when mom knocked on the door, she was pissed off.

"I called the doctor's office from the receipt you left downstairs," she said, followed by the unmistakably raised and stern voice demanding, "Unlock this door!"

I'd forgotten about the pharmacy receipt in my purse, which I'd accidentally left on the kitchen counter. Whoops.

I had nothing left to give. I was an empty shell of myself, reeking of cheap wine and floating in the sea of Demerol.

"Mom," I stood up to go and open the door. Blood dripped from the inside of my right wrist from the key in my left hand that I was digging into my skin. I had wanted to give myself a scar as a forever reminder of the murder I had committed.

"Oh, honey," Mom said. She wasn't shouting any longer. She opened her arms and held me close before noticing my wrist. She gasped. "What did you do?"

"I'm so sorry, Mom," was all I could say.

After cleaning me up and holding me a little longer, my mother shared a story about herself and my dad.

"Before we were married, I got pregnant," she explained. "We weren't ready. I had one, too."

I stopped crying and looked into her eyes. "You did?" I held my breath in shock.

"Oh, honey, I'm so sorry you had to go through this alone. Why didn't you tell me?" She held my chin gently in her palm.

"I'm sorry," I assured her. My words were sincere.

I never felt as close to my mother as I did the day I chose not to be one.

# CHAPTER SEVEN

# DOWN THE RABBIT HOLE, I GO.

The first time I did cocaine, I was with my friend Leslie; both of us were sixteen, unbeknownst to the two guys in their mid-twenties we'd met at Bobby McGee's on the South side of Waikiki.

Earlier that night, Leslie and I entered the nightclub with our fake IDs, dressed in skintight miniskirts and mischief. We felt like sexy royals. The bouncers at the front door sported tuxedoes and let us in without paying the cover charge or waiting in line.

We stepped up the red-carpeted hallway trimmed with gold chandeliers and mirrored walls. The laughter and clinking glasses coming from the room were familiar and welcoming. It sounded like my mother's parties muffled through the bedroom door when I was a kid.

We chose a spot next to the dance floor as soon as we picked up our drinks. I was a vodka-and-cranberry girl. Leslie was always Jack and Coke.

It took a second to realize he wasn't Rod Stewart, but between the hairstyle and tight jeans, this guy was a dead ringer. I laughed as soon as I heard his voice. Of course, he had a British accent. His friend had one, too.

A couple of hours and a few double vodka cocktails later, Leslie and I were in the dynamic duo's bachelor pad.

"It's not pink," I insisted, "Coke is white." I was such a snob, pretending I knew what I was talking about because I had seen the movie, *Scarface*, and nowhere in that movie did I witness people snorting pink powder.

"This is Peruvian, darlin'," came the reply. That accent just killed me.

I took the bill in my hand, rolling it up like a tiny Peruvian rug, and snorted one nostril and then the other. There was no hesitation, no question in my mind of what was right or wrong. I knew it was wrong, and I didn't care. It felt incredible. I found courage. I found denial. I found my beauty, scarred face, and all.

More drinks and more clinking and laughter ensued until the evening ended abruptly. As soon as I told Rod my answer as to why I needed to get home ("My mom thinks I'm babysitting"), they realized our age, and we were shown the front door.

My party life escalated after that. I barely graduated high school in 1986. Like I can't remember anything before my nine years on this earth, high school went by in a haze of drugs, sex, and alcohol. Little did I know my life was about to get obliterated. The years that followed high school were worse—a revolving door of drug dealers, abusive relationships, and even more promiscuity. My life had become an endless loop of sex, drugs and tons of rock and roll. I reveled in the cliché of it all, joking that I was the star of my very own *ABC Afterschool Special*. Except my story would have to have been on premium cable, preferably HBO.

Shortly after high school, I entered an amateur stripping contest and found my new home on stage. It was a no-brainer: utilizing my sexuality, slamming body and my love of dance in exchange for the feeling of power. As a bonus, I was making tons of cash. I was all in. Plus, since I'd always wanted to be a dancer, my strip stage might have well been Broadway, and I was good with it. Dance, one way or the other, found me.

I did have a great body, and the amounts of drugs I used kept it svelte. Unfortunately, my face continued to be a horror I struggled with every day. There were specific areas, like the inner side of my eye above my nose and the right temple above my cheekbone, where the craters were so deep, children would point at me and say things like, "Mommy, why does she have a thousand holes in her face?"

This particular comment was from the son of a fellow dancer, Peaches. About a block away from Femme Nu on the north end of Ala Moana Shopping Center, we ran into each other one afternoon at Yami Yogurt. As soon as she introduced me to her little one, he pointed at me and asked the question with the innocence only a child could possess.

Peaches was mortified and kept apologizing, but I was used to this from small children whenever I was in closed spaces with them like elevators and crowded busses (and drunken assholes in bars who oddly have the same maturity level). With no filters, children are so honest.

"It's fine," I assured Peaches after giving her a hug. I mean, who can fault kids for their naïve curiosity? My face did look different, and to a child, perhaps it appeared to be covered in "holes." I felt for Peaches, though, and I wish I had given the same amount of empathy toward myself.

"See you tonight at the club?" Peaches tentatively asked, still feeling like shit.

"Yup, see you there," I replied before leaving in search of a cab. I never made it to the club that night, opting for a few bottles of wine and a shitload of blow to escort me into the land of self-anesthetization and manufactured happiness. There was no way I would muster up enough confidence (cocaine or otherwise) to try to sell my ass to a room full of drunken horndogs after taking that verbal bullet.

Nothing takes the air out of your tires like feeling robbed of your beauty because of faulty DNA. Of all the gifts my deadbeat dad could have left me, this was one I never wanted. Had I known about this disease and knew I carried the gene for it, I might have been able to act prophylactically. This was a new burden and type of pain I felt responsible for. If only I had stopped the cysts from breaking open, I wouldn't have these scars. And this was after my dermabrasion at fifteen and many more after!

How I ended up in the office of a locally renowned plastic surgeon Dr. Flowers at age fifteen for my first skin treatment was a mystery. Still, I knew it had something to do with Winnie, who I'd sometimes visit in the summer for vacation. Grandma, who I happened to like, always taught me I was a lady, and which fork to use while dining and other proper etiquette young ladies should engage. I believe she was bipolar, a term not known or used at the time, and a free spirit who loved reading the rag magazines like Enquirer and Star. On the other hand, Grandpa was quiet and kind and always put up with his wife's outbursts and abuse.

My mother was on the phone with Winnie, her mother, in Canada earlier in the month of my treatment. Her view of my skin was like that of my classmates, and to her, it was an unfortunate blow to her upper-crust image. Somehow, my facial scars rendered me less of a lady. It wasn't a good feeling hearing that, but I mean, she was right about my being unladylike, but it had nothing to do with my skin unless you count that screwing every boy in school a way to validate my beauty.

Winnie wasn't old-money wealthy, but she had the pedigree and enough dough she was willing to fork over to improve my image, so she covered the major surgery my mom had begged her to finance. The procedure was called a Dermabrasion, not to be confused with today's microdermabrasion, and this shit was serious, especially in 1985 before the magic of lasers. The process was for the surgeon to use a bristle brush, or wire burr, to sand the first layers of skin down to a raw and open wound so new skin would grow over the scab (my entire face). Patients were put under general anesthesia, and the recovery time was a full fourteen days indoors. Hurray. It also meant no school.

"I mean it, no walking outside even to the mailbox," Dr. Flowers warned.

My pre-op appointment didn't go as well as I had hoped. I still had smaller, residual cysts on my face. Dr. Flowers was adamant about me not having any cysts before our scheduled surgery date. If they weren't gone in two weeks, I'd have to postpone the operation. Dr. Izumi did what he could, but these pesky bumps deep under my skin wouldn't budge.

This left me desperate, so I decided to visit the local holistic healing center, which served as a hippy-dippy health food store, considered wacky back then. Picture the pot-loving parents in the 80s movie, *Valley Girl* and multiply them by the hundreds. But I didn't care. Bring on the patchouli and Birkenstocks. I have a face to heal!

Huge *mahalo* (thank you) to the holistic healing expert at this healthy heaven near the University of Hawai'i on the outskirts of Waikiki. Because of her recommendation, I religiously took tinctures of Milk Thistle Yellow Dock Supreme, a liquid potion that tasted like dirt and made me gag. But within ten days, my skin was cleared.

The surgery was a go.

I don't remember much before going under, but the recovery process in the hospital was an experience. I tried to speak to my mother, who had been waiting for hours for me to awaken, but my throat was killing me, and I couldn't speak. My face was covered in gauze like a mummy, with only tiny slits cut open for my eyes, nose, and mouth.

I tried to ask mom how it went.

"Oh honey, don't talk right now," she said. "You had a tube down your windpipe. Mom was a beautiful angel, as were the nurses, and my fingers, as I wiggled them in front of me. Narcotics, man. This shit was deep, and it was real. It was my first experience with heavy duty, hospital-grade pain killers, and I was in love.

"Oh, okay," I hummed, eyes closed, trying to grin, but my skin was too tight to move under the bandages.

The next few weeks were full of puzzles, board games, and way too many marathons on television. I immersed myself in classics like *Soap, Maude, Barney Miller, The Carol Burnett Show*, and *Cagney & Lacey*. I hated not even being able to see the sun outside, but I was an obedient, good little girl for once.

I'd learned my lesson when I defied the doctor's orders not to look in the mirror when I got home that afternoon post-surgery. Of course, I looked, and of course, I cried. I was not only swollen and looking like a cartoon character with an oversized bloody face; I was covered in rust-colored gauze resulting from the iodine slathered on my skin after being fully bandaged up. I immediately screamed in horror. And then, the physical pain followed. The salt in my tears leaked under the bandages and burned the raw wound and open flesh on my face.

A mistake you only make once.

After the bandages were finally peeled off, I was torn. I didn't know if I was witnessing a new and improved face or if it was the same but now shiny and red after the top layers were sanded off. What I did notice were my scars. They were still there. Sure, they were softer, but what the actual fuck?

"Because your scars are so deep," Dr. Flowers said. "There was only so much skin we could grind down. We can do this again in a few months. But with each procedure, the percentage of improvement decreases."

Thanks to Winnie, my junior and senior years in high school were filled with two more dermabrasions and another right after graduation in 1986. I was grateful because each result helped my scars become a little smoother, but after the third operation, I knew I needed to start working on healing my inner scars. This would come much later after enduring six more procedures throughout my twenties, ranging from scar excision surgery to the new carbon-dioxide lasers (CO2 laser) freshly on the market.

My scars did soften. But they were still part of me, a fact I needed to get used to no matter how many surgeries I had. If only there had been a pain pill to remove my self-loathing. With the child's innocent comment, even years later, in a moment of utter despair, I fleetingly wondered what else I had to do to make my skin not the center of my life.

Starting out in the game at the precious age of sixteen with the magical eighties drug cocaine, my party game was solid—and all before I graduated high school in '86, I'd been bold enough to strut onto the stage in my cap and gown with half a gram of blow tucked in my bra. It should've been a red flag that I was headed for (or already in) deep shit, but all I felt was a certainty. I was a budding star on the precipice of a new life packed with glamour and grownups.

In reality, I hated myself, and my scars were just another reason to remain in self-denial. Had my troubles started because of my scars...or were they from the sheer neglect in childhood? Had Shelly not given me that drink...would I have found it anyway? I don't know. All I knew was, I was a sixteen-year-old mess.

# CHAPTER EIGHT

# UNDER THE INFLUENCE

Everyone has baggage. People who say they don't are smuggling their carry ons. As far back as I can remember—from getting arrested in third grade to the Freddy Krueger years and, of course, The Pole—I required more than luggage to stash the hordes of skeletons in my walk-in closet. To be honest, I'd need a safety deposit room—an entire bank vault to fit the remnants of my bad choices, most of them made when I was whacked out of my mind on drugs. My chamber of chaos would house at its center a very insecure, misguided girl with dashed dreams who succumbed to the demise of taking illicit narcotics for as long as I did. I'd tried coke at sixteen and liked it. So did my best friend, Isabelle.

I was flipping through rows of vinyl at Tower Records near Ala Moana Shopping Center on Keʻeamoku Street, just outside of Waikiki. This was where Isabelle's exchange family mom worked as a manager, and Isabelle handled the cash register after school. A French girl who had moved to Hawaiʻi as part of a foreign exchange student program, Isabelle and I instantly bonded over our mutual hatred of everyone else.

I'd made the hour-long bus ride to Tower at Isabelle's request one Friday afternoon, and since she was busy at the register when I arrived, I thought I'd check to see if they had the latest Siouxsie and the Banshees record to kill time. I had some cash from my sweet sixteen birthday earlier that week and was ready to splurge.

"Crees! Crees! Come meet Thane!" I didn't have the heart to tell Isabelle how much I hated being called "Chris" because, with her accent, it was adorable. "Crees!" shouted Isabelle again from the front of the store over Bananarama, singing about how cruel the summer was through the thumping sound system.

We'd met in high school during our junior year on one of the rare days I attended. Isabelle was learning to navigate her new school on an island worlds away from her Parisian home and upbringing. She'd noticed me eating lunch alone on the steps of the library and approached me. A teen model back home in France, she spoke perfect English with a darling accent. A stunning natural beauty with Russian, Armenian, Dutch, and French DNA swirling throughout her body, she was who the boys paid attention to.

Much to my shock, Isabelle hated the high school scene in both France and America as much as I did, but for very different reasons. I wanted to evaporate, feeling like the Elephant Man with my skin disease, and Isabelle despised anyone fake, which pretty much summed up everyone in high school, no matter where in the world you lived. But she liked me, and I adored her. We hated the same clique bullshit and cracked each other up constantly.

At first, I was shocked that someone so beautiful would want to be seen with me—Freddy—let alone be my new best friend.

But Isabelle was my own Marvel Comic superhero vigilante. She was aware of how badly I was bullied in school and of the rumors about me screwing around with any dude I could find (which were true). She became the kind of friend who had your back and with whom you'd laugh so hard that you end up crying, having no memory of what made you start laughing in the first place. Isabelle was my first true friend and someone I would take a bullet for to this day. Sometimes it only takes one person to hold your space, and Isabelle was mine.

There's a Hawaiian word that was made for people like Isabelle: *'ohana*. It means "family," and in Hawai'i, and anywhere in the world, really, people we consider family without sharing blood are considered *'ohana*.

"Okay!" I replied from the back of the store after picking up "Purple Rain" and rummaging through the bottom of my purse for cash.

"This is Thane, the one we spoke about!" Isabelle said, reminding me of our conversation on the phone the night before when she gleefully explained how she sold a Sex Pistols record to some hot stoner dude who sold coke and recently graduated from our rival school Kalani High.

"At first, I thought perhaps this boy is flirting," Isabelle explained on the phone. "But then he came out with it, asking if I like to do coke-ayyyne!" Her voice went up an octave. I was pretty fucking pumped, too.

"That's so cool!" I chimed in. "No more treasure hunts from babysitting jobs!" I referenced the few times I babysat for friends of friends of someone who knew my mom. The first thing I'd do after whatever kid I was watching fell asleep was to raid the refrigerator for snacks and call anyone around asking if they wanted to come party at whoever's house I was babysitting.

Sometimes, I had guests. Most of the time, I hung out alone watching television shows like *Cheers* and *The Cosby Show*, sucking down whatever booze was in the house. If the parents were gone for a while and I got bored with Johnny Carson, I snooped. No area was left unsearched. I'd try on sparkly shoes, spritz fancy perfume on my neck, and steal whatever pills I could find from the medicine cabinet.

Then there were the special nights. It wasn't common (and chalk it up to this being the eighties), but every so often, I'd find a secret stash of cocaine in the parents' bedrooms. And the Babysitter of the Year Award goes to....

"Yes!" Isabelle was laughing over the phone. "Salut, babysitting treasures!"

Thane introduced himself right after Isabelle did. "S'up, I'm Thane," he mumbled and lifted his chin like a typical nineteen-year-old baller. His grin peeked through a thick surfer's mane of shoulder-length blonde locks, which occupied most of his face, covering his sun-kissed freckles and emerald eyes. Standing six feet tall in tan corduroy OP shorts and wearing a Black Flag concert T-shirt, he was a vision. Plus, he smelled like the beach and *pakalōlō*, and all of it was working for me.

Then again, Thane could've smelled like dog shit, and I'd have been cool with him. He was now Our Guy With The Blow.

"Hey," I replied while leaning in for our kiss-on-the-cheek exchange. *Kama'āinas* are like Europeans when greeting one another—except we kiss only one cheek. It was a fact I needed to share with Isabelle because she always went in for the second cheek and couldn't understand why people in Hawai'i didn't follow suit.

"So...," Isabelle smiled at Thane and me, starting the conversation about why we were both there to meet up while she was working. "Sheet, hold on, yes?" Suddenly a bunch of customers walked in, and Isabelle trotted toward the register.

"So…," I chimed in to fill the awkward silence one typically encounters when being introduced to their new drug dealer. Thane lifted his index finger and placed it over my mouth, motioning us to move closer to the speakers further back in the store. It felt like we were spies about to break a drug case wide open. An older, hot dude with blow who ordered me around while sharing a secret? I wanted his pants off immediately.

"Iz told me," Thane whispered. "You partying tonight?" I liked that he was already on a nickname basis with Isabelle, having just met her.

"Yup. Iz and I will be at Pinks, you?" I gave him my best "business transaction" serious voice.

"Right on," Thane replied as he reached into the back pocket of his OP shorts. "Nah, not my scene."

Well, fuck, that was it. If he weren't already my new favorite drug dealer, I would've walked away right then. How could I possibly hang with someone who didn't appreciate Pinks?

"Cool," I nodded in solidarity, still shocked he'd dissed our favorite dance club and smiled. Here I was, shooting the breeze with and about to purchase drugs from this guy who had my panties in a twist, and he didn't like Pinks! The excitement of it all had my blood rush to my head. This was some serious *Miami Vice* shit going down. I thought about how cool it would be to hear "Smuggler's Blues" by Glenn Frey through the speakers at that exact moment. But alas, our drug deal would be accompanied by Kenny Loggins, which is probably why I have yet to see *Footloose*.

"So, what, a half?" Thane dropped a folded square of a magazine corner into my side purse pocket. My stomach flipped, and I felt like throwing up from the excitement. "There's a bindle for you ladies."

Before I paid Thane and was about to say goodbye, I surprised myself by whispering, "You got another one?" as I casually rifled through the P's, trying to figure out what the word "Synchronicity" meant and why The Police were singing about it.

"Yeah, for sure." Thane happily obliged and reached for his pocket again as I tried to pay him as discreetly as possible. "So, is she single?"

There it was. The question I was always prepared for whenever I hung out with Isabelle.

"I think so. I'll put in a good word for you," I assured, feeling like I now had a special task from my new, hot drug dealer dude, hoping sales for future purchases would be discounted if I pimped out my hot French sister-friend.

"Just drop it in the sleeve of this one," Thane ordered, pulling out a used Pretenders record. I placed the cash in the sleeve and walked away feeling invincible. I left the store while throwing Isabelle a discreet thumbs-up sign.

"Call me when you're off!" I gestured to Isabelle, my hand mimicking holding a telephone, which looks exactly like the Hawaiian sign for "shaka," meaning, "What's up?" or "Hang loose." She nodded, and I headed for the bus stop with two half-grams of blow in my purse.

Sitting on the bench, I turned my Walkman on, covered my ears with the plastic headphones and pressed PLAY. As I sat there waiting for my bus, my Depeche Mode cassette sang to me about how "People Are People," and I began to mentally assemble the outfit I would wear at Pinks later that night, wondering what dress goes with fabulous.

Maybe whoever they were singing about should do some lines together, I thought. Surely, they'd get along then. But it was none of my business, and I didn't care. I turned up the volume as the bus pulled up, trying to conceal my delight after finding a seat at the window. I had just turned sixteen and was in a dreamlike state of euphoria and excitement: I had just scored blow from my new personal drug dealer. This, I thought, was grown-up glamour.

It didn't take long until partying on the weekends turned into a daily routine for Isabelle and me. We started snorting lines in between classes during our junior year of high school, straddling the backs of toilet seats and snorting off the lids of porcelain tanks. That's in addition to smoking and drinking after class, something Isabelle was used to doing from her partying ways back home in France.

I wondered if Isabelle's exchange program was a family shame code for "living with a friend of the family" because she'd become "too much to handle." Whatever it was, I didn't care. She was perfectly fine to me.

In addition to the intense feelings of confidence and general badassery cocaine gave me, I learned quickly that having this glorious white powder on me at all times served up something I never had prior: party friends from every high school clique imaginable. Isabelle wasn't affected by this newfound social status, but I reveled in its wonder and considered it payback for being ostracized because of my skin. Apparently, cocaine wins every beauty contest—and everyone wanted a piece of my crown.

Senior Prom was a hoot. It was hard to squeeze into my gold lamé strapless dress because I had been unaware I was pregnant for a couple of weeks. I bragged to my classmates I was packing an eight-ball (three and a half grams of cocaine), and suddenly the event was all about me: where I was, who I was with, and how much I had to share.

Thrilled with the attention that wasn't accompanied by me weeping on the bus ride home after school, I shared my not-so-secret stash with anyone who wanted a bump. The punk kids who listened to The Ramones and PiL were the first in line, followed by the goths who looked like police lineup clones of Robert Smith and Siouxsie Sioux.

Eventually, the stoner-surfers were curious, so I shared my party powder with them, in addition to the stragglers who came late to the party in our hotel room because they were busy slow dancing with the cheerleaders and jocks in the main ballroom of our hotel in Waikiki. Even my prom date, who I didn't really know but asked to accompany me because he was younger and prettier than I could ever be, was impressed. I'm sure he only said yes because of my willingness to share my crown.

On the morning of graduation, Isabelle and I agreed to stuff a baggie of blow in our bras and laughed about how cool it would be.

"We should do this!" she squealed at my suggestion.

"We'd never forget this day, that's for sure!" I replied.

Since I graduated high school at seventeen, I would not be of legal drinking age in Hawai'i for a few more months, which at the time was eighteen but was later changed to twenty-one. Isabelle was busy applying for a permanent American Visa and researching ways to attend KCC (University of Hawai'i Kapi'olani Community College), and I was on my way to being a bikini dancer at a topless bar in Waikiki.

# SECTION TWO

# IT'S SHOWTIME!

CHAPTER NINE

# ROCKIN' ROBERT

If no Thane, there is always another.

It was three a.m., and in my mind, I was about to bang Scott Baio, the actor who played Fonzie's younger cousin Chachi Arcola in *Happy Days*. He'd been my childhood fantasy boyfriend. At seventeen, my dream of consummating our love was coming to fruition by way of a twenty-seven-year-old doppelgänger who had free cocaine, a huge penis, nightclub connections, and more free cocaine.

As a graduation present from high school, mom bought me a used Toyota Tercel she picked up for $400 from one of Dick's work buddies. What a game-changer. I was already a reckless party girl, but now I was mobile. My new chariot served me well, carting me to nightclubs in Waikiki, where I met my fantasy boyfriend from television and lured him to my love den. Tears for Fears serenaded our newfound romance through the dashboard cassette in my beat-up Tercel as the warm tropical breeze swept through the opened windows, tousling his perfectly feathered hair. I struggled to keep from swerving when his hand disappeared up my skirt. I stepped harder on the gas.

"Damn, how much longer until we get there?" he asked hungrily. Waikiki is a mere three miles long, so any place outside of the city seemed far.

"We're almost there," I lied.

I still lived with my mother in our adult-free weekend townhouse, twelve miles away. Laurie was on the mainland for her first year at college, and Mom was with Dick at the Poipu house—like she had been every Saturday night for years. Mom-free weekends were pretty great. Other than my sister walking in on me giving a blow job after too many wine coolers on my sixteenth birthday, my unsupervised experiences were tame in the beginning. But after Laurie left for college, my social world exploded.

Saturday nights were spent living in a smoke-filled cigarette bubble of booze-and-blow where I pretended the house was mine, my four-bedroom castle with wall-to-wall shag carpeting, a swimming pool, and a fully stocked bar.

I had more friends than ever in my senior year. Even though I knew they were using me, I didn't care. I was getting attention for something other than my face. No longer was I the scar-faced girl. I was Party-Pad-Chris! The power of having something the other kids wanted and being able to make it happen was intoxicating.

Mom rarely checked on me when she was with Dick ten minutes down the road, but it was always with a phone call when she did. Telling her what she wanted to hear was easy, and I ladled on the lies. The juxtaposition between being Mommy's little angel and who I really was provided a rush that fed my inner devil perfectly.

When we pulled into the driveway, my childhood dreams of finding my love started to come true.

"This place is the bomb!" Chachi observed, duly impressed.

"Thanks! Come in; it's all ours!" I announced while taking his hand and walking him inside, frantically unbuttoning his shirt. He kissed me deeply and with force. My knees buckled, and I inhaled his Paco Rabanne. "Let's go upstairs," I whispered, nibbling on his neck.

"Got a mirror?" he asked, grabbing my ass, and peeling off my skirt.

I nodded, pulled a mirror from the foyer wall, and tucked it under my arm. Now naked from the waist down, I motioned for him to follow me upstairs, where we ran to my mother's bedroom. It was twice the size of mine, with a king-size bed and grown-up furniture. The walls were free of Tower Records and Richard Gere posters, and no dirty clothes or record sleeves were blanketing the floor.

On top of mom's maple dresser were bottles of Chanel N°5 and Shalimar, a silver antique Parisian jewelry box, and her cherished collection of porcelain Lladró lady figurines. The massive piece of wood held nine drawers and stretched alongside the louvered glass windows. One could see coconut palms flickering with the crescent moon and bright stars through them. Framing the length of the dresser was a large wooden mirror watching our every move.

"So, your name is Robert?" I asked, handing him the foyer mirror. He sat on the edge of the bed, reached inside his pants pocket, and pulled out a gold razor blade, a McDonald's straw cut into a third, and a tiny paper envelope. He unfolded the bindle and dumped a mountain of cocaine on the mirror. My mouth watered as I nuzzled behind him, my legs and arms wrapped around his waist, my chin perched on his shoulder.

"Yeah," he replied. "But everyone calls me Rockin' Rob." He snickered, chopping the powder with the blade, licking his lips.

"Nice!" I said. I was dying to know more but kept my cool.

"Yeah, that was my stage name in LA. Did I tell you I worked at Chippendales before coming here?" he asked casually, snorting three lines quickly. He shifted his seat on the bed, allowing me access to the mirror, and he immediately realized his faux pas.

"Shit, my bad! Ladies always go first." He shook his head and kissed me, handing me the straw.

My little devil and I were in heaven. A Chippendales dancer—so much better than Chachi.

"It's all good, and who you callin' lady?" I flirted.

As I leaned over the mirror for my turn, I suddenly caught a reflection of my face. I was mortified. The light from the nightstand behind us cast an eerie shadow, and my crevice-like scars looked even worse than usual. I wanted to leap across the room and smash the bulb but instead shook my head, fluffing my hair to cover my cheeks.

This wasn't my first-time manipulating shadows that highlighted the deep craters on my skin. I usually had friends around to warn me when the lighting was bad. Our code word was "fluff." That prompted me to move from the harsh lighting and fluff up my hair to cover my cheeks as a protective shield. I was alone this time with Robert, freaked out but grateful my party mirror understood the code.

I carefully and quickly pulled my hair to one side and held my breath with my eyes closed. I inhaled all three lines as fast as possible, praying Robert didn't notice the shadows on my skin.

"That's my girl!" he observed, impressed I could ingest three lines as quickly as he did without gagging. "You're a pro, baby."

He placed the mirror on the floor and kissed me.

"Hang on," I said. I stood up and walked over to the hallway outside the bedroom and switched the dimmer on low before heading toward the nightstand to darken our corner.

"That's better," I said, feeling a body rush, my head tingling. The coke was moving through me, and I was vibrating with confidence. Our togetherness was intense, and at that moment, I was convinced our bodies were two pieces of a Kama Sutra puzzle, custom-fitted for one another. Our heavy breathing synchronized in perfect rhythm. My lips were numb from kissing, and this was a most delicious mix of sex and blow.

"I am your girl," I proclaimed. I had fallen hopelessly in love.

Hours later, when the cotton balls in the sky morphed into amethysts on fire born from the rising sun, I dropped Robert off in Waikiki. A wave of panic came over me, watching his reflection fade in the rearview mirror as I drove away and turned the corner. My nose started to tickle, and I fought back the tears, struggling to breathe. How would I survive an entire week without seeing my new man again?

I turned on the radio, and "Slave to Love" by Bryan Ferry was playing.

"Yes!" I thought. He's running with me! Our hearts are restless! We aren't chained and bound! This was true love to which I was, blissfully, a slave.

I was in a trance the entire way home, reenacting our love story frame by frame. Had I found love at last?

When we met, I'd been with friends at Pink Cadillac (Pinks), an alternative music nightclub in Waikiki that catered to the eighteen-and-older crowd. We were a group of teenage misfits, some of us with fake IDs (mine Laurie's), who embraced our inner weirdo, waving our freak flags wildly. Some of us used egg whites to spike our mohawks, while others painted black eyeliner and lipstick on our faces, inspired by Siouxsie Sioux.

That night I was channeling Molly Ringwald's character in *The Breakfast Club* and Lisa from *Weird Science*, wearing a skintight tube skirt and stilettos while donning a wavy mushroom bob styled with too much mousse ("I have more than mousse in my hair, I have Bullwinkle!") and a shaved nape underneath my fluffy pouf.

Pinks was the place to be and my home away from home on Saturday nights. It was a two-story building that took up half a block and was located just off Kalākaua Avenue, one of the three main streets in Waikiki. The entrance wasn't hard to miss, with the front end of an actual baby-pink colored '59 Cadillac poking out from the wall above the entrance on the second floor. Next to that was a neon pink sign flashing the words "Pink Cadillac" in cursive. Simply standing on the steps waiting to go inside was an event in itself. We'd smoke cloves and greet friends who went to different high schools, all basking in the pink neon glow that bathed us with acceptance.

As the line moved forward and the music grew louder, the bass under our feet propelled our excitement. The DJ was our pastor, and his music was the gospel of New Wave. Nobody understood us the way bands like The Cure, New Order, Yaz, The Smiths, Blondie, and The Clash could.

Once inside, I noticed Robert immediately. Tall and drop-dead gorgeous, Robert was a Mexican American from Inglewood, CA, who passed himself off as Italian—John Travolta in *Saturday Night Fever* Italian. He was guarding the entrance of the VIP room at the back of the club near the bar. Managing the velvet rope, he had some power. He wasn't dressed like the waiters and bar staff, who wore black jeans and hot pink '50s-inspired bowling shirts with black lapels. Robert was in a tux. His black tux with a glittery-gold cummerbund and bow tie, which I'm sure he picked up during his Chippendales days, made his Chippendales body even more delicious.

My two girlfriends, Kimmy, and Dany had helped me polish off a bottle of Boone's Farm Tickle Pink wine earlier in the car, so I had some liquid courage when I walked over to the sexy man in the golden tux.

"You're new," I said. Like he needed this information. It's Chachi, right?

"You're not," he shot back with a wink, lifting the latch of the velvet rope, allowing us access to the private room.

"Do you know that guy?" asked Kimmy, impressed. So was I. She and I had met recently through Dany, a girl I'd met sweating on the dance floor. Dany and I bonded while dancing at Pinks to Robert Smith and New Order a few weeks earlier. It turned out that Kimmy and Dany went to the same private school, La Pietra Hawai'i School for Girls, in the lavish neighborhood of Diamond Head overlooking Kapi'olani Park just outside Kahala.

Dany's black hair was short and slicked back, and she chained smoked Parliaments and chewed black gum. She dressed in black tights with an oversized wide-belted white Haynes t-shirt and flat white leather boots with tiny daisies carved into the ankles. Her mahogany skin was luminous against her cat-green eyes. She looked like a Middle Eastern punk rock princess.

Kimmy was a professional model with sun-kissed skin and a bleached pixie haircut. Her almond eyes sparkled with mischief and effortless sex appeal. Always in strappy Spandex dresses and sheer black pantyhose with a vertical line tracing the back of her legs, Kimmy's signature fragrance was Obsession, which was fitting because she looked as if she jumped off the pages of a

Calvin Klein magazine ad. Kimmy and Dany were the types of beautiful girls who strangers ask you if they're single when you are out with them in public. But neither of them had a shred of conceit. They were just silly and fun and wanted nothing from me other than my friendship. I was humbled and grateful for our newly formed sisterhood and proud of my sudden street cred in the Hot Girls Club.

The three of us chilled on the black velvet couches sipping our $5 Long Island Iced Teas and enjoyed feeling special from inside the rope. I pulled out a clove from the inside pocket of my purse, and a lit match magically appeared before my eyes.

"You party?" Robert asked, leaning over with my light.

My stomach was full of butterflies. He wasn't talking to Kimmy or Dany but to me!

"Thanks," I said. I inhaled my smoke and blew out his match, looking into his dark brown eyes. "Why, do you have any?" I asked, exhaling from the corner of my mouth, and turning my head away from his face. I loved that we already had a secret language; "party" meant cocaine, and I melted in his words.

He handed me a tiny envelope. "Take your friends to the bathroom," he ordered.

"Planet Claire" by The B-52s sang through the speakers, and my heart was thumping in tune with the flashing lights illuminating from underneath the dance floor in the center of the club.

Kimmy smoked a little pot but was afraid of cocaine, so I leaned over to Dany and smiled. "Oh my God!" I said, pulling her up from the couch. "Come with me!" Dany's face lit up, and we giggled while holding hands to the bathroom, feeling like rock stars with blow.

The three of us danced until last call. When the lights came on, we started walking down the outside stairs, and I felt a hand tug on the back of my elbow.

"See you next week?" Robert asked.

I told the girls I'd see them later. "No," I said, leaning away, hiding my face from the floodlight just outside the entrance. "I'll wait for you downstairs. I'm not done seeing you tonight." Cocaine Confidence: The newest fragrance by Chrissy Klein.

After dropping Robert back in Waikiki, I pulled into the driveway and saw mom's car, so I knew she was already home from her weekend with Dick. I heard her on the phone as I walked into the kitchen through the back door and was so relieved, I'd washed her sheets earlier that morning. I wanted her to hang up the phone to free up the line so Robert could get through when he called like he said he would.

When I got to my room upstairs and closed the door so I could dance to my records in celebration of finding true love, I had a minute to think. I suddenly felt like I was kicked in the gut. Shit. Robert didn't ask for my number. Really, it was time to find my own place.

# CHAPTER TEN

# THE OTHER WOMAN

Robert was truly hot, and he knew it. Often, he'd lean into the mirror and say, "Damn, I'm so good looking. Thank you, God." He was cocky and self-focused. He knew he had an amazing body from his years as a Chippendales dancer on Sunset Boulevard in California and jumped at the chance to showcase his hotness in Waikiki after Joe Camacho, the owner of Pinks, flew him to Hawai'i to help promote his club.

A few months later and Robert was officially my guy. Or so I'd thought. Meanwhile, I had now moved, living in the city (Waikiki), away from my hook-up castle and mom's bedroom. Wrapped up in my new relationship with Robert, who was kicking ass in his career of dealing blow out of his pedicab during the day and managing Pinks' VIP room at night on the weekends, I was in bliss. My love for Robert had become the driving force behind my moving. I had no idea how I'd managed to get an apartment despite being only eighteen, but somehow, my bullshit charm and $600-a-month hotel receptionist gig helped make it happen. It was a shoebox-sized shithole apartment crawling with roaches, but it was directly across the street from Robert's club (priorities), and it was mine.

We moved in together.

"Just for a couple of days," Robert had assured me.

"Of course, baby," I replied, "stay as long as you need."

A couple of days turned into over a year, but who's counting? Robert and I were living together! This had to mean he was my boyfriend, a concept as foreign to me as a flat iron was to Chaka Khan. Apparently foreign to him as well.

My template for toxic men had long solidified. Robert was abusive and emotionally damaging, furthering my basement bottom self-esteem, but being an addict, unbeknownst to me at the time, I held on to him for dear life. His emotional and sometimes physical abuse I would own as something I deserved. As usual, when we were out, he walked five steps in front of me, his way of telling the world we weren't together. His vanity rejected my imperfections. The scars on my face didn't sit well with him, and he made a point of telling me so. He could do nothing to push me away, so I kept my pace behind his back, feeling the uncomfortable sting of unworthiness deep inside my longing for his attention. Knowing he and I were together behind closed doors kept my feet moving in his direction and my life in silent chaos. In my mind, we inhabited an exclusive club, one where dark shadows and secret liaisons borne of shallow complexities were coveted. In this underground world, I was worthy, beautiful even.

After our Royal walk, when we arrived back at the apartment, Robert chopped me up a line of coke before jumping in the shower to get ready for work. He was starting his shift as a pedicab driver at noon. A born salesman, he never had a problem getting fares, and as a party boy, he always found plenty of customers for his side job: selling cocaine out of his cab.

He motioned for me to do the line. "Those jeans are getting tight."

I looked down at my belly and slid my fingers inside the waistline of my size 2 jeans. Taking a dollar bill and rolling it, I agreed. My jeans could be baggier. Standing five feet, seven inches and weighing 115 pounds wasn't good enough. So, I stayed with my cocaine diet like a good little girl.

After snorting the line on my dresser, I noticed the clutter piled in front of me. Random pieces of our lives were strewed about, including drugstore receipts, empty paper bags with beer bottle caps piled inside, and loose papers with different women's phone numbers on them. Robert never hid the fact that he picked up women. Sometimes I called the numbers to tell them he was with me, but it never stopped the numbers from coming.

One day, I'd finally had enough. After Robert went to work, I ripped off a piece of the paper bag and used the hand I don't write with, my right, to scribble a fictitious phone number and man's name down, just to even the score and hopefully get him jealous. I left it in plain view.

The next morning, Robert found the note, and I was questioned.

"Who's Steve?" Robert asked angrily.

"No one–just a guy I met." I loved his attention and played coy.

He grabbed me and threw me on the bed. "Where'd you meet him?" he demanded.

I felt the birth of bruises on my arms as he picked me up and shoved me against the wall.

"Did you fuck him?" Robert kept his grip while shaking me and screaming.

"No, nothing like that!" I suddenly realized I was in danger and felt shame for bringing this on myself. Still, I'd never felt so alive. He was jealous.

"Don't fucking lie to me!"

Burying my face in my hands, I allowed tears to trickle down my cheeks to the curve of my smile. Only a man who loved me would care so much.

Robert would've been a real catch if he weren't such a drug-addicted, abusive, cheating asshole. And if his profits weren't snorted up his nostrils sooner than you could say eight ball, I'm sure he'd have been a fabulous salesman, loaded like his idol Tony Montana in *Scarface*. The irony that he was boning a girl with scars on her face was not lost on me. Maybe he'd not be Miami mansion wealthy, but he would've had more dough than the spare change I managed to find in the pockets of his MC Hammer pants.

But that's where I came in. I provided shelter and sex, what he needed most. Robert moving in, supplying me blow and hot sex in exchange for rent-free digs, was a match made in codependent, drug-addicted heaven. Having started bikini dancing in 1987, I was living large on my own, thanks to my cocaine-fueled work ethic and tenacity for performing on stage.

Table dancing at The Lollipop Lounge was a natural hustle for me. We sold personal dances on the floor for five bucks a song. CDs played at the club ranged from Mötley Crüe, Poison, and Def Leppard to Madonna, Terence Trent D'Arby, and Love and Rockets.

My favorite song to dance to was "So Alive" by Love and Rockets because not only was the tune straight-up sexy, the lyrics felt like he was speaking directly to me: "I don't know what color your eyes are, baby, but your hair is long and brown." Indeed, I had long brown hair and hypnotic blue eyes.

A year had rolled by, and I was now nineteen. If there was one part of me that was beautiful, it was my eyes. I have gorgeous blue eyes. There. I said it.

I wasn't dancing on Broadway, but I get a thrill when table dancing. Whatever songs the other gals and I picked; they serenaded our seductions beautifully. The crowd would get in the spirit, singing along to every song in groups. Oh, how I curse you, Billy Idol, with your "Mony Mony" (pronounced "Mow-nay, Mow-nay") song. The men were in heaven as we ground their laps using both sides of our bodies, wearing only bikinis or lingerie (and L'eggs pantyhose pinned to our G-strings).

At The Pop, there were no separate rooms for private shows for which I was grateful, having learned what goes down in private VIP Rooms at other strip bars. So, we danced for our young military boys stationed on the island with their buddies waiting for a turn watching from the main floor. A natural salesgirl, I'd line up my next customer by mouthing the words, "You're next," to the guy right behind my customer. I would get a kick out of the drooling man before me, even for a woman who was burying her cleavage-less double A-cups in his face. If my customer gave me a $20 bill, rarely was there anticipation of change. I simply kept dancing after the first song was over and didn't stop until the fourth tune ended. Then, I'd kiss my customer on the cheek, thanking him for the cash and ability to keep his hands to himself and move on to my next mark.

My table dancing helped me rake in cash. Robert and I were knee-deep into our poisonous pairing when I moved into a new high-rise rental apartment on the North end of Waikiki. He hung out at my place so much that I believed we were a real couple. I didn't think about how he never pitched in any money for rent or bills. Or how I tempered my anger when he'd fuck around on me constantly. Or how I sucked it up when he'd tell me I was getting too fat, then too thin. My life was like walking a tight rope with the unpredictable Robert. All the free cocaine and multiple orgasms I could want were no longer cutting it, but I couldn't leave. I was addicted.

"So, you say, when you were a crack whore…" a therapist once began.

"No, no, no, coke whore," I corrected. "Big difference."

Even after a year plus, Robert continued to be Robert, still not wanting to be seen with me. He constantly warned me never to call him "The b-word," but I had convinced myself he was my boyfriend no matter what he said. When he managed to stumble home, he'd be happy sleeping in my shoebox shithole, on my mattress on the floor, and getting Taco Bell delivered and his whites separated. If that wasn't domestic bliss, I didn't know what was. He was king of my new castle in our high-rise apartment my money paid for.

It was no surprise to me that he was popular with women. He never hid it. I knew about them but remained in denial. And then, it happened. I always thought it would be a treat meeting the other woman who is screwing your boyfriend until you realize you're the one screwing hers. It was the first time I could put a face to the "other woman." I'd found a full-length bikini photo of her with a perfect ass while rummaging through my "boyfriend's" shit. I don't recommend snooping but knock yourself out if you want to prove your partner is cheating and you're high off your ass.

After the initial heart-stopping shell shock of finding the bikini broad's photo during my frenzied cocaine-fueled poke-around, I reeled in my breath and read the handwritten love letter saying she was moving to Oʻahu from Los Angeles. Her aunt lived just outside the city in the town of Kahala and she couldn't wait to see him. "Every time I see the teddy bear in that Snuggle fabric softener commercial on TV, I can't help but think of us," the note began.

He's an "us" with someone other than us? It's one thing to snoop blindly because you're suspicious of your lover *shtupping* other babes, but to have concrete proof in your trembling palms, to see the flesh of the other woman, while fighting every urge to picture them grunting naked, is to finally swallow the lover's poison swirling around in your mouth ever since you felt that first pang of fear.

As the bitter venom slowly dripped down my esophagus, I tasted its concoction of two parts bitter, one-part relief. I'm not fucking crazy! He is the bastard I suspected (because he was an absolute prince otherwise)!

As painful as it was, seeing Angela in Technicolor was the first step in cracking the code and finding the combination to the emotional padlock that kept me prisoner in my very own straitjacket of denial when it came to Robert.

At the bottom of the page at the end of the letter was a local telephone number. Before I realized the receiver was in my hand, I heard her voice and then spoke.

"Is this Angela?" I was trembling.

"Yeah." She sounded confused.

"Um, you don't know me, but do you know Robert Lazar?" Breathe, Christine, breathe.

"Oh my God, yeah?" Now, she sounded like she was shaking.

"Well, I'm Christine. I don't know if you've ever heard of me, but, um, Robert lives with me. I mean, we live together. He's, my boyfriend." I was this close to pissing on the phone and marking my territory.

After an eternity of silence, Angela replied, "Oh fuck. I knew it. I knew he was with someone! I'm so sorry, Christine—this is NOT who I am. You have to believe me. I had no idea. What are you doing right now? I just moved here and am staying in Kahala. I can be in Waikiki in ten minutes. Meet me for a drink."

"Uh…" I wasn't counting on her being so nice. I panicked. What outfit goes with "Back off, sister, that's my leopard-printed Chippendales G-string-covered penis?"

"Please," Angela urged, "we have to meet. There's a lot you need to know."

I landed on my favorite black mini tank dress from Contempo Casuals and hula hoop-sized silver earrings.

"Give me twenty," I said before hanging up.

CHAPTER ELEVEN

# PEAS IN A PARTY POD

Before there was Thelma and Louise on the big screen, we had Laverne and Shirley on television. During the years in between, Angela and Stephanie were all the rage, lighting up the streets in Waikiki. (More about my name change later.)

If those palm trees and coconuts could talk…well, that would prove whoever was witnessing that shit was tripping. What I mean to say is that we left our mark.

Ang and I blew onto the scene in the late eighties and were a pair of crazy fun party gals whose photo together back then could've easily been placed next to the word trouble in the dictionary. From the moment we met, we were sisters. I had just turned nineteen, and Ang was five years my senior. So, she was non-judgmental and adored me.

"Shit, girl, I have so much to tell you!" Angela said. She bought us a round and was squealing with energy while pouring our first pitcher of margaritas. After our second, I learned about Robert's secret life as a drug mule and that he and Ang had a history I only thought went down in the movies.

I never felt so young and yet so close to another person. Not only did we share a man every other month while he flew to L.A. to pick up his product for Rick (cocaine for his drug lord boss), but we also clicked organically. The Hot Mess leading The Hot Mess.

It was easy to forget we were both The Other Woman because we had so much in common (in addition to Robert's penis). Never ones to shy away from booze and blow, always the loudest and funniest ladies in the room, and we loved, loved, loved to dance.

Angela shared my obsession with Bob Fosse, and I developed a hardcore jealousy crush when she told me she and Robert worked as background dancers on television shows like *Soul Train* and *Dance Fever* back in Hollywood.

I basked in their juicy showbiz stories and was in awe that I knew people on TV doing what I had dreamt of since I was eleven watching *Solid Gold*. This is why I couldn't end all ties with Robert. Plus, he had the blow.

After Angela and I met, I found the balls to kick him out of my apartment. And even though it felt foreign to stand up for myself, my spine grew stronger thanks to Ang. She wanted us to create a united front regarding Robert and our little conundrum, and I agreed. Hoes before Bros, fellas. Vagina always beats Rock-Paper-Penis.

Neither one of us was surprised about Robert being with us both, and because we got along so well, it became more of a fun party story instead of a reason to hate each other. Angela and Robert, I soon learned, had ended their romance, and Ang was madly in love with someone she had met on the beach. I invited Angela to move in shortly after Robert left. Although there was no animosity, I still wish I could've captured the look on Robert's face when he saw us sitting on the couch together one night, which is how he learned we'd discovered one another. Had cellphones and the internet existed back then, you bet your ass I'd have blasted that shit online.

I was still working the reception desk at The Ilikai Hotel. Ang was studying for her pedicab license so she could pedal her flawlessly fit body all day and rake in cash, which is why she ended up on the island. She was inspired by Robert's bragging about how much money he made doing it before his nightly shifts at the club, not including the coke he sold to tourists from his cab.

Unfortunately, the pedicab industry was outlawed that same year, leaving Angela unemployed. I took her out for Bloody Marys at the Tahitian Lanai next to The Ilikai to cheer her up. Later, we decided to work on our tan lines and talk about her job options while chillin' on the sand in front of the Royal Hawaiian Hotel.

Little did we know how profoundly that afternoon in Waikiki would change our lives forever.

Nobody dreams of becoming a stripper. Little girls aren't sitting around playing with Barbies, sharing visions of clear heels. They don't swing on the monkey bars thinking about the pole, and they're certainly no high school career aptitude tests that prepare you for table dancing.

I made my stage debut in 1987. At nineteen, wearing nothing but a neon G-string and a smile, I was a mere hopscotch and skip away from Easy Bake Ovens and Lee Press-On Nails. My new best friend Angela and I were lying on the beach, cultivating our cocoa-buttered tans, when we were approached.

"You ladies want to make an easy hundred?" His oiled-up pecs, hot pink Speedo, and curly gelled mullet were mocking him. He was recruiting us for a wet t-shirt contest.

A hundred bones. That's the amount one of us stood to win, and it represented a huge wad of cash I could throw down for a gram of coke, my portion of the rent now that Angela was helping out, or that white jacket with the suede fringe I'd been eyeing at North Beach Leather. And all we had to do was dance in a bikini and water-soaked t-shirt.

Where do I sign up?

Walking into the strip bar later that afternoon was an adjustment. It took a minute for my eyes to adapt from palm trees to stripper poles, but I immediately pegged the smell of coconut tanning oil, stale beer, and cigarettes. Having spent my childhood weekends at The Elks, a watering hole where Bloody Marys are a perfectly acceptable breakfast choice, I was familiar. The scenery may have been different, but the vibe was the same. Nothing screams Waikiki Happy Hour like crispy boozers who dig their Marlboros.

Traces of sand decorated the floor, and Jon Bon Jovi's "You Give Love a Bad Name" serenaded my entrance. Angela, who'd raced home from the beach to get ready for our debut, had gotten there before me. I'd stayed behind, suddenly on the fence about going at all. My trepidation was not so much about wet bikinis but how to cover my scars under those bright lights on stage? I decided to give it a shot, so I headed to the club after an hour of hairspray and styling gel and a couple of shots of liquid courage.

As soon as the contestants learned the winner would be chosen based on audience applause, the girls were all over it, hamming it up with the boys in uniform. I took a more laid-back approach though I was oscillating between the butterflies in my stomach from the excitement and nausea from the fear. I skated past the rowdy crowd of mostly young military boys, ordered a Bud Light, and quickly found the dressing room.

"You here for the contest?" a tall Black woman with stoned eyes inquired.

"Uh-huh," I stammered.

"Well, okay, honey, put your name down. You got a shirt?" She handed me a clipboard. Her long pink nails mesmerized me.

"Yeah."

I chose Stephanie, my middle name, as my new stage name because it was easy to remember. Stephanie also breathlessly rolled off the tongue a lot better than Christine. Besides, "Christine" was way too Catholic and represented nothing about me.

As soon as pink-nailed House mom handed me the pen, I was all over it. I signed my new name before you could say Frederick's of Hollywood, using an oversized S for effect. SSSteph-an-ie.

So began my stripper transformation. The only girl I knew, the bullied scarface with the skin thing Christine, was fading into the dressing room rearview mirror to breathless Stephanie. What a big Fuck You to all the cruel assholes in high school.

Changing my name was the first of many yellow bricks I'd lay down while blazing the road of my journey to Oz. I paid no attention to the DJ selling drugs behind the curtain. Woven within the space between obligatory applause and the pounding in my chest, the guitar intro to "Wanted Dead or Alive" (Jon Bon Jovi ruled) escorted me on stage. Before I knew it, my stage name was called.

Ladies and Gentlemen, coming to the stage, we have the sexxxxyyyy Stephanieeeeeee.

I loved the sound of that. And what a brilliant young man for pointing out I was sexy. Cloaked in adrenaline and a heavy beer fog, I turned it out, quickly discovering I was a stripping natural.

It's all the same. Only the names have chaaaaaanged.

I was suddenly in my own music video, and he was singing directly to me:

"*Every day, it seems we're wastin' away...*"

(I know, Jon Bon...I know.)

The crowd lit up as I whipped around my over-teased drag queen hair and shook my ass with unabashed purpose. I fed off the whistles and hollers from the sea of buzzcuts poking through the cigarette smoke and caught a glimpse of myself in the mirror as I spun around the tiny stage. My unkempt hairy caterpillars above my eyes (Brooke Shields had nothing on these babies), orange and gold-sparkled shadow, flammable bird's nest hair, and neon yellow bikini G-string bottom were all working for me. I was dancing.

Right around Richie Sambora's guitar solo, I realized my white tank top was soaked, and you could see straight through to my A-cups. But I loved it. No shame, just showmanship. Fosse, Fosse, Fosse. While I was performing, I had flawless skin. As I worked my rockin' bod, it was love at first set. And Stephanie was born.

On stage, I was perfect, channeling a mix of Tawny Kitaen in every Whitesnake video and the Solid Gold Dancers I used to dream about as a kid while mimicking their every move in front of the TV. Only now, instead of encountering Marilyn McCoo, the announcer was a skinny kid named Rob who was called The Weasel.

The Weasel was a handsome Irish dude with the sharpest mind and great sense of humor. The way he spoke, his mannerisms, and even his looks had me convinced Michael Keaton was going to storm the club one night in search of his missing younger brother whom he just discovered was living in paradise, speaking into a mic for a living, and partying with naked centerfolds. He was everything you wanted in a strip club DJ. He played the hottest hair bands for us while making side deals with customers about which girls would give hand jobs under the tables. I wasn't one of those girls, but I immediately had a crush on him. I mean, to parlay his DJ gig into a little pimping on the side...what an entrepreneur. Since he tended to rotate between a few clubs, I was always happy to reunite with The Weasel. He understood me and knew I was insufferable when it came to music choices for my sets. Plus, the extra cash I threw him didn't hurt.

After my set, Angela and I hung out with the crowd, drinking watered-down draft beers and listening to the guys' stories of how they ended up stationed at various military bases on the island. It was a frat party without the school, and we were the hotties on campus. They adored us for showering them with attention.

We sold table dances for five bucks a pop, and every hour or so, we'd sneak away to the dressing room for a bikini change and a coke bump. Before we knew it, The Weasel called us back to the main stage, and the glamorous merry-go-round of debauchery continued. I couldn't believe this was an actual job. You got paid for dancing on stage, partying, and being told how hot you were. What was not to love?

For the first time in my life, I felt completely beautiful and, more to the point, accepted. I was worlds apart from hiding my face behind my scribbled-on Pee Chee folders and textbooks. I didn't want the night to end. I savored every morsel and inhaled every accolade as if it were the breath of life itself.

Who's Freddy Krueger now, bitches?

To add celebration to elation, I won the contest. Crowned with a tiara of drunken adoration and a new personal sense of hotness draped across my chest, I floated away that night with a wad of cash, a new job, and a brand new me.

I couldn't wait to go back. I was home.

Working at the club was a little different from shaking my moneymaker for a contest. Like all the girls, I had to double as a waitress. It all added up to tips, however—tips for dancing, tips for waitressing and tips for selling watered-down alcohol. There was a small fry-cook stand next to the back tip stage area where customers could feast on greasy fries and chicken wings while watching girls strut our stuff on stage.

Since we served food in addition to alcohol, wearing pantyhose was required by law. It took a certain skill to master the assembly of wearing sheer hose underneath a G-string, but I was a problem solver, and I mastered the technique of attaching my nylons to my G-string.

Soon it'd be my turn, and so, there I was, on stage. Fabulous Stephanie. Perfect everything. Hip popping, Aqua-netted head-rolling, ass-kicking, moneymaking Steph. I was having a blast while channeling every Bob Fosse move I could, bending over, taking a tip, head up, and moving on. The customers seemed like they were flocking to me, staring at my ass, and smiling.

Cha-ching, baby. I'm a rock star.

After Mötley Crüe sang their last note, I saw Angela upside-down through my legs. She waved me down, and we walked offstage to meet in the dressing room.

"Honey, come here," she said with a look of concern.

"Take a look." Angela placed my back to the floor-length mirror and made me bend over, looking at my reflection through my legs.

Holy shit.

I gasped in horror. I never shaved or groomed. Ever. Add that to the visual of my pantyhose smashed up to my G-string; I was Chewbacca from *Star Wars*, only hairier. A bushel of pubic hair flattened out like a dead spider under my pantyhose. It looked like my money maker was robbing a bank.

"Oh my God!"

I couldn't believe I was on stage bending over with my bank robber business hanging out for all the world to see, smiling, and asking for money! And all the time, I thought customers were flocking to me because I was hot.

I needed more than a razor. I needed a cocktail.

I took the rest of the night off, sneaking out the back exit.

After scampering home in shame, I ran a hot bath and grabbed a pair of scissors, a razor, and a hand mirror. I very carefully started lady scaping, and with every stroke of the razor, I tried to weed whack the horrifying vision I couldn't erase from my mind.

It would be the only mistake from my nine years on the pole that I needed to learn from, and just once. If only the rest of my life were that easy.

# CHAPTER TWELVE

# MAID OF DISHONOR

No bride expects her maid of honor to be high on drugs on the Big Day, especially when it's her younger sister in the supporting role. After church, photographs, and the limousine ride, we arrived at the reception. Between greeting the guests, gift-giving, and more photo sessions, I found a pocket of time to slip away to meet my dealer in the hotel lobby. Armed with a half gram of cocaine, I locked myself in the bathroom stall. Lifting my strapless, floor-length bridesmaid dress, I straddled the back of the toilet with my dyed-to-match pastel pumps. I held my over-teased hair with one hand and snorted through a rolled-up dollar bill in the other. In other words, it was just another day, but with less make-up and more patience needed to pretend I wasn't a hot mess.

Within seconds, my heartbeat kicked up a notch, and the music echoing through the hall began to thump a little louder. The subtle vibration of the metal stall reminded me where I was, but I wasn't in a hurry. I knew I had time as long as I heard the cheesy Top 40 pop music from the ballroom. A couple of more lines, pantyhose adjustments, and lip-gloss reapplications later,

I was ready to head back. Before reaching the door, I cursed the fluorescent lights framing the mirror, surveyed my nostrils, and wiped away any residue evidence of my secret.

Stepping closer to the reception, I couldn't escape thoughts of my upcoming toast. I was bubbling with cocaine confidence but still had no idea what I would say about my sister Laurie and her groom. As her sister and maid of honor, I knew I had to say something.

Barely out of high school, I had little life experience, so Mom served up a crash course in wedding etiquette the night before the big day. My toast was to be lighthearted and personal, a trip down relationship lane I never had about my sis and soon-to-be brother-in-law.

"Just share a nice story about them," she consulted.

The problem was, I didn't have any stories, nice or otherwise. Short of the pre-wedding hullabaloo, my sister and I barely spoke. "Okay," I nonetheless agreed.

"Oh my, you two could be twins!" is a statement the two of us often heard growing up, but Laurie and I couldn't have been more different. She knew nothing about my lifestyle, and she was so normal. I'd never stop to think of how Laurie experienced childhood and how it affected her. I know it must have because when things were tense between mom and Dick, she asked if she could go live with our dad, which she did for a year. Our relationship hit the skids for good because of my reckless behavior.

When I graduated high school in 1986, my sister was away at college, so she had no idea how much of a mess I was by then. I'd moved away from home in Hawai'i Kai to Waikiki before the ink on my diploma dried and was shacking up with Robert. There I was in my dump of an apartment unpacking my things when I came across my sister's old checkbook for an account that had been closed. I don't know what possessed me. Well, yes, I did know and immediately called Kimmy.

"We're going shopping," I squealed.

"What? Where?" Kimmy was excitedly confused.

"Contempo Casuals, North Beach Leather, Benetton, anything you want!" That checkbook was our VIP pass, and we were headed to every store in Ala Moana Shopping Center with cheap leather and bolero hats. Using my sister's driver's license, which she thought she'd lost when I had swiped it a year earlier for bar hopping, I wrote a half-dozen checks from her closed bank account and gifted my friend and me a new wardrobe. I knew it was wrong, but not once did it ever occur to me that I'd get caught. Never had logic. When your head is this far up your ass, they never coincide.

A couple of months later, I received a phone call. "What were you thinking?" My mom's voice was shaking with anger. "Your sister wants to press charges. Do you know what they do to women in jail?"

Scared shitless, I begged and pleaded for mom to help me pay back the money, in between wiping my tears and apologizing over and over.

"Don't tell me. Tell your sister," Mom wasn't responding to my tears.

Laurie's and my relationship had been strained since, so I was surprised I was invited to the wedding. I was to throw Laurie a bachelorette party and did. I assumed everyone hired a male stripper for these occasions (because, well, I partied with those dudes). When Laurie answered the door, her hunk-for-hire was dressed as a cop and pretended to be arresting her for check fraud. Clearly one of the worst ideas of my life, by far.

"No, that would be her," she said to the mock cop, pointing to me. She was not amused.

The ballroom was packed. When my time came to toast the happy couple, my eyes wrestled with the spotlight (wondering how visible my scars were in the harsh brightness) and landed on my mom sitting in front. She was smiling and nodding with nervous encouragement.

I took a beat, cleared my throat, and out it came.

"Well, Mom, you always wanted me in the spotlight, and now I'm here!"

What the...? Shit...just keep talking. This isn't about you, girl.

I looked over at my sister, who was just as confused as I was. In an attempt to undo my coked-up narcissism, I babbled about how happy I was they'd found each other, how I wished them well, and blah, blah, blah, get me off this stage. Now!

After that speech, I didn't expect, or receive congratulatory remarks from anyone, especially my sister. The night carried on, and I continued my bathroom liaisons, chalking up my maid of dishonor toast as just another feather in my overstuffed, disappointing-sister cap.

Shortly after her wedding, Laurie graduated college, began work as a middle school teacher, and got pregnant while I was sailing through life on cocaine and booze, go-go dancing at a topless bar. You know, not exactly six of one.... While she was stocking up on booties and burp cloths, I was collecting tips on stage, saving up to go backpacking through the south of France with Guy, a one-night stand-turned-boyfriend in between one of Robert and my breakups, which were many. Guy had just moved to London, where I saved enough cash at The Pop to meet him. Before making it to France, gypsy kids in Madrid ambushed us and took off with everything in our fanny packs.

Three years later, my sister called after opening her mail (the old-fashioned kind, as email wasn't a thing yet).

"Why do I have a letter from the American Embassy in Spain?" she questioned.

Here we go again. One of the kids who'd taken my wallet in Madrid used my sister's driver's license!

Once again, I found myself trying to clean up the awful mess I'd made, begging my sister for forgiveness. It's been decades since I've thrown Laurie on the chopping block, but we're still navigating our way through sisterhood. We connect mostly through emails and texts when we must and frankly, I'm amazed we communicate at all.

I never meant to hurt Laurie. Looking back, I'm shocked by my unfathomable behavior. I'm sure all the psychology books will say I acted out of revenge for the seemingly unfair cards I was dealt with my skin disease, but that's not true. Laurie had her way of dealing with our childhood trauma, but my sister isn't the type who likes to revisit the past, and part of me is grateful. But when it comes to bringing us closer, I wonder if we should. Some years later, she divorced her husband, who ironically reminded me of Dick with his six-pack-a-night drinking and verbal abuse toward his daughter, and found the church. I called Laurie once when the Katie Couric talk show, *Katie*, called after reading the essay I wrote, published in a popular online magazine. They wanted me to come on the show for their sibling rivalry episode, but I had to get my sister to agree. Laurie, of course, categorically refused and offered me a title for my next book: *Living in the Present*.

# CHAPTER THIRTEEN

# IGNORANCE IS THIS

The eighties were coming to a close, and shit was goin' down. By the fall of 1989, my imaginary love affair with Robert was the cherry atop my overindulgent and highly delusional sundae—complete with eighties-era party residue. On the rare occasion when he took me out to dinner, it was always at a five-star restaurant, but we didn't let that intimidate us. Like any proper date ten years older and wiser, Robert taught me how to snort blow off the back of my hand, the back of your palm corner where the bottom of your thumb and index finger connects. This way, we didn't need to scurry to a bathroom stall alone and be forced to do lines by ourselves in private, like animals.

Robert disappeared shortly after our last dinner together at Nicholas Nicholas, a posh steakhouse overlooking the city from 39 floors above The Ala Moana Shopping Center. Somewhere between smuggling four kilograms of cocaine taped to his body under his clothes in Los Angeles and boarding the flight home to Hawai'i to deliver the packages of blow to his boss, Rick, Robert went missing. He never got off the plane, which means Robert somehow exited the aircraft at the last minute after Rick's L.A. boys left the gate to see him off. My guess is that he already had another ticket for Mexico, but who knows? I was just glad I didn't.

After Robert vanished with Rick's product, I was used to being followed and questioned almost daily. I understood why Rick thought I was in on Robert's disappearing act (we were in love, remember), but it simply wasn't true. "You can tap my phones, break into my place, and keep following me," I said, looking Rick squarely in the eye. "I still have no idea where he is."

"I know you know." His eyes were menacing.

"I really don't," I answered, with zero fear, knowing I was telling the truth.

Rick and his muscle men clearly didn't believe me. My place was broken into and rummaged through every week or so, and I was afraid my phones were tapped. Rick and his boys quickly snatched what few belongings Robert left behind in my apartment.

The fact that drug lords were following me didn't scare me as much as it should have. I wasn't lying, so I welcomed their prodding. I felt like I was on a Hollywood set: Drug Dealers and Strippers: The Movie. The true depth of the danger I might have been in never dawned on me. I was happy Robert was gone even though I missed him terribly. I felt alone and worthless without a "boyfriend." I never saw Robert again.

*       *       *

Drug lord drama aside, I was getting used to sleeping through the night alone without Robert and his middle-of-the-night insanity. Walking to the front door in disbelief, I checked the lock to see if it was still bolted. Pulling the curtain to one side, I hadn't seen the police all night and didn't notice any women lurking in the bushes next to my three-story walk-up, another apartment he and I shared.

Robert was gone, and I was learning to breathe again.

I don't remember the exact moment it happened, but something inside me changed with Robert's disappearance. I always imagined I was nothing without him—a piece of garbage left on the street. His departure, and my standing up to his drug dealer boss fueled a shift inside my spirit. I suddenly realized I was only as weak as I chose to be. I'd allowed Robert to throw me around and treat me like a piece of trash. It was my choice.

It took years of therapy to realize my choices were my own. That I could change my mind. That I was better than the life I was living. The bar of my self-esteem was low, but I finally understood I had the power to raise it.

# SECTION THREE

# FOR MATURE
# AUDIENCES ONLY

# CHAPTER FOURTEEN

# SIXTY SECONDS

It was six years later from the first time I did cocaine with Rod Stewart's doppelgänger from Bobby McGee's, and I was about to start my set. The first song that played was just too perfect: Rod Stewart's "Hot Legs." As usual, before my name was announced, I went to the bathroom stall and chopped my coke into tiny little pieces on the back of the toilet. I smoothed each fluffy grain of white powder into perfectly straight lines with practiced sophistication.

"Aaaaaaalright, laaaaaadies and geentleeeemen…."

I had sixty-seconds.

The ceremony of cocaine was as much of a rush as the actual act of snorting it. The sound of chopping. The rolling of the dollar bill. The secrecy of it all. It provided a different kind of intoxication.

My breaths grew louder as the burning numbness electrified my nostrils. The inside of my brain was an itch, and with every snort, I scratched. It was nirvana laced with beauty, dipped in control.

"Put your hands together for the sensaaaational Stephani-eeeeeeee!!!!!"

I quickly straddled the white porcelain with my miniskirt, hiked up around my waist and pulled my hair to one side while filling my brain with the euphoric burn. I tilted my head back, checked my nose for powdery residue before leaving the dressing room, and headed for the stage.

Trotting up in my six-inch stilettos, I surveyed the room. One of my regulars was standing next to the DJ booth with his arm extended. I grasped his hand to help steady myself up the four steps to the stage. I smiled, pulling down my Spandex to ensure my ass was fully covered. I never wanted to be falling out of my clothes when walking the floor. I was a lady.

Even though I was still adjusting to life without Robert, I was too busy falling in love with a newcomer to be heartbroken. My love affair with blow had become a threesome the night I discovered MDMA (Molly, Ecstasy) on my twenty-first birthday in November of '89. Like with cocaine, feeling the effects of that capsule of uncut molecules swimming in my bloodstream was love at first high. What blow gave me in terms of moxie, Ecstasy provided overflowing amounts of unconditional love and pure beauty. I was loved and in love with everything and everyone, including myself. And all I had to do was take a pill to feel it.

I was all grown up, twenty-fucking-one, and moving on and away from Robert and The Lollipop Lounge to the Big Girls Clubs, the nude strip club Club Femme Nu, just up the street from The Pop on Kapi'olani Boulevard. With my body full of MDMA, booze and coke, I had found my holy grail of happiness. And it was all thanks to Kiley's birthday present.

Kiley was a new girlfriend who'd just moved to Hawai'i from the stripping scene in Hollywood, Cali. Kiley had introduced herself to me in the dressing room at Femme Nu and was thrilled when I invited her to my twenty-first birthday bash at Hernando's Hideaway, a local pub in the middle of Waikiki only locals knew about. For that reason, industry folks (from bartenders and servers to strippers and bouncers) hung out there to get away from military crowds, random tourists, and college kids from the mainland who frequented Moose McGillicuddy's, or The Jazz Cellar clubs on Lewers Street, a couple of blocks away.

"You're gonna love this shit," Kiley promised as she handed me a large clear capsule filled with MDMA. "Happy Birthday, girl!" She was more excited than I was.

"Thanks!" I said, happily accepting her birthday present and swallowing the capsule with a glass of champagne.

"Oh, perfect timing," I said to our small table of guests after looking at the time on my new Swatch watch. "Our limo should be outside now!"

I motioned for us to head out from the Hernando's lanai to the sidewalk on Kūhiō Avenue where I had arranged for a white stretch limousine to escort us to dinner at The Black Orchid, a new restaurant in downtown Honolulu just north of Waikiki. One of my friends was screwing the bouncer there, so we had VIP connections. And all of us were dying to explore the new restaurant *Magnum P.I.* had built. (Tom Selleck was one of the owners.) As soon as we piled into the limo, I started to feel the effects of my present.

"Wow," I purred.

"I told you!" Kiley chimed in.

Isabelle was with us but opted to stick with her standard cocaine-and-vodka cocktail. The rest of our little crew was strictly into booze and weed, so Kiley and I latched onto each other as soon as we started to roll.

"It was just made illegal," Kiley explained. "Marriage counselors used to prescribe this shit to couples in Texas, but people started abusing it because it feels so fucking amazing."

I nodded and asked the driver to roll down the window so I could feel Mother Earth's fingers through my hair by way of her tropical trade winds.

"Fuuck meeee…." I tried to handle a conversation but was paralyzed with pleasure, and words seemed too complicated. No matter. I was in love.

As soon as The Cure's "Lullaby" started playing, I asked our driver once again for a favor: turn up the volume! The melody was percolating inside me, and it felt like I was an instrument in a crazy Ecstasy Orchestra, and Robert Smith was our conductor.

"Jeeeeeezusssss…," I sang, moving my hands in the air as if dancing the hula. I was tingling everywhere like I had fallen asleep on my whole body (like we do with our arms sometimes when asleep), and I needed to touch every part of my skin and move around to wake it up.

"I can't wait to dance," I shared with Kiley, my teeth starting to grind, chattering from the pulse of whatever was happening inside of me.

"Mmmmmm, yesssss," Kiley replied. "Your teeth, sweetie. Come here." Kiley pulled me close to her inside the limo and planted a kiss on me. My friends cheered, and our driver tried to watch us through the rearview mirror.

There was a live band at The Black Orchid, and thanks to my friend's hoo-ha, we were seated directly in front of the stage. I sipped champagne and melted into the booth while Isabelle and the rest of our crew grazed on crab cakes and fresh poke while guzzling champagne. Knowing I had zero appetite, Kiley pulled me onto the dance floor.

"C'mon, Stephanie!" Kiley urged, excited we were on the same level. Her dark tan complimented her bottled-sunset-red-dye-job and hazel eyes, a look only she could pull off. I took her hand and wanted to smother myself in her skin; it was so soft. We moved to the music and started kissing again in front of everyone at the restaurant and on the dance floor. With my eyes closed, anything other than Kiley's lips didn't exist.

"She's dressed in yellow, she says, 'Hello, come sit next to me, you fine fellow!' You run over there without a second to lose, and what comes next? Hey, bust a move!"

After what felt like an eternity, I opened my eyes to find the lead singer of a cover band singing in front of me, "If you want it, you got it. If you want it, baaaaaby, you got it!"

It took me a second to adjust to the fact that we were dancing to a live band instead of the real Tone Loc, which is ironic because a couple of years later, I ran into Mr. Loc at a club on Sunset Boulevard in California while—shocker—rolling on E. I could barely see straight, but as soon as I heard him say, "Hey, baby girl," I was reminded of my night at The Black Orchid while busting a move to his song.

After Magnum's Musical Adventure at the Orchid, our party jumped back into the limo, and we were off to Wave Waikiki, a nightclub so insane I still get thrilling flashbacks when hearing Peter Murphy, PJ Harvey, Ministry, or Nine Inch Nails, to name a few.

While Pinks gave us high school seniors a home for self-expression and love of eighties alternative music, The Wave turned everything up a notch. Both were the Sodom and Gomorrah of our time and dripping with debauchery as the fabric that made up our young lives. I've never been more grateful to have experienced my twenties pre-smartphones and internet.

Located just a block away from Pink Cadillac, The Wave, also known as The Grave, The Slave, and The Cave, was another two-story dance club (and live music venue) that catered to alternative music lovers and general misfits and weirdos. It closed at four in the morning, so industry folks piled in there after our shifts wrapped at one or two in the morning.

There was no such thing as waiting in line for us. A quick flash of our LC (liquor commission) cards, and we were entry-stamped on the back of our hands like local royalty. Strippers also had LC cards, but ours were stamped with "EXOTIC" on the front.

License to strip? Right this way, Sistah.

I used to joke around with Jack, the owner of The Wave, I should get my mail delivered there. This was, of course, back when Apple was something we ate and Microsoft, a swatch of tiny velvet. Naturally, I was referring to snail-mail, something that's rarely used now since paying bills online became a thing.

"Ha-ha, yeah. There are a few of you regulars I should build mailboxes for," Jack said with a chuckle. He was like everyone's favorite gay uncle (guncle?) who knew how to throw the wildest parties. In addition to owning Wave Waikiki, he also owned and operated Hula's Waikiki, the hottest gay bar on the island, about a mile away from The Cave on Kūhiō Avenue.

One of Jack's wilder events at The Wave was Love-In Night, a hippie-themed party complete with sugar cubes masquerading as LSD and queen-sized beds upstairs in the VIP Room. Technically, there was no official VIP Room, but we industry kids claimed our territory at two every morning.

MDMA was made for these nights, and if I had a dollar for every person I played tonsil hockey with and groped on those upstairs couches in that club, I'd own a house in Maui on the beach paid for with cash.

But after nearly six years of hedonism (nightly partying until dawn), all the blow, pills, booze, and pot swirling around my body started to turn on me. Something about waking up with dried vomit on my lips and fuzzy memories of who I was lying next to or where I'd parked my car just didn't feel sexy anymore.

I didn't recognize my reflection in the mirror with my eyes half-closed and pupils the size of saucers. I was a long way from being in the strip clubs with all of us rolling on E and flashing the "X" sign with our forearms from the shower and tip stages as our little gang sign. It was so much fun until it wasn't.

Here's the thing about drugs: they feel fucking amazing. But what nobody tells you when you're partying is that as high as you can get from whatever you choose to elevate your soul, the lows are so much more intense.

The last time I woke up from partying with MDMA (by then, I was up to six pills a night due to half a decade of built-up tolerance), I felt in a state of dream-sleep while being fully awake. I later learned that this is called lucid dreaming. Whatever it was, it freaked me the fuck out. I saw myself sleeping but couldn't tell if I was ever going to wake up.

When I finally managed to open my eyes, I saw myself standing in the doorway staring at me in bed. I never told anyone, but that experience scared me straight out of my nearly six-year Ecstasy addiction.

The coke, however, was delighted to have me all to herself again.

# CHAPTER FIFTEEN

# PEACHES AND CREAM

On my first night at Femme Nu, I met a goddess. Her name was Red. She was an Annie Lennox look-alike with a fiery mane redolent of vanilla and coconuts that swept across her perfectly round ass. Her almond eyes lit up from under a canopy of bangs and perfectly applied liquid eyeliner as I peeled open the crimson velvet curtain to the dressing room.

"Oh hey!" she belted over Madonna's "Vogue" rattling through the speakers outside the room. "How's it going?"

Red took a drag of her Virginia Slims and hugged me, standing naked and tall in six-inch, gold-spiked-heel stilettos. There was a garter on her upper thigh filled with dollar bills. Her lily-white skin was soft and covered in chicken skin, still damp from the shower stage, I assumed. She was paler than me, but I knew she was a fellow island girl. Kama'āina's greet strangers with a hug and kiss on the cheek—mainlanders, a friendly handshake.

"Hi!" I said with a shy smile during our quick embrace, sneaking a glance at her perfect body in the mirror. I witnessed it but still could not believe my eyes: a real-life Playboy-type beauty was welcoming me into her lair.

"I'm Red! There's an empty locker over here," she said. Red sniffed and wiped under her nose with the back of her hand, smiling at me while motioning to a spot next to her.

"Smoke?" she offered, fidgeting with half of a crinkled pack.

"I'm good, but thanks!" I replied. "Oh, and I'm Stephanie."

As soon as my words touched air, I regretted not accepting her cigarette. Who turns down a welcome smoke from a naked starlet?

Sitting on the stool next to her, I unpacked my bag, reminding myself I belonged there. I took a sip of my vodka cranberry and surveyed the space. Besides Red and me, the dressing room was empty and looked like what I imagined a college dorm room would be. But instead of textbooks and backpacks, it was saturated in neon Spandex, Aqua Net hairspray bottles, empty cocktail glasses, overflowing ashtrays, and tackle boxes.

The boxes covered most of the red linoleum countertops and were decorated with stickers, varying from Hello Kitty bunnies and surfing logos to Metallica and Mötley Crüe concert swag. I knew about the fishing boxes from my time at The Lollipop Lounge, as they were the perfect make-up cases for us performers. The tool kits were big enough to hold our beauty tricks yet travel-friendly and durable, with built-in handles and hard plastic shells. I placed mine on the counter in front of me.

"Allllllright, guys! Make some noise for Peeeeeaches!" the DJ announced as Madonna faded away and a wave of applause echoed in the distance. "Coming up next to the main stage, give it up for the Delectable Dallasssss!"

Aerosmith's "The Other Side" began playing, and I nodded to the beat, vibrating the mirrored walls.

Red pulled a miniature glass vial of white powder from her purse. "Like the devil in the deep blue seaaaaaaa," she sang. "Fucking Steven Tyler, man." She popped open and tilted the vial, tapping it gently on the counter. She used a VIP coupon card to chop the grainy powder and continued, "He's so fucking hot but ugly hot, you know?"

She was a master chef working the edges of the card, smoothing out the coke like a sexy samurai. She pulled a dollar bill from a laundry bag in her locker and began to roll it like a tiny carpet.

"These are dry," Red said, referring to the wet bills in her garter from the shower stage. "Want a bump?" She waved the rolled-up bill at me.

Take me to the other side.

I smiled yes and turned toward Red, gathering my hair to one side in preparation for my turn to snort. "Yes, please," I replied to her bump offer. My heart raced with anticipation, and Red threw me a knowing smirk that could only mean, "Of course you do."

She carefully divided the coke into two lines, both as thick as my pinky. Red snorted hers. Now it was my turn. After inhaling my portion, I tilted my head back, looking up my nostrils in the mirror.

"You're good," Red assured. She sized herself up in the mirror, adjusting her C-cups, pulling the front of her dress low enough to showcase her cleavage but high enough to cover her nipples.

"How about me, anything?" she asked. She sniffed and tilted her head back in front of me. I gave her a thumbs up.

I loved the secret society that came with cocaine. How we always had each other's backs, whether it be standing guard while the other prepared lines or confirming our faces were powder-free after snorting.

Since high school, I'd been a card-carrying party girl, so I welcomed the familiar camaraderie with anyone new. But something was different with Red. My seat at the cool kids' table felt magically reupholstered with tufted velvet cushions and Victorian legs dipped in gold.

This shit was strong.

"Wow, thanks, girl!" I chirped happily, kissing my new friend on the cheek, and opening my tackle box. As I applied my lipstick, the coke continued to work her magic. Waves of acceptance and happiness lapped against my self-doubt, and I felt completely present and valid.

I brushed some color on my lids before opening my eyes for a moment. Staring back at me was a kaleidoscope of blue and gold flecks surrounding my pupils, and I was hypnotized, drunk on debauchery.

This was it.

I was about to dance nude in one of the hottest strip clubs on the island. I was hanging with a real-life centerfold, dishing about which celebrity freaks we wanted to bang and doing lines of her rock star-quality blow.

You're gonna kill it!

My set was coming up, so I walked the floor in search of customers sitting at the tip stage who responded to my smile. Peaches was now dancing in the shower stage, which was in an actual Plexiglass stall with a jet steam runway at the edge that stretched half the length of the club.

Peaches looked like the girl-next-door and reminded me of Julia Roberts; only Peaches was prettier. She wore little make-up except for pink lip gloss and mascara, and her strawberry blonde waves looked amazing even when wet.

The DJ started playing "Wild Thing" by Tone Loc, and the jet-stream crowd went crazy. I made my way to the bar to get a better view of Peaches' show, and when I saw it, I was left in disbelief. Wholesome, lovely Peaches, with her natural beauty and demure smile. I just couldn't believe it.

"What the fuck?" I spoke into the air with my mouth wide open.

"Oh, that's Peaches!" the bartender shouted to anyone who asked. "She just had a baby! So...."

As Tone Loc sang, "Rollin' down the street, I saw this girl, and she was pumpin'," I started laughing nervously with a follow-up question.

"Did she choose this song?" I inquired in disbelief. I was mortified and officially freaked out, wondering what I had gotten myself into with this new club. Red saw the expression on my face and was laughing. The song continued, the crowd cheered even louder, and Peaches kept doing it: squeezing out breast milk into the crowd of men waving their money.

"Don't worry," Red said, putting a reassuring arm around my shoulder. "She's our only squirter."

Red wasn't the only goddess I met at Femme Nu.

High on E and coke, anything can happen, and it did at my 21st birthday party with Kiley. I'd kissed a girl before, but I always felt straight until I met Tara. She was in a goddess category of her own. How I handled this one very isolated event with this girl would navigate my heart's compass throughout my twenties and even to this day. Gay, straight, gender-neutral, asexual, or bisexual was never a problem with me. I simply loved nature's magical potion of intangible chemistry, no matter what flavor its desire.

However, I considered my first lip-gloss lock with Tara a defining moment in my sexuality. It was a karmic occasion, and

I still enjoy its ripple effects. Allowing myself to push through the walls built around who I thought I was to lay the foundation of who I truly am was a game-changer. So, if ever a goddess-like Tara leans in to kiss you in the bathroom of a strip bar where you both work, you pucker up. High, sober, comatose, straight, or not—just do it, even if you're not a stripper.

"Your set was amazing," my little Michelle Pfeiffer look-alike, circa 1989 from *The Fabulous Baker Boys* said, coming into the bathroom. "That last song? Fucking WOW." For someone so tiny, she had quite a mouth.

"Oh, thanks," I replied, startled by her entrance. I was flattered but annoyed she'd halted my plan to snort my perfectly set up cocaine-filled fingernail. After dancing on the main stage for about twenty minutes, I had just run in for a quick re-charge. Sweaty and flushed, I rambled on, "You think so? I wasn't too much? I just love that song. Have you seen the movie? They're both so hot." I rambled on, realizing she made me nervous.

"You are the fucking hot one," Tara interrupted, placing her delicate index finger over my lips.

A little embarrassed, I wondered just how I looked up there, crawling around completely naked on the stage, gyrating to the club lights blinking as "This City Never Sleeps" by the Eurythmics filled the room through the loudspeakers, the bass rattling every glass on the bar. Toward the end of the song, I did my usual maneuver: roll over on my back, push my hips up while grinding my pelvis like the ghosts of stripper's past were inside me. I guess it looked good. At that moment, I was picturing a young Mickey Rourke tracing Kim Basinger's belly button with an ice cube while he gently used an ivory-colored silk scarf to cover her eyes as "This City Never Sleeps" by the Eurythmics played in the background." (And yes, I agree. *Fifty Shades of Grey* will never hold a candle to *9 1/2 Weeks,* the origin of this song.)

"Oh, my God, girl, are you kidding? You were great!" Tara cheered.

"Thank you." I struggled to believe her, which is why I wanted more blow.

"You're welcome!" She continued as I visualized her shaking pom poms wearing a mini skirt and pigtails. "I've never seen anyone move to the music as you do. You're like velvet up there!" Tara purred.

Great. Now I wanted Ecstasy. I was high enough already but not rolling like Tara. I could tell she was marinating in her own vat of heaven, filled with excessive serotonin and dopamine fun, and it was breathtakingly palpable. "Wow. Thank you so much!" I said again like a grateful puppy. I was uncomfortable but simultaneously aware of her impeccable taste. If she had a *schlong*, I'd know what to do because my flirtation game with dudes was solid. But…wait, was she flirting?

I had never encountered such angelic beauty as this woman possessed. She looked far from my mental image of what I thought an angel would embody; she was beyond breathtaking. More than angelic and, at the same time, devilishly luscious. Plus, she smelled like bubble gum and trouble. When you think about it, it isn't fair. Devil or Angel. Pick a side.

With my spiked heels on, my six-foot frame towered over her pocket-sized sexy. So, even though I was on the receiving end of her advances, I still felt like the traditional dude. So…velvet, you say? What the fuck was happening?

"I just want to…." There she was, inches from my face whispering to me, telling me what she was about to do while gently tugging the back of my hair. I closed my eyes instinctively and tasted her lips. I discerned notes of strawberry sprinkled with sultry-flavored innocence. And bubblegum. Our tonsil hockey session lasted for half a song, but it melted my kneecaps to gelatin. That moldy, ciggy-smoke-filled cloud of the club, with the image of my goddess, is where I remained in my mind for the rest of the night.

I've since gone on to smooch a handful of other women, mostly to gain the attention of guys I wanted to bang. I've even slept with some gals, usually with other men involved. But as amazing as those experiences were, they didn't compare with Tara. Maybe it's because she was my first fancy new color in the larger crayon box I never knew I wanted. Either way, she helped me understand how beautiful it was to cast a wider net when it comes to physically connecting with someone. No longer do I prevent myself from following my gut instincts, feelings, and desires.

What a gift. What a kiss.

And what a fucking night.

CHAPTER SIXTEEN

# DON'T I KNOW YOU?

As the fourth and final song faded, The Weasel worked the crowd for applause. I was happy to see him again in this new club. I made my way off the center stage; the balls of my feet were throbbing. I couldn't wait to release my toes. Beads of sweat tickled the small of my back, and my cocaine-fueled heart thumping inside my chest served as a reminder I was alive.

I kicked off my shoes and prepared for my final set in the shower stage. That always drew in a big crowd. A nude chick, sudsing up, hair dripping wet, strutting up and down a jet-stream runway. What's not to love? The audience was seated directly on each side of the jet stream runway and always filled with the foot fetish gang. They'd sit just waiting for us to shower and walk that runway, the water shooting from the sides of the three-inch Plexiglas in front of them like a fetish sneeze guard.

The foot thing wasn't my jam, but who was I to judge? If they wanted to tip me for wiggling my toes over that railing, I wasn't going to kill their buzz. Still naked from performing earlier on the main stage, I grabbed the bills from my thigh, popped each garter off, and tossed them onto the floor. I covered my loot with my dress already near the shower stage. After exchanging non-verbal assurances that my stash was safely guarded by my favorite bouncer, Tuli, I stepped into the shower and turned on the water inside the clear stall.

Flashing a smile at the audience, I began to sponge up with the bottle of Prell shampoo provided by management. Prell gave this cool neon green glow under the black lights. We all looked like The Hulk, but with better hair, slimmer waists, bigger tits, hairless vaginas, or its hair shaved into landing strips.

Deana followed my set center stage. I loved her taste in music, which meant I had a blast performing my wet-n-wild show while she worked the main room. I threw her a smile from my corner, nodding in appreciation as Faith No More sang to us through the speakers. We both mouthed the words to the crowd:

"You want it all, but you can't have it. It's in your face, but you can't grab it!"

Teasing customers was a blast, even more so when the music was rad.

Receiving tips in the shower differed from collecting them on the main (dry) stage. Customers loved slapping the bills on our wet bodies. Never one to disappoint, I always bent over, standing on my tippy toes with my ass in the air, inviting spanks with every dollar bill. The guys took such pleasure in sneaking a touch. I took pleasure in their cash. Some girls hated the spank tips, but I didn't mind. As long as they stayed on my ass and didn't travel south of the border, I was cool.

As the final song began, my ass-slappers started to thin out, leaving me alone to survey the crowd. My hips swayed to "Fire Woman" by The Cult—another ass-kicking Deana choice. I was all smiles and in tune with the guitar riffs until my eyes landed on a familiar face from high school walking through the black velvet curtains.

Motherfucker.

My eyes bolted off the runway to the dressing room, and I thought of running, but my body was frozen. The smoky air served as equal parts drama and suspense. I inhaled deeply, seeking comfort, trying to control my breath as I watched him walk straight toward me. A man who was once the sixteen-year-old boy who pushed me further down my distorted yellow brick road was heading in my direction.

Pretending not to see him, I spun around, whipping my water-soaked hair like I was a backup dancer in a Poison video. My world was suddenly moving in slow motion. The butterflies inside my belly were choking on the reality of his presence.

"Hey! Hey!" he said, trying to grab my attention.

I knew he was talking to me, but I kept dancing.

"I know you. Christine, right?" He pushed.

Christine? Nobody called me that. Not in this world. Nobody even knew me as her. Here, I was Stephanie. Christine had long been buried in the chaos that was my childhood. Realizing he wasn't going to stop, I replied with the same volume as the thumping in my chest and the bass vibrating the walls. "Nope. My name is Stephanie." My voice was shaking, and my knees struggled to support me.

"No, it's Christine. I know you." His smirk was the same as I remembered.

"Wrong girl," I shot back without blinking.

Suddenly, I wished I really were The Hulk.

"No, you went to Kaiser High School!" he insisted.

With unabashed purpose, I lowered my body level to his eyes. I was still trembling, but there was no way he would win. Not this time. "I don't know what you're talking about. My name is Stephanie. You got the wrong girl." I looked him square in the face, determined to reclaim that night eight years before when I was a thirteen-year-old girl away at camp on the beach.

He shook his head and threw me that smirk. He knew I was full of shit. And I knew that he knew. And I didn't fucking care. It was my turn to ignore him. As I straightened up and walked away, The Weasel began to speak, and I was saved. I grabbed my towel from the floor, leaving my cash, shoes, and dress on the side-stage. I bolted past him through the crowd to the dressing room. He tried to block me, but I quickly navigated myself to safety.

In the dressing room, where the other girls were getting ready for their set, I pulled in a deep breath from the well of my pain and audibly began to let go. As I did, I started to tremble, and my soaked body shook in unison with my breath as I hyperventilated through my panic. I clutched onto my friend Alison, who was lining her lips in front of the mirror. I couldn't speak.

"What, honey? What is it?" Alison asked while holding me close and rubbing my back.

No words emerged.

"Did someone try to touch you?" Her tone was firm, and I could tell she was ready to kick someone's ass.

Shaking my head, I untangled from her embrace, opened my locker, and pulled out my purse. I couldn't stop gasping.

"Holy shit, Stephanie, what the fuck happened?" She went from pissed to deeply concerned.

I dumped some blow on the dressing room counter and snorted my angst.

Alison kept rubbing my back. "It's okay, sweetie," she reassured, shifting her voice to maternal.

Sitting naked on the stool with a towel draped around my hips, I wiped tears from my face and finally found the words.

"I saw him," I said firmly. My breath was heavy. I bent over and sniffed another line the size of my thumb.

"Who?" she asked, offering me a cocktail napkin as a tissue. I didn't know if it was for my nose or tears, so I used it for both.

"The motherfucker who raped me."

# CHAPTER SEVENTEEN

# BREAST INTENTIONS

Ah, tits. Nature's answer to "Where can I lay my face?" and a fascination since the beginning of time when Adam took one look at Eve and reportedly observed, "Nice apples."

Venerated in timeless pieces of art, women's breasts deserve all the accolades and spotlight that hold them in the highest regard and appreciation. What's more fun to play with than a woman's breasts? Whether you're a watermelon, a juicy apple, or cherry tomatoes type fan, we've all invested time at some point in our lives thinking about women's curves. And who wouldn't? I defy anyone to show me something as beautiful, natural, and customizable to each body type as the human breast. Those beautiful orbs with their magical powers to bestow the continuation of life, upon which a nourishing child depends. C'mon! (In my most passionate Gob Bluth from "Arrested Development" voice).

When I hit puberty, I was fixated on my chest. When was I going to get boobs? How big would they be? When would I need to wear a bra? I needed answers because boys seemed obsessed with breasts, and I was obsessed with boys. No matter how long I waited, I never grew past the cherry tomato stage. Life was a tad different when I started dancing in a bikini for cash tips at age nineteen, but I was still fixated on the opportunity to dance for money. Dancers with big racks got more tips, but mine never grew beyond a double AA. I started asking new questions. Should I get them done? If I did, would they be numb? Are implants safe? The shelf life of my internal dialogue about getting breast implants expired in roughly two years. In the stripper game circa 1989, boob jobs were often occupational side effects if you weren't already packing, so they were everywhere. Unlike celebrities forced to get veneers to upgrade their smile, use narcotics to keep their figures or get plastic surgery at the urging of the industry "pimps," no one makes strippers get their tits done (aside from manipulative partners). There's no lanky, cigar-smoking, greasy-haired dude doused in Drakkar Noir sitting on a stool in the back of the club promising treasures of diamonds and gold if we only go under the knife.

Our pimp was in our head, between our ears, telling us absurdities: if only we had bigger tits, we'd hustle more cash, find true love, be happy, or finally feel complete. I've kept that mantra on a memory loop for so long because it's my own story. My life experiences, however, didn't always mirror other strippers with natural chests who had no desire to go under the knife. So, it's truly a personal choice whether to get fun bags or not.

It was a packed Saturday night and also the 15th of the month. This meant that in addition to our local boys, random married guys and tourists, our trusty military buddies had fresh paychecks, and they were ready to party. I was surprised to see so many buzzcuts in the crowd. I soon learned more were being stationed on the island again after Iran-Iraq. It was nice to see their crazy asses admiring our naked asses again, especially since they'd soon be deployed to Desert Storm.

Our tiny dressing room was packed and overflowing almost to the floor outside our stripper sanctuary. It was insane—wall-to-wall customers with cash and horny energy to burn were on the other side of the door waiting for what we had to offer.

"Thanks," I exhaled as Red made space for me on her chair in the crowded dressing room. I had just rushed off the front tip stage and was dripping sweat. "Oh shit, sorry!" I continued, noticing I was sitting on her dress.

"It's all good, sister," she replied, popping up from our seat.

"I'm going back out." Red pulled two bushels of cash from her left and right garter (about $100 a thigh) and shoved it into her locker at lightning speed. She wanted to hop back on the tip stage as soon as possible. Stripping 101: Never leave a hot stage unless completely necessary to go to the bathroom or empty your garter to make room for more cash. If you'd been in the garter game for even a little while, you got used to mentally counting your cash on each thigh. I could tell just by feeling the cash how much was accumulating within five or six songs. Okay, that's about $50; this leg has $80....

"Still jammin' out there, yah?" Red asked as she unhooked her lime green neon lace bra, which complemented her striking mane of natural red hair brushing up against her tramp stamp of a plumeria flower. Most of us gals donned neon colors on stage because we looked like Electric Porno Barbies under the black lights. Stripper Barbie—sold from our catalog only. Free Shipping with Coupon Code: XXX.

The blacklights also highlighted our crispy, tan-lined bodies perfectly. A stripper's day job back then in Waikiki was to bake our skin in the tropical sun for hours while floating on cheap blow-up rafts from the corner ABC Store. Later, we'd compare tan lines over sunset cocktails at Duke's, a new outdoor restaurant and bar on the first floor of the Outrigger Waikiki Beach Hotel. Wearing our bikinis and *pareus* (pah-day-ohs), we danced to live music on the sand every Sunday. There's nothing as freeing and enjoyable as slamming a few libations while watching a fiery island sunset turn lavender against swaying palm trees, all the time dancing to amazing music and hanging out with your stripper-sisters before a money-making shift.

As soon as Red's neon underwire allowed her chest to breathe in our smokey, perfume-reeking dressing room, I happened to be looking in the mirror and standing naked in front of me was a woman with the most perfect rack I'd ever seen. At attention, nipples hard and her skin blindly pale against her sun-kissed shoulders, my eyes froze on Red's perfect curves. I instinctively looked down at my chest, feeling nine years old again.

Red saw the look on my face and offered me her fingernail full of blow. "Here, doll," she offered.

I smiled and took her by the wrist, guiding the tip of her pinky finger into my left nostril. "Thanks!" I replied after a quick sniff and an instinctive nose check in the mirror. Still mesmerized by Red's perfect figure, I said, barely hiding my veiled hostility, "And you're such a bitch, look at you!"

"Oh, baby, if you think these are real…" she shouted over the music thumping through the speakers.

I didn't respond. Kiley was finishing her set and the crowd's excitement was so palpable, it reached us in the dressing room. It was hard to hear anything but "Let's hear it for Ka-Ka-Ka-Kaaaayley!" The Weasel was saying in his best Stripper DJ voice.

"Fuuuuuck!" Kiley stormed into the room, shouting. "That Weasel dude never gets it right! It's Kye-Lee!" She lit a cigarette and sat down after pulling her purse out of her locker. "There goes his tip!" she griped.

Poor Weez. He was probably just as fucked up as we were and sitting alone in his DJ booth in his hypnotic state, looking at dozens of naked bodies grinding on the stages below him. It was a miracle he could even speak, let alone get our names right.

"Well, at least he doesn't call you "Steph-Horny!" I replied, laughing. It suddenly dawned on me that fucking him may have been a mistake.

"Wait, what?" I turned back around, looking at Red. It finally registered that she told me her boobs were fake.

"Those aren't real?" I asked with a gasp.

"No, girl, they're totally real and mine! Compliments of Doctor Lozada!" Red was laughing and shimmied closer to me. "Feel 'em! Try and find the scar. I dare you! LOZADA, man–he's the BEST!" Red boasted about her plastic surgeon like he was her hairdresser.

I placed my hands on Red's tits and tried to locate her incision scar. Most of the boob jobs I was used to seeing at The Lollipop were on the older dancers, and their scars were visible, lateral, and just under each breast or under their arms. It all depended on the surgeon's choice.

"I can't find your scar, and what the fuck, they're so soft!" I mused in amazement.

The other girls in the room chimed in, and my Boob Job Lesson had officially begun.

I learned that the newest way to implant fun bags was through the nipple. Most doctors traced the areola, and a small scar could be detected. But not Red's, or Jessica's, or Cherrie's. They were all Lozada's girls.

"Yeah, I should've gone to Lozada," Cassandra said. "Mine are so fucked up." Her boobs were nice, but you could tell they were fake in the same way you could see two balloons under your shirt. I touched them and lied.

"No, yours are fine," I reassured.

Cassandra rolled her eyes, took a shot of tequila, and snuffed out her cigarette. "Thanks, Steph. I'll see you bitches out there."

Cassandra opened the door, and more cheers and music thumped through the entryway. A couple of young dudes would always hang outside our dressing room door, trying to steal a peek whenever someone walked in or out.

"Save it for the stage!" Red shouted at our latest voyeurs and kicked the door shut in their faces with her spiked metal heel. (Clear heels weren't invented yet, so our shoes were strictly Leeds metal-heeled spikes with a strap around the ankle.) As usual, her timing was unplanned and perfectly synchronized to the beat of the music. The sound of the slam-door-kick hit a note that was spot-on with this Aerosmith gem of a song "Love in the Elevator."

I pulled out my blow dryer and started to style my hair, shouting over the noise, "I still can't believe all of your boobs aren't real!"

By now, my hands had gone five ladies deep, touching their tits, and terms like "400 cc's" and "The Snoopy Effect" (it's an over vs. under the muscle thing) were being thrown around by the girls who were happy to share their stories. I kept nodding, not having a clue about what they were saying.

"I need to see this doctor," I finally concluded. If I had the worst of what I saw and felt standing in front of me, I'd still look amazing.

"Yes!" Red said while lighting a cigarette and spitting out her gum. "I'll give you his number after this set! Oh my GOD, Stephanie, a set of double Ds on you would be perfect! Waddaya think, Velvet, 500 cc's? Okay, see 'ya!"

And she was off.

Velvet was a newcomer like me and another stripper I thought was organically endowed, but alas, she was a Lozada girl.

"Maybe 450?" Velvet asked. "I have 400; come feel."

Lucky Stripper Number Six.

That's the thing about women (maybe men, too?). You hang out naked together long enough, and it feels totally normal, not sexual at all.

Velvet was the polar opposite of Red. Her voice was as soft as she was quiet. She was a schoolteacher during the day and, like Peaches, started working the pole to make ends meet so she could feed her new baby. We were never close (she didn't party), but I always enjoyed her company. She was so reserved that I took her inviting me to feel her up as a personal honor.

Later that night, Red and I had a chance to talk shop, and I got the skinny on all of it. "CC" stands for cubic centimeter, and it's a way to measure liquid. Also, another tip, and yes, I did this: I bought a bag of birdseed, measured the cc's to various recommended sizes ranging from modest (200 cc's, depending on the natural size of breasts you have to work with) to 800 cc's (Dolly Parton territory), put them in a pair of pantyhose cut off at the ankle, then put the bags under my bra to see what the best size for my body type was.

I even tested out size effectiveness at the grocery store, shopping with three different sizes stuffed in my bra on different days within one week. I was sold the day I walked out of the grocery store with a full C-cup worth of birdseed in my bra, hoping not to have a

Tippi Hedren moment. Placebo effect? Perhaps. All I knew was, I wanted a pair, given how confident and balanced I felt.

Dr. Lozada greeted me with a warm smile, his kind eyes visible from behind his reading glasses. When he asked me to give him a written letter about why I wanted breast implants, I assumed it was because of my age at barely twenty-one. I was an exotic dancer and wanted to balance my figure with larger breasts. I was tired of looking like a boy and felt insecure among my coworkers. In other words, I told the truth. What I didn't tell him, if I'm being totally honest, was that I also wanted a distraction from my face. But I spared him my scar-face pity party even though he was a plastic surgeon. We were there to talk tits!

"Okay, you know this surgery will not be a tax write-off, yes?" His Puerto Rican accent was adorable, and I loved him from the moment he asked me to write the essay. His wife was the receptionist and his surgical nurse, so between them both, I knew I would be well taken care of.

"Yeah, I know," I replied. "But honestly, this will help so much with my self-esteem. I won't lie. I do think I'll make more money on stage with bigger boobs. I'm sure that comes with self-confidence, but this boost will come from my new figure."

"You are certain of this, that is for sure," Dr. Lozada answered.

I agreed, and we went forward with the procedure.

Did I flash my new fun bags like a maniac at The Wave as soon as I could? You're damn right I did. They served me well for thirteen years (I had them removed in my thirties), and I'm so happy I captured professional photos with them so I can look back on my Lozada curves all those years ago and smile.

# CHAPTER EIGHTEEN

# THE INVITATION

I walked on stage as if strutting on a fashion runway. Pockets of perfumed dancers blended with the familiar intoxicating aroma of dirty minds and money. The music carried me as the heavy baseline vibrated the speakers, each thump pulsing through the Plexiglass, tickling the bottom of my feet and traveling up my calves to the backs of my knees. The six-inch spiked metal rods under my heels tapped along to the music with each carefully balanced step.

Walking in these shoes took practice, but once I mastered it, I was transformed. Something about dancing on a four-foot-high stage in these shoes turned my attitude up a notch. I could kick any customer's ass with one push if they tried to cop a feel, but at the same time, never have I felt more delicate.

The second song began, and I made eye contact with an impeccably dressed Japanese businessman seated front and center on the tip stage. His salt-and-pepper hair was full of shiny gel and meticulously combed to one side. Like most of the businessmen from Japan, he was smoking.

He commanded the room with his presence, sitting confidently in his gray Armani suit. We locked eyes, and I strolled toward him, envisioning his introduction: "Miyagi. James Miyagi." Instead, he simply nodded and summoned me over with his eyes, not smiling.

Standing tall in my black spaghetti strap, baby doll mini dress, I slowly peeled off my panties, and he was now able to peek at my hairless moneymaker from his seat at the edge of the stage.

He liked what he saw. But his dollars weren't moving.

I smiled at him coyly and swayed my hips to the beat, turning around while pulling up my dress above my ass. I spread my legs for balance, tightened my stomach muscles and slowly bent over, my red acrylics tapping the stage and the flashing lights underfoot. Through my legs, my eyes focused on his stack of dollar bills next to his rum and Coke and pack of cigarettes. As I waited for him to tip me, I heard him speak and saw his moves. "Open! Open!" he commanded, making hand gestures like he was swimming the breaststroke.

What? I couldn't believe he was showing me how lovely it would be if I were to spread for him, as if bending over naked inches from his face wasn't quite enough. I nearly lost my balance but kept it together, still bent over and smiling—not moving, waiting for him to place a dollar bill in my garter.

"Open! Open!" He was insistent now, dragging from his cigarette, blowing smoke directly between my legs.

Jesus! What am I, a dog and pussy show? I wanted to be fluent in Japanese so I could ask him. Instead, I propped myself up, brushing off my head rush while still smiling and dancing. I pretended not to understand his request.

Still moving, no tipping, blank stare. Realizing he wasn't going to throw me any cash and that I was wasting time on him,

I grew more pissed off. For a second, before walking away, we had a stare down. He gave me the "elevator look," peering at my naked body from head to toe, stopping on the second floor. I suppose he was waiting for the doors to open.

Smiling through my defeat and anger, I glided away quickly to the opposite side of the stage, determined to rally, and make the most of my set.

Third and final song. My tongue felt like shriveled sandpaper. I was desperate for another drink, but I was a trouper and stayed on stage. I wasn't about to cut my set short because of a little cocaine cottonmouth.

For many reasons, Hawai'i is one of the most popular tourist destinations for Japanese travelers, and strip bars are often on the agenda. Tour buses would deliver flocks of these dudes along with their mistresses. These types of customers were the hardest to dance for (unless you liked cigarette smoke blown on your puss). I don't know if it's a power-trip/subservient thing, but you had to work for your tips with these guys. Commands of, "Bend over" and "Open! Open!" were common.

My next target was a younger Japanese tourist with shaggy hair, dressed in a Black Members Only jacket and khakis. Still shaking "Open, Open" out of my head, I positioned myself in front of him and began to flirt, lifting my dress.

"Hi!" I said plaintively, sounding like a drunken cheerleader. Mr. Khakis shot me a sly grin, and his fingers reached for his stack of bills.

I started to lip-synch with Guns N' Roses, and I felt a rush looking at his pile of money. Even though I was naked, I still worked my eyes into the program, bending down on my bare knees this time. We were now eye-to-eye. As Axl Rose belted out being taken down to Paradise City, I pulled him into mine and watched him tip me repeatedly. I lost count when the ones turned into twenties. Before long, my right thigh was full, and my new best friend started to occupy my left garter. Jackpot!

Just when I thought things couldn't get any better, he pulled out five-hundred-dollar bills and presented them on the stage in front of me. My face lit up, and he kept gazing into my eyes. Butterflies spun inside me as I mentally tallied up the total I would pull in on this set.

"*Dōmo arigatō*!" I said. "Thank you very much," was all I knew in Japanese, and I said it perfectly. I smiled and nodded, lifting my garter like I was opening my front door at Christmas. He didn't budge. I wondered: was he torturing me? Going to buy me champagne? Having a stroke?

Then I saw it. His hands made their way to his pile of money, and I braced myself for the largest cash tip of my career. My hand extended to accept his kind donation to the arts, but my bubble was suddenly burst with the reality of his touch.

"No, no, no, no, no." He gently wiped my hand away. I knew he didn't speak English by the sound of his accent, but he certainly knew the word "No."

I wasn't giving up. My knees began to shake with the weight of my body, and I clung to my patience. The power game between customer and dancer was always draining, but with half a grand in front of me, I covered any restlessness while throwing him my best puppy-dog eyes. He responded by reaching for his wallet, and I just about fell onto his lap.

More money? My thoughts quickly shifted from the idea of a grand in cash when I realized he'd pulled out his hotel room key.

"Oh!" My heart was racing. All I could do was flip my hair and caress my breasts as I processed the fact that I was being propositioned to fuck for cash. The song was ending, and his hundreds still weren't mine. I kept smiling, keeping my thumb under my garter, hoping he was kidding. However, I knew he wasn't. In a split second, I heard a voice inside me telling me to take the key. My next thought was: could I sleep with a customer for money? How did this become my life?

Like a flag breaking free in the wind, the sound of applause filled the room, and I knew my set was over. I pulled myself up, smiled and gave him my answer. "No, thank you." My fingers grazed the cash I did have on my thighs, and I was grateful for it.

I made no judgment of the other dancers who slept with customers for money. I was already using my body visually for tips. What difference did it make to take it a step further? In the end, I couldn't do it. If I had, I would have lost the ability to protect myself from the most dangerous parts of me. The parts that always touched the wall under the "Wet Paint" sign, that always swallowed pills from random strangers at a party and then asked, "What did I just take?" that snorted mountains of cocaine until dawn but, when asked to try heroin, was offended. That shit'll kill ya (sniff)! Something in me always pulled back from the ultimate dive over the cliff. There would be no turning back if I'd lifted the veil and took customers home with me.

Later that year, I did take a customer home, but it was on my terms. No money was exchanged. I felt more in control that way. After I kicked him out with cab fare, I plopped back into bed, watching the pink tropical morning clouds peek through the glass louvers down the hall of my studio apartment.

What a waste, I thought. The sex? Mediocre, at best. Maybe I should have charged him after all.

# CHAPTER NINETEEN

# THE CUSTOMER IS ALWAYS TRITE

There are many misnomers about what strip clubs are. A place of ill repute, a red-light district. It's neither. It's a business like any other. Strippers dance for myriad of reasons: the mother who needs to feed her child, the occasional student to pay for their education, and some lost but harmless souls. The customer's reason for coming is also varied.

Strip club customers are like used cars in auto malls. There's always a variety of inventory, and each wants you to test ride them. (Thanks, I'll be here all week.) The majority of this hodgepodge are harmless horny dudes or lonely men who need to feel belonging. Not surprisingly, I describe my old stripper-self the same way. Perhaps both ends of the stage simply wanted an escape. An escape from war, a nagging wife, an unfair boss, or just sheer entertainment for those not burdened by society's duplicitous morals.

Always making for an interesting adventure, the different characters in the audience never disappoint. Though they varied in looks, career, style and needs, it was easy to categorize the kinds of people who frequented strip clubs. It pays to know who 'who' is because if you're dancing for tips, they're what a stripper lives on. No tips and life could be messy, so picking your target is crucial.

A stripper's job is to separate the customer from their money, hoping it lands in their garter belt or comes from the quadrupled marked-up bottles of libations served, as the proceeds are shared with the house 50/50. Knowing your customer can help you make bank, i.e., make your monthly quota and not worry about paying bills. The most I've raked in on a night was around $2,000, and the amount of money I made determined how often I went to the club to work. Even in the 90s the price of living in paradise was not cheap, so I made it my business to know my customers and took to the stage accordingly. Allow me to paint you a picture of just a few of our clients.

## The College Guy

This type of customer is the classic example of a wolf in sheep's clothing. On second thought, they were more like boys in men's clothing. As a novice back in the day, I'd think, "He's young and clean-cut," so I would rest easy working my way up to them on the stage. Once positioned and face-to-face with the darlin' scholars, I'd smile, dance a little, and lift my garter for them to place a tip. More often than not, College Guy smiled back, kept staring at my ta-tas but made no attempt to fetch his wallet.

At this moment, every stripper realizes that College Guy is a euphemism for Poor Guy—not to be confused with Cheap Guy who is much lower on the stripper tolerance scale. Barely able to afford the cover charge to the club, College Guys are there for free visuals.

If College Guy really liked you, and if you had the patience or were just a glutton for punishment, you could get a dollar bill from him after about four songs (roughly 20 minutes). It was a lot of work for a buck, but you had to respect a guy for squeezing in midterms with strip bars, not to mention fitting in a stripper tip on a ramen noodle budget.

## Drug Dealer Dude

Steadfastly calm and rarely perched directly under the lights on the stage, Drug Dealer Dude is a subtle and loyal fixture within the walls of stripper debauchery. Although neatly tucked in the shadows, spotting him in the club is never difficult. D3 is not there to ogle your goodies; he's there for his clientele. Drug Dealer Dudes are usually surrounded by a bevy of beauties donning not much more than a G-string and a smile. Count me in as one of the gals in line to schmooze for some mind-altering merchandise.

In nineties Waikiki, the hot substances in the skin trade were cocaine and Ecstasy (now called "Molly"). Occasionally, you'd smell pot backstage, but the real action was in pills and powder.

Always the consummate salesman, Drug Dealer Dude was a blast to hang out with but not the greatest customer. Unless he had a crush on one of the girls or was lost in a girlfriend fantasy, they could get more than a peek as some gals banged them for free drugs. Drug Dealer Dude never really tipped. So, you learned to put your earning potential energy elsewhere unless you needed money to cop drugs if you're not willing to sleep with D3.

## Mr. Married

Here's a group who always made me feel like I was on the witness stand in the proverbial Justifying My Life trial. These are often successful men looking for a diversion. The 'Wall Street' corporate types discussing stocks between dances. They're more there for the power trips with us gals than donating to the arts via dollar bills. And let's not forget about the glamor drug—cocaine. Nearly all the Mr. Marrieds were hopped up on blow, which was obvious to me because I was right there with them, secretly partying with whoever else was high with me. More secret society stuff.

But Mr. Married was never cool. It's safe to assume dancing for wedding rings wasn't my favorite pastime. It was a constant reminder that I was a cliché. I'm not sure if it's because Mr. Married had kids of their own, and they'd feel sorry for me, but this group of men always made me feel judged.

Always.

"What does your dad think about your doing this?" he'd ask.

"I don't have a dad. He left when I was two." What's my stage name? "Stripper Cliché."

"Okay, then how does your mother feel about you, stripping?" he'd try again.

Without missing a beat, I'd reach over to his left hand and gaze into his eyes as my fingers touched his ring. "I don't know. How does your wife feel about your being at a strip bar?"

Silence.

I usually received that uncomfortable touché look, and the subject was immediately dropped.

They were big enough tippers…kind of like tipping the waiter for a drink. So, like it or not, if you need to make bank, you danced for Mr. Married.

## Japanese Tourist

Most of the tour groups came in big numbers. Positioned quietly beside their men, the petite mistresses would sit and smile, looking out of place and bored. In giving them attention, I realized I could get them to tip me if I simply made the ladies feel present.

Stripping for their mistresses was different from tolerating the men. I preferred it. Instead of being provocative, which made them uneasy, I created a little game. I took one of the bills piled in the stack in front of them, folded it and placed it in their hands. I then took my breasts and scooped the bill up with my cleavage right out of their fingers.

They all giggled while covering their mouth. They loved being a part of the show rather than just sitting there and watching their men enjoy it.

I taught each mistress at the tip stage how to "high-five" with their hands and made a point to clap and cheer each time they tipped me. Before long, those gals were having a blast, waving their dollars, eager to play the booby-tipping, high-five game. I not only provided some erotic fun to their evening, but I also doubled my money.

**The Girlfriend**

Now and then, a couple (gay or straight) would come into the bar and, after some cocktails, venture up to the tip stage for a closer look. I don't know about the lesbian tribe, but one of the most popular fantasies of straight dudes is to watch two hot chicks bump and grind. I always had fun playing the part. I felt comfortable, respected, and adored when dancing for a woman. Women are competitive by nature, so it's no surprise I considered their tips to be one of my highest compliments. I always wished more couples had come into the club. I think it's a blast if both parties respect one another's boundaries.

**Military Boys**

Oʻahu is a military stomping ground, with every service base and reserve station on the island within an approximate 50-mile radius. You'd find your share of servicemen spending their hard-earned cash at the strip bars on any given day. Payday for them was always the 1st and 15th of the month, so you knew to work a double shift on those days if you wanted to make bank.

Outside of some isolated drunken nights involving fistfights and police arrests (usually when they were in large groups), military boys brought out the gratitude in me. They drank impressively and tipped even better if they took a fancy to you. However, you also had to be careful not to break their young, starry-eyed hearts.

# CHAPTER TWENTY

# SISTERHOOD

In the "underworld," you meet many memorable people. Some of the most interesting were the women I met dancing. As I said earlier, women danced for various reasons: their survival, their education, etc. However, some danced because they could or just out of plain curiosity. Michelle was one of the curious ones, a demure, corkscrew-curled brunette who worked as a recurring Victoria's Secret Catalog model. It puzzled me why she wanted to dance in a nude strip club. Originally from Seattle, Michelle was a natural beauty with a button nose and sweeping lashes perfectly framing her crystal blue eyes. She wasn't planning to be a regular because she was passing through Waikiki en route to New York, her hometown after working in Sydney for an Australian Vogue cover shoot. For some reason, Michelle always wanted to know what it was like to be an exotic dancer, as much as I could pretend, I was a Fosse dancer on the strip stage of Waikiki. So, with her layover, she thought fuck it and was ready to satisfy her curiosity. That night, I was sharing the stage with Michelle.

"Hi, I'm Stephanie," I offered as soon as she walked into the dressing room. I could instantly tell she was not a stripping pro like us. She was such a knockout, so, naturally, I needed answers.

"Oh hey," she answered, barely looking me in the eye. She was wearing a long, flowery Elaine-from-Seinfeld dress with sexy spiked heels and white lace thigh highs peeking at the room from underneath. Michelle was more than a little apprehensive once she learned from one of the other gals that Hawai'i was the only all-nude stripper state in the country that served alcohol.

"You dance nude? No bottoms?" Michelle sounded like a five-year-old asking if she had to eat her broccoli.

We were paired up for the next set, so I took the opportunity to chill her out before we walked onto the stage. Hugging her reassuringly, I held her hand and told her she didn't have to do anything she didn't want to do. "None of us will judge you if you bag this set."

"No, I'm okay, thanks," she assured, nodding, and squeezing my palm.

"Hey, we're all sisters here," I replied, happy to provide some organic aloha her way, even if she was only in town for a couple of days.

We shared a three-song set, and each time we passed one another, I threw her a smile, and she nodded, her lips curved, showing me her warm smile. Her body was breathtaking. Lean and strong, her curved back swayed as she moved, so deep it almost seemed an unnatural arch. She moved like the tides during a full moon, but this was sexier.

The final song of our time on stage together was U2's "So Cruel" from their 1991 album, *Achtung Baby*. I was obsessed. Bono and I, well, we had our imaginary thing, so I was in pure bliss up on that stage, but his lyrics…man, how did my fantasy lover know me so well?

Michelle noticed a couple of teardrops escape down my face as I bent over to receive a tip. Although I loved the song, tears always fell as soon as I heard the lyrics.

Michelle knew I was fine. I was fine but still triggered, thinking love would never be anything to me other than violent and desperate. It's a bummer to feel alone and blue, but to be naked on stage while drugging through the darkness? Well, sometimes the tears just fall.

After our set and back in the dressing room, the two of us rested our feet and shared stories of the Pacific Northwest and the Hawaiian Islands, what we hated, and boys we loved who broke our hearts, and her favorite restaurant in New York.

"I've never been to New...," I started to say.

"He's probably not ever gonna change, you know," Michelle interrupted. She was so sweet and pretty sharp in picking up how that final song got to me there on stage.

"Yeah," I nodded. "I know." Not an ounce of bitterness or victimization in my voice, which surprised me. "Thanks."

It was true. I'd long since gotten over Robert. Our customized chaos and toxic pairing had been an aphrodisiac fueled by co-dependency and addiction, and it had gotten old, fast. We'd been the stale pretzels at the bottom of the plastic container behind the bar and weren't ready to throw them away. Yet, I kept expecting him to fill the bowl. My choice of men didn't improve for a while, even after our sister talk.

Decades later, as I listen to this same old song, I feel the same tickle in my nose. But my tears are no longer numb. They're filled with joy in knowing myself and feeling free from the overwhelming need for validation from anyone to feel loved. Tears still trickle down my face, but today, instead of falling onto a stripper stage, they touch the keyboard of my laptop. When this happens, I think of what I told Michelle all those years ago, "You don't have to do anything you don't want to do, and no one will judge you if you walk away."

Self-worth may take a long way to find us, but it reminds us we are worthy of so much more when it finally does.

\*         \*         \*

Show me a broad who had her shit together at age eighteen, was fearless and free, smoked Marlboro Reds, and tooled around in her red Miata like she owned the streets of Waikiki, and I'll give you Layla. She knew what she was worth from day one and danced because she could. If you lived in Waikiki in the early to mid-nineties, we were inseparable. Layla and I together were a dream team.

When we joined forces, the Layla and Steph combination was fierce. She was younger, petite, and a dark-haired vixen with traces of Māori in her veins (she has family ties in New Zealand). Layla was a blast to hang with, so unbelievably beautiful, a rebel who was clueless about her magnetic powers. Her curly, chestnut locks were wild, grazing her bra hooks down her back, and her deep brown eyes sparkled with every laugh, which were many. Layla was both passionate and adventurous. Her street cred went up a notch (or ten) with me after she shared news of her love affair with a member of the band, The Red Hot Chili Peppers.

"Wait, WHAT?" I was instantly tingling with a thirst for more of the story. "Really, you hooked up with him?"

"I mean, yeah, we kind of hooked up when he was here getting sober," Layla dropped casually as she was putting on her makeup in the dressing room. Her lover boy was a partier, too, and started his journey down his yellow brick road in his early teens, just like us.

"We used to take showers together, and he'd sing to me." Layla continued.

"This was around when their album *"Blood Sugar Sex Magik"* came out," she added.

"Oh my God, and?" I couldn't' contain my excitement. Layla was amused by my reaction because she couldn't see what I saw. She knew a Rock Star I was lusting after. I was dying.

"Go on," I urged. I had no idea what I wanted to hear, but this was as close as I'd come to knowing him personally.

Working in the clubs through the years, I met a few A+ celebrities who'd stop by the club while in town filming for a movie. Movie stars were a little more laid back and nestled in VIP rooms, which was the opposite of sports figures who were more outgoing. These dudes tended to order never-ending bottles of champagne. As dancers, we cashed in, as the price of booze was split between us and the club 50/50. You bet we plied it on, especially since the markup was so high.

One night, some of players from The Lakers, popped into the club, and I hung with them. These encounters were thrilling. I also met a well know British singer once in the upstairs "VIP Room" at The Wave. However, none could hold a candle to my crush on Layla's man. I'd have given up any of those experiences for one night with him. At least now, I was living vicariously through Layla, who never said a bad word about the man. Just as I suspected, she confirmed my assumption that he was a true romantic and a kind human being.

I reunited with Layla some twenty-plus years later and still introduce her to people as my friend who fooled around with the singer from RHCP. She rolls her eyes in friendly humility and honest perplexity because she still can't understand my excitement, even all these years later. I usually follow up with "I promise to stop...," and we share a laugh, knowing full well I'm never going to stop bragging about my sorority sister who got to be naked with my dream crush back in the day.

\*       \*       \*

Navigating six-inch heels on stage with smoke in your face takes practice. Sporting a smile while dancing to "Me So Horny" in those heels requires a cocktail. One of the unique challenges I faced during my career as a stripper was pretending to like certain types of music. It's like suffering through a bad date when you realize something isn't your taste but smile politely and muddle through.

A typical Saturday night set on the main stage was shared with three other women, each providing the DJ with very specific song requests. I was always the Enigma or Nine Inch Nails girl with an occasional PJ Harvey thrown in for good measure. Pair that with the Bel Biv DeVoe and Naughty by Nature gals, and let the squabbling ensue. It's not that I didn't appreciate a little Ice Cube with my INXS; I just didn't feel sexy dancing on stage with them. I always felt like an extra on MTV's *Beach House*.

My taste in music was a bit more edgy and alternative than what was played on mainstream radio. In classic narcissistic fashion, I took full credit for introducing the local masses to PJ Harvey's "Down by the Water." The song made absolutely no sense to me at the time, but dancing to it made me feel sexy as hell. My style on stage was ALL Bob Fosse-inspired, so the percussions were the perfect backdrop for the wannabe Broadway dancer in me.

Some may be surprised to learn that a few of us strippers cared about what music we danced to. I can't speak for the gals today, but most of us were known for our performance sets back in my day (it's official, I'm old).

Mind you, the American Ballet Theatre wasn't banging down the door; but the costumes and choreography were damn amazing. I used to sit in awe with my twenty-one-year-old eyes popping in wonder at such beautiful women and their talent. Greta and Loretta, a couple of the more seasoned gals in their late twenties, come to mind.

Greta was a petite but solid blonde who walked on stage donning an old granny mask, baggy clothes, and a cane while Jan and Dean's "Little Old Lady from Pasadena" blasted through the speakers. The audience would cheer in excitement mid-song as Greta peeled off her mask, revealing her stunning face. The raucous applause continued as the body of a goddess emerged from the granny clothes, and money rolled up in balls would literally fly onto the stage as men stood in awe. Greta was the embodiment of classic blonde beauty with a killer physique. Think Brigitte Bardot meets Jessica Biel.

Loretta, a raven-haired vixen from the island of Kaua'i (and a February 1983 Penthouse Pet of the Month), was another showstopper. She was a Feature Dancer performing just a couple times a year. The buzz in the air surrounding her arrival resulted in the club being filled to capacity. I don't know if Loretta invented chair show choreography, but she kicked serious ass with it on stage. I remember being star-struck by this exotic beauty who loved her weed and was never shy about it. If the smell of a burning joint bothered you, you knew not to hang out in the dressing room when Loretta was in town. I was mesmerized each time I watched her show. In addition to Loretta's flawless ivory skin and thick wavy hair (think Dita Von Teese), the oversized tattoo on her left thigh drew my gaze. I remember thinking only someone really hot could get away with a tattoo that large on their thigh. She made it work. Few women could pull off flawless with half their leg marked in ink in 1990. One night in Hernando's Hideaway, some random guy came up to me asking if I had a large tattoo on my left thigh. I almost blew him at the bar for the compliment.

Stripping is the ultimate sales job on and off the stage, and I was one talented bitch. The dressing room walls were shaking with each thump of the baseline. After a quick garter and G-string check in the mirror (assuring everything was in its place), I pulled open the door and headed for the stage.

Strolling past the customers, my eyes adjusted to the smoky darkness while my brain played catch-up to the sudden shift in the music's volume. The audience would never know I wasn't down with the DJs song choice because I worked the problem like every good sales pro.

I navigated my towering stilettos onto the neon flashing Plexiglas. My hips curved around each thumping beat, and my smile served as a beautiful mask of my internal disdain. I was not a fan of the Eighties rap group 2 Live Crew, but no one would ever know. After the performance I gave, the crowd really did think, "Me so horny, me love you long time."

"God, you're such a bitch—you have zero cellulite," Shayla whined as she spanked my ass at the bar. "Great set, doll." She sized up my body with her hypnotic gaze. "I hate you." Her energy was wickedly salacious.

"What?" I laughed off Shayla's digs in between deep breaths, still recovering from my Oscar-winning performance on stage. I played along, pretending to understand. "Oh right, thanks!"

Strippers are sorority sisters without midterms. Instead of libraries and lecture halls, our campuses are smoky bars with 2-for-1 shot nights, yoked-up bouncers, and horny DJs with drug connections.

But no matter the layout, we had each other's backs—and never missed a chance to throw out a good dig in the name of envy. Shayla was in her late twenties and carried faint traces of cellulite around her hips which made her self-conscious. But to me, she was a stone-cold fox.

Later that night, alone in my apartment, I broke out my mental measuring tape. Standing naked in front of the mirror,

I inspected each body part. It was true. Unlike my face, my 22-year-old body was casualty-free, spared from the damage of the rare blood disease I was born with that left my face covered in deep crater-like acne scars.

My stomach was toned and flat, my Lozada C-cups were perky, and my ass was solid and plump. I knew my body was stripper-worthy, so why didn't I feel beautiful?

On the heels of being labeled Krueger in high school, being envied was foreign to me. Anyone looking at me through a complimentary lens immediately tossed me into a sea of uncharted territory. I was desperate to catch Shayla's life raft that night in the club, but there were too many leaks in my self-esteem to believe I could.

When you're young and peppered with wisdom from anyone older, it serves up nothing but reminders that we still have time. The delicious irony is, nobody in their twenties truly understands the concept of youth being on their side until it's gone.

I'd been stripping for nearly five years, and thanks to people like Shayla, I was starting to feel something new seeping into my consciousness. I was still in the thick of my underground lifestyle with no ending in sight. But bleeding through the cracks were rays of light, patches of radiance I began to feel when accepting compliments like the one Shayla tossed out with veiled snark. Stephanie may be a 'bitch' for not appreciating her perfect ass at the time, but Christine was there to balance the vibe. Both these women had each other's backs, and for the first time in her life, she knew they were both fucking awesome.

These were just a few of the many women from my dancing days who helped my inner goddess emerge purely by inspiration. They were all my stripper sisters, brave warriors in the trenches of life, incredibly talented and so wonderfully unique.

Eating sand at the beach,
and always eating my feelings.

The Spirit of '76!

Ah, the 'tween years. Before boys, braces,
and the boulders on my face started forming.
(And haircare products, apparently.)

Surfer Girl with just a hint
of Kristy McNichol in Little
Darlings.

May Day is Lei Day in Hawaiʻi. My grandmother, Winnie, marked an X under me dancing hula in our seventies school's May Day celebration.

After braces I tried piano lessons one summer but because of my dyslexia (unknown at the time), I quit in frustration trying to read the notes.

My Drama Queen poses, however, remained flawless.

WHITE LADY

I AM ATTACHED TO A FEELING
I NO LONGER ENJOY -

EVERYTHING IS SO INTENSE,
WHEN YOU USE IT AS A TOY.

I AM SINKING -
  YET FLYING
AT AN UNCONTROLLABLE SPEED..
I AM LAUGHING -
  AS I AM CRYING
ITS NOT A WANT,
BUT A NEED.

SOMEONE GIVE ME STRENGTH
TO STOP THIS DRUG AS A WHOLE -
STOP IT FROM GOING INTO ME,
CORRODING MY SOUL.

A Poem I Wrote - Late eighties.

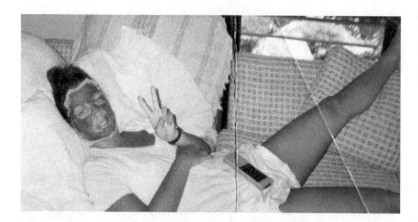

Post full-face dermabrasion (under full anesthetic), feeling zero pain and 100% in love with being high on Demerol. My face was wrapped in gauze and covered in iodine. I promised the surgeon I would not look in the mirror, but of course I did. And the salt in my tears burned as they fell down my cheeks.

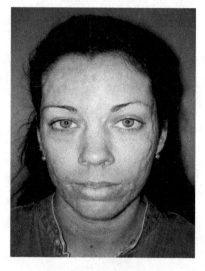

Pre-op photo for scar excision surgery. You can see how deep the crater-like scars were, especially near my left eye. I promise, it's not a mug shot.

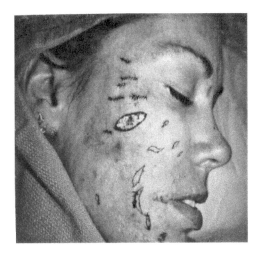

Scar excision surgery. The surgeon circled, with ink, which crater-like scars would be removed. He cut around the holes and stitched them up, one by one. I was awake and dreaming of being anywhere else.

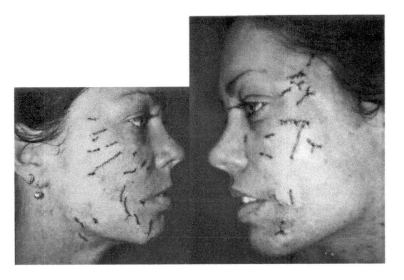

Post-op profile photo after scar excision surgery. The procedure took over three hours and I was awake on local anesthetic. A numbing agent was injected into my face before each slice of skin was removed.

North Shore of Oʻahu dancing hula for a friend's wedding
and striking a pose at Makapuʻu Beach Park.

1987 and 19 years old. Before my first night working
The Lollipop Lounge—ready to take a shot of tequila for courage.

Working my Elaine from Seinfeld dress at my sister Laurie's college graduation. Five hours later, I was on stage at work.

Days were spent in Waikiki Beach sailing on local catamarans.

Liquor Commission Card stamped with the word:
EXOTIC: License to strip.

I'm nineteen; late eighties. My first
night working at The Lollipop Lounge.

Working on my tan lines and posing with a friend's two parakeets
in front of The Hilton Hawaiian Village.

Many of my friends and co-workers in the clubs were dancing in Tokyo, and this is my own audition Polaroid. Nothing screams "Tokyo Stripper" like a bedazzled rhinestone G-string.

Halloween in the late eighties, waitressing (and dancing) at The Lollipop Lounge in Waikiki.

Dressing room at The Lollipop Lounge, 1987.
I love my Madonna "Desperately Seeking Susan" boots.

Halloween, early nineties. 6:00 am
after party, high on MDMA
and cocaine.

Wearing Robert's Chippendales emcee fedora, holding a Budweiser beer
can and cigarette in my left Swatch Watch-wearing hand.
My first apartment, which was a three-story walkup where Robert
and I lived. We shared that mattress on the floor.

Christine Macdonald - 2022

*I'm such a work-in-progress, I should wear orange cones for earrings.*
                                                              *- C. Macdonald*

# CHAPTER TWENTY-ONE

# THE OTHER SUNSET STRIP

After years of the same routine, things became stale; the scene got old. Waikiki is small, and my yearning for worlds outside of Honolulu became top of mind when I met Michela who further piqued my curiosity. A five-foot, ten-inch glamazonian from San Francisco, she had migrated south for the stripping scene in L.A. because she declared, "You don't have The Whisky or The Veil up north." Michela had taken a week off from her usual club on Sunset Boulevard in California to hang out in Waikiki and began working a couple of nights at my club to pay for the trip back home. As we shared tales of our stripping lives, I had no idea what she was talking about, but the Los Angeles vibe was a trip. It sounded like Waikiki on steroids.

It all sounded exciting as she talked about The Rainbow, The Roxy, and Whisky a Go-Go, the hot bars on Sunset Boulevard and The Seventh Veil, the club where she stripped. It was even more so when she told me she'd met and partied with band members from Mötley Crüe and Poison. I'd first learned of the infamous Seventh Veil strip bar through Mötley Crüe's music video, "Girls, Girls, Girls." It'd become a stripping anthem at The Lollipop. As soon as it came on, all of us dancers used to hop on stage promoting The Goods. By the end of Michela's stories, I was dying to check out her world on the mainland.

I was awakened by the captain's voice. He instructed the rest of the passengers on the plane to buckle up and lift our tray tables back to their original, upright position. By the time he announced the weather forecast over the extra-loud-when-hungover speaker, I was fully awake. I immediately craved a stiff cocktail and fat line. Knowing I'd be partying within the hour, I chilled out and sat up in my seat. Lifting my window shade slowly, like a six-year-old sneaking a peek through the seam of a poorly wrapped present, I stared.

There it was. Los Angeles: The City of Angels in all her glory. At last, we'd meet. The window shade wasn't the bright lights of Broadway, and there were no Fosse dancers in sight, but I didn't care. This was Hollywood! Metropolis to us dreamers. This was the land of the Stars. Movie stars: Hepburn, Astaire, Monroe. I couldn't stop smiling: Elvis, Liz, Katherine…Classic. I was finally here and soon to be in the thick of it.

The plane taxied to our gate, and I wondered if my fellow passengers could hear my heart thumping with glee. I donned my Ray-Bans, played it cool, and hoped my friend Michela had listened to my answering machine message reminding her to set her alarm clock and write down my arrival gate number.

As soon as I exited, my anxiety disappeared as I heard Michela's unmistakable voice. When I spun around and saw what she was carrying, I laughed and turned off my Walkman.

"Stephanie!" Her double Ds were bouncing out of her crop top, and she was holding a handmade cardboard sign full of glitter and DayGlo letters that spelled out, "Welcome, Bitch!"

Her frizzy auburn mane was swept up with a velvet leopard scrunchie, and it looked like she was wearing last night's makeup.

A small part of me was embarrassed, but since I saw Michela as 'ohana, I didn't give a fuck what people thought. The stares prompted my 'move along, people, nothing to see here' response, but I get why they were staring. We were a hot mess, dressed like porn stars and smelled of Aqua Net and Jean Nate, wafting in a smoke-filled cigarette cloud of debauchery and bad decisions. It's the neon-laced potpourri of mixed messages we strippers send into the universe. We dress like we're on display, but when disrespected, we lash out. For some strippers, insecurity and self-protection are fingers laced together, no matter how much the rings may clash.

As soon as we locked eyes, I exhaled and hurried over to her. We squealed like excited schoolgirls, annoying everyone around us even more.

"You bitch! How are you?" she screamed in my ear way louder than Axl Rose could.

"I'm good," I replied, taking her hand, and walking us away from the crowd. "I slept most of the way, and I'm ready, girlie. How are you?"

Hawai'i to Los Angeles is a five-and-a-half-hour flight. I was thrilled to have zonked out for most of it, and I was ready to party.

"Better now," Michela whispered in my ear, taking my other hand, gifting me a folded-up magazine corner full of cocaine. With the same precision cheating classmates have while passing test answers back-and-forth under their desks, we made the exchange, and I headed toward the bathroom.

You never know how life will play out. We'd met only a month before at Femme Nu while on stage. There's something in general about strippers who connect. We're sorority sisters, each other's cheerleaders rolled in one. If one person's damage matches yours, you're instant best friends. Trauma Bonding 101: hanging with someone as fucked up as you are, life becomes less normal when chilling with others who aren't like you. Michela was a rock star. Most of the time, anyway. But I was privy to her flip side. She was more fucked up than most of us who found The Pole. We clicked immediately because I was just as emotionally broken, which is why I saw pieces of her that no one else could. With each other, we felt normal.

When Michela was dolled up, my frizzy-haired friend owned the stage, putting the audience in a sexual trance with her perfectly tanned and toned body and wicked smile, like a punk rock Liz Taylor. She'd throw you a look from the stage, making you feel you were in on the joke with no idea of what was so funny while effortlessly making the crowd want to bang her.

We hung out in the dressing room, at the bar while working, after work in the clubs, and at each other's apartments in the early morning hours, snorting blow and slicing emotional veins with each passing hour. When damage finds damage, there's no magical fix. Accepting our flaws together made us feel less alone.

Like Michela, I had to work at least a couple of nights to earn enough cash for my airfare back home to Hawai'i. It didn't take long to find myself auditioning at The Seventh Veil, a topless club on Sunset Boulevard. Topless only wasn't my usual jam, but I had to make it work with just my tits. It was The Seventh Veil!

"You audition? You come with me," the owner commanded. His name was Sam. Traces of Drakkar Noir and body odor left sensory landmines in his path. Mr. Noir and I went into his office where another Middle Eastern man was smoking a cigar. They spoke in Farsi and then English.

"Your top, take off," they ordered.

I smiled nervously and obliged. I knew many of the bars with strippers on the mainland were topless, so I was glad for Dr. Lozada's C-cups.

"Turn around," they said next.

I did, but wondered, Did Katherine Hepburn have to do this? "You pick one song. You go next," Sam said after blowing cigar smoke toward me.

I came out of the office and called Michela into the dressing room. It was early enough in the evening that only a handful of girls were there, and I could tell they weren't down with some nude dancer infiltrating their space. I didn't give a shit. I was only there for the cash.

As The Cure's "Lullaby" began to bleed through the speakers, I had to remember not to take my bottoms off. I just needed to make my plane fare home in a week or so, so I wasn't sweating a long-term gig. I could see small groups of strippers talking about me, but I stayed on my game. Stripper hierarchy.

A couple of nights later, after our shift, Michela insisted we go to a Hollywood party before I headed back to Hawai'i. I'd already hit the Rainbow (where Nicholas Cage refused an autograph) and The Whisky, so why not a stranger's party? Besides, I'd yet to see the glitz and glamour of the city I'd heard so much about. All I'd experienced so far were homeless junkies and filthy sidewalks covered with the lives of showbiz hopefuls.

We arrived at the party, and within the hour, I was riding on the back of a motorcycle with Marco, a fresh-faced Italian, twenty-something soap actor hoping to cross over to the silver screen. We tooled around town and ended up having sex on the balcony of his condo. It was fun, and I had a great time, but to be honest, I was bummed, mostly feeling bad for him. Marco didn't possess the one thing we gals (and some boys) enjoy: a decent-sized piece. By the end of the night, I should have earned my own Hollywood Boulevard star for the way I screamed and moaned. Call it codependent tendencies, but I wanted him to feel good, so I embellished a little.

Weeks later, after arriving home, I was at work in the dressing room applying my mascara and sharing the story of my Hollywood TV star hunk with the girl sitting next to me.

"Marco Walter?" she asked. "What about him?"

"Oh, just that I met him in L.A., and we hooked up on my last night there. I feel so awful for him because his thing is so small," I said. "Why, have you seen him on that soap?"

"Um, no," she said, quickly standing up to leave the room. "He's a good friend of mine."

# SECTION FOUR

# SHIT'S GETTING REAL

# CHAPTER TWENTY-TWO

# I'M WITH THE (HAIR) BAND

Being a friend's wingwoman can be a pain in the ass. It usually consists of hanging out at a bar or nightclub alone while your homie plays tonsil hockey all night with their hookup du jour. Katie was a gal from Texas and a Feature Dancer at Club Rock-Za, located across the street from Femme Nu. The owner of Za was much nicer and a welcome change for me from the owner of my old club, who was always riding my ass for me to cover my face with my hair. I instantly took to her and took an auntie's interest in her daughter Tracy, a senior in high school who helped manage the club.

Katie and I met while having drinks at the bar before our set. She was a platinum blonde bombshell and well-known centerfold who made a killing touring strip clubs all over the world, performing as a Feature Event performer. She reminded me of Tawny Kitaen. To be honest, I felt unworthy in Katie's presence, but she adored me and my balls-out sense of humor. So, when she asked me to leave the club for a bit and be her wingwoman at The Cellar, I happily obliged.

I was cool until I realized my friend's new squeeze had brought a friend for her friend, and I was to be their hookup. No stranger to this, when the feeling of revulsion is mutual, this is when I either feign interest with small talk or head to the dance floor alone. Since my date is exactly like hearing nails on a chalkboard (but thank you, Jägermeister, for the valiant effort), I opted for dancing solo on this night of mutual revulsion.

"Awesome. Cool. Will you excuse me?" I'd asked, pulling myself up from the barstool as Brett Michaels from Poison began singing about how he wanted us to talk dirty to him. Since we weren't at The Wave where I knew the layout of the lights and shadows, and I didn't have my usual group of girlfriends there to remind me to "fluff my hair" to cover my facial scars, The Jazz Cellar threw me off my game. Still, I danced anyway to pass the time, patting myself on the back for being such a great friend. Supporting Katie's sexual conquest wasn't like supporting famine relief or finding a cure for AIDS, but it was solid. Unfortunately, I had to dance to Glam Rock and NOT for cash on stage!

It's not that there was anything wrong with The Cellar (The Jazz Cellar) and their music scene, but it wasn't my vibe. Still, it was a cool dive bar that hosted up-and-coming rock bands from on and off the island. Located just a handful of blocks from The Wave in the heart of Waikiki on Lewers Street, The Cellar's regulars were mostly military boys and diehard glam-rockers with long hair, guyliner, and Madonna-looking black rubber bracelets stacked to their elbow. Some of them were cute, but like Kimmy and I have said ever since watching *About Last Night* together (quoting Elizabeth Perkins' Joan), "I refuse go out with a man whose ass is smaller than mine."

Cute or not, those rocker dudes needed a burger (this, coming from a coke fiend who could've used that meal). So, there I was, shaking all I had on the dance floor, happy to be buzzed. And then it happened. Like the flash of a spotlight—poof— the night went from blah to ohmyfuckinggawd.

Nothing turns up your dance game like noticing a hot person watching you with That Look. The wall-sized mirror next to the band's stage gave me the perfect view of him checking me out without turning around. He was zoned in on my ass, tits, hips, and finally, my face. I was sure to fluff my hair and turned up my game, moving my hips enough so he wouldn't notice my face. Fosse, Fosse, Fosse.

I'd always fancied myself an equal opportunity sex maniac. The second I laid my tits on this dude, I realized I'd yet to swim in the Hair Band Pond. I thought about how it was 19-fucking-90 now, and by God, it was time. After flirty introductions, complete with hair flips and giggles, I learned his name was Reece. He was from the San Fernando Valley and was the bass player for the featured band, SLAM. That's right bitches. A rock star thinks I'm hot.

"Reece? Like the candy?" I quipped. My subconscious witty banter test had begun. I wondered if his shoulder-length chestnut curls were real and if he was a good kisser with those juicy lips flirting back at me.

"So, I've been told," he volleyed back, peeling off my panties with his smile. "Hey, you hanging out for a while?" my candy man asked while touching my shoulder.

I was tingling in all the right places, trying to keep it cool and feeling like the groupie allowed backstage, a whole new type of high.

"Yeah, my friend Katie is pretty happy over there," I said, motioning to my friend with her dude at the bar in the corner by the cigarette machine.

"There he is!" Reece declared, throwing his perfectly lean, rubber bracelet-covered wrists in the air and walking away. I was shattered, my abandonment issues unknowingly triggered. I thought he was gone forever and had a moment of silence for the orgasms that would never be. I headed for the bar, and within minutes, Katie sat down next to me, sans her new man.

"That was him!" she validated. "Fuck, Steph. I'm in deep," she continued. "Who was that other dude, his drummer?"

I was confused. "His what?" I asked, realizing Reece had been looking for the lead singer of his band, which coincidentally was Katie's guy.

"Yeah, girl. My new guy is the lead singer for SLAM!" she bragged, high on hormones and blow, pointing to the SLAM Flyer taped to the entryway door.

"Oh fuck, girl, I just met the bass player!" I screeched. We both giggled like horny prom dates eager to put out. Reece was a happy and unexpected bonus, like being ordered to traffic school and getting to seduce your hot instructor.

For the next few weeks, Reece and I were inseparable. He was stoked he'd met a local girl who loved his jokes and was riding his *schlong* multiple times a day. I took him to places off the map, and we shared adventures only locals knew about. He was also hooking up with at least one other stripper—my friend, Tanya, who was cool, so it didn't matter to us as long as everyone was safe and respectful.

One day, Reece, Tanya and I found one another on Waikiki Beach, and we started playing paddleball and frolicking in the water together. It was the strangest sexual energy I've ever felt. I knew they were into each other, and Tanya knew about Reece and me, but none of that mattered while we played on the beach.

We took photos of our asses in G-strings while Reece stood between us.

What a fucking God he must've felt like.

That is, until the night I spit in his face.

It wasn't my finest hour, and providing the backstory may make it worse, but here goes:

It was early evening. Reece and I spent another day together fucking around and exploring waterfalls and then fucking in waterfalls. After saying our goodbyes, I showed up for work at Rock-Za a couple hours later and heard the news. One of the other girls told me "someone was just here looking for you" as she casually set up makeup camp from her tackle box in her space in front of the mirror.

"What?" I was all aflutter, feeling like a sexy witch whose potion was hard to forget.

"Yeah, he asked for Stephanie and described you as the girl with the scars all over her face," she said blankly.

The other girls in the dressing room stopped talking and turned around to look at my reaction. I raised my eyebrows in disbelief as the room fell silent.

"He said what?" I asked.

"He asked . . . ."

"No, no, no, I'm fine, it's fine. I got it," I insisted, interrupting her mid-sentence, and standing up.

"Did he say where he was going?" I asked, slamming my clothes back into my dance bag in a rage.

"Stephanie, what are you doing?" Katie asked, worried I was going to lose it.

"He was with his band. I think they're headed to The Cellar," the other girl replied, enjoying that she delivered such hurtful news.

The five-minute cab ride was a blur. I was blind with rage and in disbelief that my lover of two weeks, the dude I felt such a connection with, would describe me as "the girl with the scars all over her face." How could I allow one human being to make me feel like the sexiest and most beautiful woman in the world and then call me Freddy Krueger behind my back within hours? It had to be all his fault.

I found Reece at The Cellar, where he and his band were rehearsing.

"What's up? Whatcha doing here?" he asked. He tried to kiss me hello, but I pulled away.

"Can you take a break for a minute?" I asked.

Confused, he followed me up the stairs and outside to the sidewalk. Another purple and pink Hawaiian sunset was bragging as the surrounding palms flapped in the breeze to bow on stage after another breathtaking performance of a day.

"I heard you came into the club looking for me earlier," I accused.

"Yeah, we all came in for a beer before rehearsal, and I asked if you were there," he answered, suspecting he was in trouble.

"I heard." My breathing grew heavy. "You described me by my scars!" I exploded. Before I allowed any time to pass, I left my body, and the coked-up monster in me took over. I spit in his face and started sobbing, the adrenaline racing through me.

"What the fuck?" Reece exclaimed in shock. "You spit in my face!" he shouted while using his palms to clean himself.

"I know, I'm sorry, but that really hurt me," I replied evenly.

"You spit in my face…," Reece kept saying as he walked away. I hailed a taxi and headed back to the club, feeling terrible and embarrassed.

A couple of nights later, I heard from Tanya that Reece's girlfriend from California had flown in to surprise him, so he was technically off the market for her now, too.

"No way!" I shouted. "Of course, he has a girlfriend!" I shook my head, laughing.

I never spoke about my fight-or-flight, Scarface spit-in-the-face moment regret, but after I learned about Reece's girlfriend, that shame pill was easier to swallow.

I wish I could say that my spitting incident was the defining moment of my time with Reece. That proverbial trophy goes to our first post-coital morning. It was eleven o'clock in the morning, and I left Reece's Waikiki hotel room, a tiny studio apartment that he shared with the rest of his band. Having worked the night prior, I had only my mini tank dress and spiked heels to walk the five blocks home while watching families headed to the beach. Reece gave me his band's t-shirt to wear to soften my walk of shame.

So, there I was, barefoot with heels in hand and raccoon eyes from my makeup the night before, my mini-dress pulled down to the knee, attempting to resemble a normal (not-slutty) skirt. That sight alone was enough to make a gal cringe. This is exactly what I did when I arrived home and re-read the band t-shirt, my new parting gift: "I Got SLAMmed in Hawai'i."

"Perfect," I said, laughing. I collapsed on my bed, giggling. "He's a fun one." I thought, comparing my connection with Reece to other dudes I'd meet on the island. Who knew just how fun?

# CHAPTER TWENTY-THREE

# THAT SHIT'LL KILL YOU

I used to be a rock star, too.

I didn't tour the world belting my heart out in stadiums, but I worked the pole to the tunes of AC/DC, Guns N' Roses, Def Leppard, Poison, Mötley Crüe, and Jon Bon Jovi for the better part of a decade and was treated just as well, but on a much smaller, very tropical scale. It was better than littering the streets of Hollywood, all those hopeful stars.

In the nineties in Waikiki, strippers were golden. We had celebrity status. There were no lines to wait in, no cover charges to pay, just champagne kisses and caviar dreams waiting for us to party on the other side of the velvet rope. In 1991, I made great money. I lived large in a luxury high-rise apartment boasting panoramic views of Diamond Head and the Pacific Ocean. Waikiki was the backdrop to a lifestyle I milked with every VIP pass and full moon limousine ride. I took taxis everywhere and enjoyed monthly facials, weekly massages with manicures, and two-hundred-dollar haircuts.

I'm not kidding about the limo rides. I had a driver named James (his real name) on retainer for monthly full moon excursions around the island. My friends could set their watches by James pulling up to The Wave at 4 a.m. In addition to a handful of strays (lucky tourists in the right place at the right time), my gal pals and I would sip champagne and act every bit the Rock Star Stripper Posse as we tooled around the island until sunrise. And party we did. James was paid well and never complained once about standing by while we skinny-dipped in the warm glow of the Hawaiian sunrise. Go figure.

The 'in' drug for dazzling people was cocaine. I always had a bump or two in my purse and never turned down a trip to the ladies' room invitation from a fellow dancer. "Wanna go to the bathroom?" was code for "Come do a line of blow with me." Breaking the rules is much more fun when you have a partner in crime.

We always flocked to the stalls when not lounging on the couches gabbing away in the "VIP" Room at The Wave. There were nights spent snorting lines of coke off the swankiest bars after hours, with famous actors and rock stars in tow. It was common to see girls making out with one another and even more so to see mountains of white powder in the room.

One night at work, I got to chatting with Teresa, a stunning dirty blonde with sun-kissed freckles and green eyes. She was in town on hiatus after touring for Australian *Playboy*. I was in awe of her beauty. Always smiling and happy to be at work, Teresa was even happier this time. I sat next to her at the bar as we waited to be called for our set.

"You're so beautiful," she observed, swaying to the music, and smiling at me.

"Thanks, T, you are too!" I was flattered and knew she was high.

"Do that Frank Sinatra thing," she begged.

Long after the clubs had closed, Teresa and I were still partying back in my apartment at six in the morning. We played music, and I performed a little one-woman show to Sinatra's "Fly Me to the Moon," complete with Fosse dance moves. She loved it.

She wasn't her normal self, and I wondered if she was on coke or something else. She seemed way too mellow, far less alert than if she were high on blow.

She leaned in to kiss me and whispered in my ear. "Do you want some?" she purred, melting with the melody of Enigma's "Sadness" playing in the background.

"Blow?" I asked. I pulled back, kissing her on the cheek.

"No, this is H, love. I just snorted some." She slurred while sporting the biggest Cheshire grin.

Heroin. Holy Shit. I suddenly broke from our connection and took a step back.

"No, hon, that's okay," I said, now officially freaked out.

Picking up my drink, sipping and staring into her eyes, I continued, "I'm up soon." And I walked away.

I was scared shitless.

Things were getting hardcore.

Heroin was something we learned about in middle school. It meant dirty needles and strung out, homeless people with scabs on their faces. I had no idea you could snort it or that beautiful models like Teresa did it.

I wondered how many other girls were snorting heroin instead of coke back in the dressing room. Was this the new designer drug? Was I considered old school with my blow?

I had one song left before my set started. I took my purse, waited my turn for the bathroom stall, and placed my coke on the back of the toilet. I chopped the powder methodically but couldn't stop thinking about Teresa. Rolling up a dollar bill, I placed it under my nose, leaned down and snorted.

How could she do heroin? I thought.

I snorted again. That Shit will kill you.

Something in me changed that night. I was beginning to feel the fray, the tattered edges of my life coming into purview, and I was not happy. The glamour, the drugs, and life in the fast lane were getting old.

# CHAPTER TWENTY-FOUR

# MARLEY

Every now and then the universe throws us a bone. And if we're lucky, it has a beautiful face and hilarious personality; Marley was this gift to me. In addition to being adorable and fun, he was the most talented guitar player I'd ever seen and caused my fangirl body parts to tingle in all the right places. But as amazing as he was, Marley wasn't perfect (who is)? His presence in my life was wrapped with a huge bow made from addiction, convenience, and betrayal. Which is why we were so attracted to one another, duh.

It was 1995, and my twenty-four-year-old ass was wiped from a long but lucrative shift at the club. Barely 1:30 in the morning, the night was young. I was off work but wouldn't be heading to The Wave to meet up with my regular party posse. I was flustered after being stood up earlier for happy hour and naked playtime with this new dude I'd been hooking up with. High on my usual elixir of booze, pills, and blow, I was on a mission for answers.

I jumped into a cab after quickly tipping the bouncers, bar staff, and Weez. My cab driver was pulling up to Moose's when I freaked out from the backseat, but quickly remembered I'd locked my dance bag filled with loose bills, a pair of spiked heels, and all but one of my costumes in the dressing room. I wasn't comfortable carrying around so much at a nightclub that didn't know me as well as The Wave did. As if any of management's relationships with its regulars (like my sloppy ass) could keep us safe from would-be thieves and druggies. It was an especially hilarious thought because I was one of them.

If The Wave on Kalākaua Avenue was my home away from home after work, Moose's (Moose McGillycuddy's), just blocks away on Lewers Street, was my fictitious cousin's crash pad with live cover bands and horny dudes. I always knew it was there, but between the heavy tourist crowd and military vibe, it just wasn't my jam offstage.

There were only two reasons you'd find me sipping cocktails at Moose's: friendship (wingwoman duty) or sex. This time it was the latter, and even though my ego was still licking the fateful spoon that scooped Marley and me up just weeks ago, I still wanted to know why he blew me off—me, a sure thing who was excited to blow him off (the fun way) after sunset cocktails at my place. It was much too early in our drug-induced roller coaster of ecstasy and trauma bond for such blatant asshole-ary.

We were still in our passive-aggressive honeymoon phase, not having spent enough time together yet to truly appreciate each other's damage so we could use the information to manipulate what the other wanted. Plus, I had to see if he were still alive. My insecurity level then was at an ATL (all-time low, not Atlanta, thanks, Bo Burnham!), so I clung to the one reason that made sense. The only way Marley could've ghosted me was because he was killed in a horrific car accident. This was a completely normal thought process for me at the time and the definition of narcissistic delusion. Drugs are fun.

Enter my pissed-off ass walking up the stairs at Moose's to see he was still alive and jamming with his band on stage to a cover song from the Gin Blossoms. I didn't know him well, but I knew he was up there with his guitar, hating that setlist. Nothing against nineties pop tunes, but we were more Mazzy Star and Nine Inch Nails people. Marley was such a free spirit who also loved to rock and then swoon you with his Flamenco talent. So, yeah, I was happy to see him using his magical fingers to play corny radio tunes instead of Zeppelin.

I surveyed the room while figuring out how to confront him. After picking up my double vodka cocktail, I slithered through the crowd and found a spot in the back corner behind one of the speakers so he couldn't see me checking him out. I'd never been so horny and pissed at the same time.

We'd met about a month before in the most romantic fashion imaginable, the way any two-party animals leaving an afterparty at sunrise do. We locked heavily dilated eyes while wanting to inhale each other immediately. Between me swooning over his long and wavy locks, perfect olive skin and almond Latino eyes, and him mesmerized by the site of my funbags winking at him over my spaghetti-strapped mini dress, we were goners. He had me at "Look at those tits!" in a voice so excited you'd think he'd discovered the golden ticket from *Charlie and the Chocolate Factory*, and it was tucked deep inside my cleavage.

I laughed nervously but was already mentally nibbling his earlobe, burying myself in his thick, coconut-flavored Paul Mitchell curls. We shared a cab to my place and consummated our attraction immediately.

Later that day, something unusual happened. Instead of bolting out the door like a typical one-night stand, Marley offered to get us a six-pack of beer from the bodega next to my apartment building on Kūhiō Avenue, just two blocks from Queens Beach. We hung out while hungover, stretching our limbs into the afternoon while listening to music like Miles Davis, Santana, and Portishead.

Pillow talk with a side of overserved-and-sexy became our thing with the typical audio backdrop of tourists walking to their hotels after a day at the beach on the sidewalk two floors below my place, mopeds whizzing by, and children whining to their exhausted parents about having to carry their own blowup rafts and beach towels. All the while, we'd be amused at the novelty (and taking it for granted) of living in such a wildly popular tourist destination, loving the euphoric phase of getting to know each other in between bumping and grinding all day.

He still wasn't my boyfriend, however, a fact made very clear to me every time I dropped him in front of his and his girlfriend's place next to Pinks on Kalākaua Avenue. I'm sure the reason Marley was a no-show had something to do with Rachel, his main squeeze. She was a stripper, too. So, not only did I carry guilt for being that girl, but the shame of crossing boundaries of betrayal with a fellow sorority sister was almost more painful than the thought of not being with Marley at all. However, I knew Rachel had a couple of dudes on the side, so the playing field was level, if not totally fucked-up. Here we were, two amazing young women who based all their worth on what other people thought of us. And to snag a lover who was spoken for? As insane as it was, it was like a badge of honor for me to be The Mistress. Somehow, if I could land someone already attached, my stock would rise because he was risking it all to be with me.

Self-worth, party of none.

Meanwhile, I slowly moved closer to the stage after my cocktail began to work, and I was spotted. As soon as our eyes locked, Marley closed his as if he were a five-year-old who shit his pants. He quickly leaned over to the lead singer on stage and whispered something. A second or two of instrument tweaking, and then I heard it: a song that was not on their setlist (I later learned) and one hundred percent directed toward me.

My knees buckled. The intro chords lifted me and carried me into a world that belonged only to me. Also, the MDMA was starting to kick in. The crowd cheered in recognition of the hit tune, and I belted out my own "Yeah!" with my hands in the air as I smiled at Marley. My ego was having multiple orgasms knowing the song was being played for me. While I wasn't a huge Nirvana fan, whenever I hear "All Apologies," I think of that moment and smile. Needless to say, Marley was forgiven.

Nearly thirty years later, I found myself back home on O'ahu to visit mom for the holidays. Flying too close to the sun is never without turbulence. When it comes to trauma survivors, it's what some of us do to make sense of our story and remind us of how far we've come. After a nearly six-hour flight from Los Angeles to Honolulu, I turned on my phone to discover a surprising text.

"Hi, Christina. Merry Christmas and Happy Holidays! Shit, my wife Aubrey checked my Facebook Messenger. Even though it was harmless, she tore me a new asshole. I guess over the years, I talked about you and how I felt about you. With that being said, in my mind, I thought we could hang out. I really want to apologize to you for everything. Aubrey is amazing and deals with my candy ass. Love you, and Happy Holidays to you and your family."

I had no idea who the message was from, but I saw it was a local Hawaiian area code. Then came another text. This time it was just one word: a name. He signed it, "Wesley." Wesley? I still had no clue who this person was.

My reply text: "Sorry about what? I don't think I know a Wesley. Please refresh my memory!" Part of me was scared of this random dude on my phone, and the other part was intrigued, thinking I must have at least made out with him, but who knows? That girl made so many horrible decisions. As I kept walking with the rest of the passengers, my brain caught up with my eyes, and my feet instantly froze; I nearly fell over. Shuffling away from the crowd to baggage claim, I reread the mystery text, and it hit me. I couldn't fucking believe it.

"It's Marley," read the third text. Of course, it was. It all made sense now. "Wesley" was a character from an Eighties cult movie about artists living in New York. I was obsessed with the screenplay and everyone in the film, particularly Wesley. He and Marley looked alike, and, in my young mind, they could've been twins. We must've watched that movie ten times, mostly due to my begging. I had completely forgotten about that, so his signoff text was priceless: a magic carpet ride back to my twenties with all the great memories and none of the drama.

As soon as I could take my facemask off outside of the terminal (thanks, COVID-19), I called him. I was too shocked to be nervous and too excited to be scared. I hadn't thought about Marley in years, so when he sent me a friend request on Facebook a week before my flight home, I accepted and was happy to see he was married and doing well. I had sent Marley a short and platonic message on FB Messenger. I mentioned I was heading back to the island in a few days and would love to meet up with him and his wife. That didn't sit well with her.

Later that night, I heard from Marley again, and we were able to talk briefly on the phone. We spoke for twenty minutes, and it was surreal.

Reuniting with someone you shared a unique experience with decades earlier is like falling down a rabbit hole dripping with nostalgia. I learned so many things about myself through his lens. I had no idea of the impact I'd had on him and how lost he was in his own life at the time. I was so far gone in my addiction and drama I couldn't see how much he truly loved me, as crazy as that may sound. But since we were so messed up, was it really love? For us, it was. I'm sure for him and Rachel, too.

I can't speak for other addicts, but I'd grab onto whomever made me feel safe when sinking in an ocean of chaos. When growing up with drama, chaos feels like home, so I created it with every relationship (platonic and otherwise). It was enough for a lover to give me the moniker: DQ. I thought it meant Dairy Queen and was confused until he explained it was an acronym for Drama Queen. He wasn't wrong. Now decades later, I realize what Marley and I shared was a beautiful tapestry of codependence, trauma bonding, chemistry, and most definitely love, even if we didn't know a healthier version of it.

I never heard from Marley after that call, nor did I reach out to him again. Aubrey put a stop to it by blocking my phone number. I respected his wife and their marriage. I didn't blame her. I'd have probably done the same thing, too. All she knew was that I was an ex-stripper who used to bang her husband thirty years ago. That didn't necessarily have platonic written all over it.

If I'm meant to reconnect with Marley again, I will. We're war buddies, survivors of our choices. I was so happy he chose to reach out to me after all these years, and we had a chance to talk. I was finally at a place in my life where I could accept the gift of knowing that I did have value, I was beautiful, and truly made a difference in someone's life back when mine was falling apart. It was a rebirth I didn't know I needed.

Let this be a reminder that everyone's memories of who you were to them are their own. But if you're really lucky, you get a chance to learn about them after a lifetime of not knowing.

# CHAPTER TWENTY-FIVE

# DENIAL, ANGER, BARGAINING, KI

The night I visited Marley at Moose's, I locked up my cash and my costumes back in the dressing room at work. All but one, my white leather G-string and bra, which were folded at the bottom of my purse. There was no way I was leaving such precious handmade cargo behind. It was one of Ki's (pronounced, "Key") creations, my illustrious friend and leather seamstress to the strippers.

Ki was a dear friend whom I never got to see enough of, but this was not a bad thing. When we got together, nights turned into days that turned into passing out on the other side of the island, wondering how we would make it back to Waikiki. So, when I say partied with Ki, I mean, we were professionals.

What began as a usual trip to The Wave for *pau hana* ("pow-hah-nah"), Hawaiian for "finished work," drinks after a shift at the club (me on stage, him working his sales mojo in the dressing room) always ended as a tragic, hilarious adventure. We were a dangerous pair. Between my loud and obnoxious self and his bleached blond curls and flamboyant vibe, I'm pretty sure we were unbearable to be around, especially if you were sober. We cracked each other up, and since he was gay, I felt safe with him as my plus one, knowing he wanted nothing from me other than friendship. Ki gave me shit about my crooked bottom teeth. After four years of braces, I couldn't bear wearing my retainer like I was supposed to. He concocted funny lyrics to songs, taking pride in his rewrite to a line in the song "Grove is in the Heart" by Deee-Lite. "Blow a stinky faaaaart!" he'd sing. A real crowd-pleaser among us twentysomethings high on Ecstasy.

We'd met a year earlier after a rave near the Aloha Tower in downtown Honolulu, about twenty minutes north of Waikiki. Feeling no pain but aware of the hour (sunlight will do that to you) and wanting to fall asleep, Ki and I bonded over free downers called Black Beauties a mutual stripper friend was handing out like a centerfold pharmacist. While shrugging our shoulders and swallowing a pill neither of us had ever heard of, we locked eyes, chuckled, and found mutual affection through our brokenness.

We were living it up at The Wave one night when Ki offered me methadone. I was beginning to roll on my usual concoction of MDMA, booze and blow, and Ki was all about his newfound drug of choice. He wasn't giving up on wanting me to try it, either. It was like he was describing the newest Enigma song but was gushing about a narcotic instead of music.

"You'll love it, girl," Ki whispered in my ear. His words slid from his lips like a Billie Holiday tune played on melted vinyl.

"Cool," I replied, suddenly feeling like a party newbie.

Ki was giving off an incredible vibe, and it was obvious he felt amazing. But it still scared the shit out of me. The only thing I knew about methadone at the time was that it was somehow related to heroin, and we all know my thoughts on that drug. So, I politely declined while trying not to sound like a snob.

"Next time, maybe," I said, raising my glass. He toasted his cocktail in solidarity, and we settled into our high.

I learned of Ki's overdose and subsequent death less than twenty-four hours later. I was just about to start my shift at the club. It was the first time in my young adult life that a friend (not an elderly family member) I was close to passed away. Unable to wrap my head around the news, I immediately ran outside to the payphone in my costume—another Ki original, a black and white zebra print leather bra and G-string. I was too out of sorts to think about covering up while standing on the sidewalk underneath the neon club sign. That night as the ominous charcoal tropical clouds hovered, damping out the auburn sunset, I dialed his number. Even the sky was sad. Ki's roommate, a fellow dancer, answered the phone. I could tell she was crying.

"Hi," I said. "Is Ki there?"

I braced myself for confirmation while trying to keep my knees from buckling.

"Um, no." Her voice was cracking as she whispered, "He's dead."

There it was. The reality I refused to believe. It still didn't feel real. I don't remember who hung up first, but I walked back into the club, and after picking up my cocktail, I headed for the dressing room. I sat in front of the mirror and wept into the palms of my hands, pulling up emotions I never knew existed. My heart was thumping between shock, fear, and sorrow so deep I couldn't believe I was still breathing. Once I regained my composure and clung to the fact that I was still alive, I felt something unexpected. A small part of me was jealous of Ki's accidental overdose. I wasn't a religious person, but I strongly believed that he was in a better place than the dystopian life we were living.

I never shared my envy of being alive with anyone while my fabulous new friend was dead.

Depression 101: when you feel jealousy toward someone who has died because you don't want to feel your pain any longer, tell someone.

I know the feeling of pleasure, and I also know the struggle of hanging on to life with bloody fingers, trying to find a reason to stay alive. After learning of Ki's death, I had to process my envy of his unexpected and unplanned exit from his pain. Distraught, I cut my night short at the club. Instead of heading to The Wave, I grabbed a cab and went home. Instead of zoning out in front of MTV music videos until sunrise, I sat alone with my thoughts. I finally pulled out a CD from my catalog, allowing myself to get lost in Robert Smith's lyrics from my favorite The Cure album, *Disintegration*. (Fitting title, yes?)

I sat with my feelings of loss, glad I'd chosen to isolate and rely on my trusty anesthetics of booze and blow to cope. It was a far better option than talking about what happened with whoever was at the bar.

Within minutes, I was transformed and felt like a cartoon of floating notes in the air as The Cure song "Closedown" filled the room at full volume.

*The real belief of something more than mockery*
*If only I could fill my heart with love*

You'd think the reality of Ki's overdose would've been enough to kick me out of my self-destructive ways, but I wasn't ready. I still subscribed to the belief that I was just a party girl. That Ki was way worse than me. He was a true drug addict, and I just did drugs. Big difference in my heavily dilated eyes. As the night went on, I swam inside a vat of denial with The Cure and cocaine by my side, singing and crying, my own celebration of life ceremony for Ki.

I'd always enjoyed writing poetry ever since I discovered Rod McKuen at thirteen, but I hadn't written creatively in years. That night was different. I pulled out a notepad and found a pen in my junk drawer in the kitchen behind the old batteries and booklet of stamps and began to write. I awoke the next day surrounded by loose papers with my feelings plastered everywhere. After reading every word, I felt a little better and was encouraged. Having projected my emotions onto the page, I realized I had a knack for this writing thing. Reading my pain didn't take it away, but it sure validated my feelings, even if they were just my own words speaking back to me. As I digested the pages, sober the next morning, I felt a glimmer of hope, wishing I could pick up the phone to call my poetic hero, Rod, to share my newly discovered talent. He wasn't for everyone, with his poetry leaning toward overkill and the sappy side, but I tucked myself in many a night with his sonnets and felt like one of his students after reading my Ki-inspired work.

I still think of Ki now and then, like when I brush my teeth and entertain the idea of adult braces or when I see a handsome, curly haired, bleached-blond man dancing in West Hollywood. And on the rare occasion when Deee-Lite sings through the background speakers of a restaurant or bar, you can bet your ass that I belt out Ki's rendition, "Blow a stinky faaaaart!" with the song.

The crowd never gets it, but I do. And I know Ki does, too.

# CHAPTER TWENTY-SIX

# ME AND MADONNA'S
# BACKUP DANCER

It was three o'clock in the morning, and my fourth hit of MDMA was locking molecules with the cocaine and booze swishing through my body. It was an unusually successful Tuesday night at the club, so I celebrated at The Wave afterward.

I was alone.

Of course, whenever anyone hit The Wave solo, it was never for long. Given the size of Waikiki, it's fair to assume when factoring in the outcasts, freaks and industry folks who loved anything alternative (from music, nipple piercings, and tattoos to mohawks, belly rings, and black lipstick), you'd run into your tribe.

In the best of ways, it was such a euphoric land of cultural dystopia, beckoning my high-as-shit ass every night after work to set myself free from showing my body on stage all night. I had at least a full hour to myself, alone on the dance floor, and I didn't give a shit who was watching. I didn't have to care if I was "chosen" for tips because it was just me and my dance…my Fosse dance. We strippers were all rock stars at The Wave, but I was still the best Fosse Girl.

After shooting the breeze with Ivan and Peter (best bartender and *Absolutely Fabulous* recapper, respectively), I was given over to "Closer" by Nine Inch Nails, its grinding guitar filtering through the speakers and into my ears like a warm invitation. I was melting in the couch cushions upstairs with some girls from the club, but before the riff to Trent Reznor's song ended, even before he sang the first lyric of his song, I was already downstairs on the dance floor.

The second I heard the beats of the sex-on-a-stick song, I was in the zone.

*"You let me violate you*

*You let me desecrate you*

*You let me penetrate you*

*You let me complicate you"*

Wearing Daisy Dukes cutoff jeans shorts, tennis shoes, and a white Haynes t-shirt, I looked like a tourist who couldn't sleep and threw on whatever was lying around the hotel room floor before heading out. On nights when I'd forgotten to remove my garter, I outed myself: Stripper! We have a Stripper in the house! Tonight, the place was dead. There were maybe ten people total downstairs, but I didn't care. They weren't customers!

I was halfway through my pretend seduction of Trent on the dance floor when from the corner of my eye and crusty bushel of Aqua Net-covered hair, I noticed this dude stripping me with his gaze. He seemed familiar, and it was driving me nuts trying to remember how I knew him. Then it hit me. He was that backup dancer from the movie, *Madonna Truth or Dare*. He was the straight dude who got so much shit for being homophobic or an ally. I couldn't remember.

*Madonna: Truth or Dare* was the new documentary about Madonna on her Blond Ambition Tour, and the big buzz was that it was filmed in black and white, of all things. No one knew how historically significant that movie would become for the gay community. Say what you want about Madge, but she's the O.G. queen who proudly wore her crown, gladly sharing it with a marginalized and shamed community for being who they were. This, for me, elevated her to Goddess status.

That movie deeply affected me and may be why I became so involved in the GLBTQI+ community. In addition to being open to both sexes (happy to represent "B"s in the GLBTQI+ community), I empathized and could relate to the community painted as outcasts and victims of ridicule and abuse, just as I have. Worse for them, they were persecuted for things out of their control. Most importantly, as survivors who overflowed with compassion and love for our fellow man, we offered something the whole world needed. Today, as a lifelong GLBTQI+ community member, I am only too happy to bow to Pink and Gaga who carry Madge's crown beautifully as they blazed their pathway to stardom. Full of love and empathy, their embrace of weird permitted so many to say I was Born This Way.

Sweaty and hot, I dabbed myself with napkins to cool off from dancing. Ready to take a short break, I went back upstairs, and that's when I saw him again. This time he came up to me and spoke.

"Hey," he smirked. He could tell I knew who he was. His black satin Johnny Gill concert baseball jacket wasn't fooling me, and he could smell it.

"You wanna go to an afterparty?" he asked, sounding like velvet (which could've been the drugs talking). All I could think about was Madonna. Even if she wasn't with him, I could get personal information about My Queen.

"Whose afterparty and where? And hi, I'm Stephanie." I was smooth and able to keep my fangirl excitement hidden.

"Right up the road," he slid into the seat next to me on the couch. "Nice to meet you," he said, extending a hand and shaking mine respectfully like I was Madonna herself.

"Who'll be there?" I asked, thinking only of Madge.

"Me."

He smiled and stood up, reaching out his hand. By then, I had played every scene he was filmed in, *Madonna: Truth or Dare*, and was beyond starstruck that someone who knows fucking Madonna was going to be mine soon enough.

"Why not!" I said happily and walked out with him. Ivan threw me a smile from behind his well, congratulating me for getting laid by Madonna's backup dancer, that's who!

"So, what did you say you were celebrating?" he asked, lifting my shirt as I kicked off my Keds in his hotel room.

"Oh," I panted. "I made bank and don't have to worry about rent for a couple of months."

He continued to undress me while Bell Biv DeVoe sang to us from the radio on the nightstand.

Once we started going at it, it was fun. I have to say that the most memorable part happened before we even got started when he refused to wear a condom. "Nah, we don't need one, baby," he cooed.

In my head, I'm thinking, this dude is crazy. First off, yes, we do. Have you read the news about this AIDS shit going around? Second, "Baby?" My high-risk behavior protection instinct took over. "Dude, what would Madonna think?" I said, looking at him like an Entertainment Tonight reporter.

There it was. The bleached blonde would have to face the elephant in the room if he wanted to play—the main reason I was there in the first place. Also, I was right: Madge would've been pissed off that he didn't want to wear a love glove. Especially since she was saturating the airwaves with her message: "Hey you! Don't be silly! Put a rubber on your willie!" How could he not when HIV/AIDS had been ravaging the U.S. since 1981, disproportionately in the world of entertainment.

He mumbled something I'm glad I didn't hear and obliged.

I left his hotel room at dawn. Purse and shoes in hand, my crusty, over-sprayed hair thrown up in a scrunchie, I couldn't wait to find my car in the hotel parking garage. The hallway was extra-long, and I suddenly felt like I was Madonna during her "Justify My Love" video. As soon as I got home, I called my BGF (best gay friend), Kai.

"Poor is the man

Whose pleasures depend

On the permission of another . . .wanting,
needing, waiting

For you to justify my love"

—Madonna

Oh, it was justified, whatever that was. But love? Only for you, Queen. #since1984.

# CHAPTER TWENTY-SEVEN

# LOSING CONTROL

I never thought about the, "Last call for alcohol!" shout-out for drugs. No bartender was kicking me out of my room. No stagehand blasting the lights up or server flipping dining room chairs on the tables for the cleaning crew. So, my apartment and I had an agreement. After the strip bar closed and The Wave kicked us out after last call at four in the morning, the afterparties ended at sun-up. If I didn't manage to get laid that night (morning), my apartment would be there waiting for my lone and exhausted ass.

I was a long way from fake I.D.s and snorting lines with Rod Stewart's doppelgänger, thanks to years and years of hamster-wheel partying. Except I wasn't partying with anyone, but me at this point. It wasn't fun anymore, and I was exhausted. One of my close friends, Connie, with whom I'd worked at Femme Nu, had since left the party scene, gotten married, and had a baby. One day, she took me to lunch at Denny's Waikiki. Over coffee, looking me straight in the eye, she said, "If you keep partying like this and flaking on me, I'll have to end our friendship."

"Wow. Okay," I responded, stunned.

"I hope you know how much I love you, but I can't watch you destroy yourself anymore," Connie continued. "I even called your mom, and she told me not to worry about you unless the cops call."

By now, Connie was crying. I handed her my napkin. Floored, I said, "What? She said that?" I was such a lost soul that I cared more about what my mother told her than that she was crying in front of me because of how much she loved me.

"Anyway, I'm gonna go," Connie said, rising from our booth at Denny's. She hugged me. "I hope I hear from you," she said softly and walked away.

Now I was crying.

"You will, I promise," I assured her. "Thank you for bringing this to my attention," I said delicately and with shame.

Half of me meant it. I was years away from really understanding what she did and how much courage was required to practice this kind of tough love in her early twenties. It astounds me to this day.

Addiction is the black magic of madness, wrapped in frivolity and apathy of circumstance. When I was high, I'd be fully aware that what I was doing wasn't healthy on so many levels. But after my Fuck It switch went off; it was anyone's guess how the night would go.

It's completely indulgent and selfish. We couldn't believe our self-harm, veiled as partying to take the edge off life, might deeply affect our loved ones. In the throes of addiction, we chose drugs over family, friendship, romantic relationships, and jobs. We'd do anything to get high. For us addicts, this warped logic somehow makes total sense. Why would we want anyone in our lives who didn't understand us? We had things under control. It was everyone else who was fucked up. In this vein, we celebrate our chaotic camaraderie by finding others who party—who get us. We develop codependent relationships and trauma bonds within our circles and encourage each other to continue the ride, keeping us all in a dramatic loop of enabling and self-destruction.

Something about a room full of dysfunctional, toxic people makes me feel at home, not judged but loved for my weirdness. Sure, we all have that look of "You party? Me too!" until the sun comes up, and we go our separate ways. But for as long as it lasts, it feels like I'm part of a community that gets me and doesn't want anything from me other than, you know, money or drugs. You know you're a party pro when you carry your sunglasses in your nightclub purse. You want to stay up? Right, this way. Ready to crash for the day? Pour yourself a glass of water and throw this back. Want to escape and feel like you're flying and being hugged from the inside? Snort this. Not into snorting? Want a faster rush and don't mind needles? Stick out your arm. Need to loosen up and forget about a shitty day? Bartender! Round of drinks! Feel invisible and wish you could own the room? Allow me to introduce you to a "bump."

That last one always got me. I didn't let go of cocaine for decades, which tells you how amazing it felt. I lost friendships, money, jobs, and health and orchestrated too many shameful scenes because of my cocaine brain. I went from owning the room to cocaine owning me, all while being completely unaware because I was so out of it. I thought I was still just a party girl even when I pawned jewelry and stole from family members to get drugs. Even when I drove myself to the grocery store in the morning after partying to buy NoDoz and Tylenol PM to chop up with a razor blade and snort them one after the other when I got home, I was clueless about how far down the addiction road I'd traveled.

"Don't know whether you're going up or down, huh?" the clerk asked.

I was too high and ashamed to answer or take my shades off. Instead, I simply chuckled and fled home to snort the pills, not realizing just how far I had sunk.

When was I gonna stop? Could I stop? I had to keep the money rolling in.

It's what we all work for. The Almighty Dollar. Cash is always king, queen and prince in a Stripper's world. It's what we need to provide for ourselves and our families. And these days, it doesn't come easy. Not having enough keeps us awake and having too much can be a dream come true. Or a nightmare. We take it for granted when we have excess, disrespect it, gamble it away, and worse.

Did I have blissful moments wrapped in laughter and comfort? Yes. Was my life one big party, full of excess and adventure? You betcha. I was also living on a hamster wheel—full of denial, self-loathing, and a warped sense of security. My drug use was the mastery of camouflage, but I was beginning to realize that no amount of money or drug was changing the fact of how far I was falling.

The older I got, the more I found myself nodding in agreement to adages like, "You get what you pay for" and "Money doesn't buy happiness." My twenty-something brain was beginning to process that you really do, and it really doesn't.

Here's the thing about clichés: they exist because there's considerable weight to their words. When I was raking in money, I did get what I paid for—numbness. I used it to usher in a life of escape and had no appreciation I was forking over top dollars to anesthetize my pain. Excess, numbness, and what I considered a fascinating life of living in the moment were nothing more than barricades to shield me from facing all I needed to work through. Believe me, I created chaos of grand proportions to avoid facing myself.

I was now nine years into my so-called rock star lifestyle, and my increasingly unhealthy choices brought more and more darkness, adding to the pile of shit I already needed to deal with. In a single moment of clarity that had been building over the years, I found the courage to walk away.

# CHAPTER TWENTY-EIGHT

# VOLUNTARY TERMINATION

I rolled down my window, giving the warm Waikiki air permission to sweep across my lap, wiping away any trace of cigarette smoke from the cab's back seat. As the breeze tickled my face, I riffled through my duffle bag.

Shoes: check. Makeup: check.

My fingers grazed the small of my back.

G-string: check.

We stopped at a light just four blocks from the club, and I took in the view. The sun was already tucked into bed, and the blue ocean lulled. The sky above the horizon was cloaked in hues of lavender and tangerine. The stoplight turned green, and we continued up the street, then turned down a narrow, unpaved driveway and stopped in front of the club.

I could tell the top girls were working. I didn't mind sharing the stage with centerfolds; it made me feel like one in a way. The room was packed, but I made my way up to the bar. I threw down a five and ordered my usual vodka and cranberry.

"Laaaaadies and gentlemen, give it up for Niki, Donna, and Amberrrrrr!"

The crowd was cheering. I opened the dressing room door with one hand, balancing my drink and bag with the other. I managed to find a seat next to the mirror and settled in, trying to tune out the other girls as I pulled out my makeup case.

I squeezed the flesh-colored liquid on my finger, wiping my cheeks slowly. Spackle—to cover every scar. My skin was uneven like melted wax, always haunting me with memories of name-calling and humiliation. After filling every crevice, I let out a sigh of acceptance and validation. I'll show them.

"All right, all right, all right! Give it up!"

The door opened, and another dancer arrived. She was young. A new girl. Someone I'd never seen before. We surveyed each other, and she made her way past me.

I shut my eyes. I saw Michelle, with her scabbed arms and caked-on makeup, talking about her daughter while taking a drag from a cigarette. I saw Cassandra and the look on her face when I told her, her boyfriend had made a pass at me. I saw the wrinkled pixie dancer who also worked as a fortune teller by day. I heard Kami yelling at a customer who tried to touch her and smelled Loretta, the pot-smoking beauty who came to town twice a year. Then there's Billie and Billy, the male and female stripper couple who liked to party and swing. Finally, I saw Robert, who used me and my home for sex and a place to crash.

The heavy base of the next song vibrated the walls, and my eyes opened to my reflection in the mirror. I saw myself, a twenty-eight-year-old stripper. Studying my eyes, I discovered that what used to be pools of blue were now dull shades of gray. Nothing scared me more than knowing I was the architect of my own demise. What was once a fantasy of fame and fortune became a harsh reminder of reputation and endurance.

Toto, I don't think we're in our Dysfunctional Childhood anymore.

Perhaps seeing the new girl made me realize I wasn't nineteen now. Nearly a decade in the making, my career as a stripper felt weathered. I wanted to live a normal life. I didn't know what that meant exactly, but it suddenly hit me: I wouldn't find it on a stage. I spoke softly to the girl in the mirror with the tired, gray eyes: "I think you're done here."

I took another sip from my drink and stood up. I brushed past the new girl. I wanted to tell her to save her money and not get caught up in the nightlife, but instead, I said, "Have a good night," and kept walking.

My head floating in a sea of uncertainty, I made my way through the crowd. I pulled open the red velvet curtains at the front door and saw the sky was now a deep purple.

I always looked at sunsets as beginnings, the beginning of my shift and a night out. But that early evening sky marked the opposite—an end to a life I no longer wanted or needed. Tomorrow would be a new day.

# CHAPTER TWENTY-NINE

# GAY PRIDE, STRAIGHT SEX,
# AND BLOODY MARYS

By the early '90s, I'd known I liked girls and boys and wanted to know more about my tribe. Embracing my bisexuality was important to navigating all of who I was. So, when my new bestie, Monroe, offered to take me to San Francisco for my first Gay Pride event, I was thrilled. The night Monroe and I landed in San Francisco, I met a gorgeous man, Michael, and hooked up with him. The next day, Michael dropped me at the Castro District in front of the café where Monroe and his friends were having brunch. As he lifted his helmet to kiss me goodbye, I heard applause from the restaurant patio. Michael and I shared a giggle before he drove off on his motorcycle into the crisp Northern Cali air.

Monroe raised his Bloody Mary to wave me over, and I sheepishly began my walk of shame to their brunch table. With disco music blaring from the outdoor speakers, I sauntered from the sidewalk to the patio entrance, through the crowd of shirtless men, dolled up drag queens, and bondage couples decked out in leather chaps and dog collars. I couldn't stop beaming. It was my first trip to San Francisco, my first gay pride, and for the first time in a long time—maybe ever—that I felt completely at home just being me.

Monroe and I had met a year earlier back home in Hawai'i. We were, at the time, newly hired food servers at the OCC (Outrigger Canoe Club) on the South side of Waikiki. When we weren't gossiping about our upper-crust clientele, dreaming up elaborate plot lines straight out of *Falcon Crest*, we'd spend our shifts quoting lines from our favorite Meryl Streep movie, *Postcards from the Edge*.

"Sorry, dear, but you know how the queens love me," Monroe whispered, walking past me with a pitcher of iced tea.

"I don't have . . . a generation," I snickered back on my way to drop off a check.

I didn't love my part-time waitress gig but working with Monroe made it tolerable and fun. We were instant friends. In his late twenties, he was a gay man from San Francisco who lived in Hawai'i with his partner Gary, a flight attendant stationed on O'ahu. Monroe made no apologies for who he was, and I marveled at his elaborate yet subtle flamboyance. He was the first gay person I didn't see as a caricature or cliché.

I grew up with Paul Lynde on *Match Game* and, later, Boy George from Culture Club, and Monroe wasn't like them. On the heels of the 80s AIDS epidemic, it wasn't nearly as socially acceptable to be out of the closet, so I respected my new friend for living in his truth and teaching me that being proud of who we are is beautiful. I was still learning who that person was (especially offstage), but Monroe was all about embracing everything about who he was with zero shame.

It didn't bother me that gay people were considered outcasts and misfits in some circles. I had been bullied for over a decade, so my heart was wrapped around the gay community in solidarity. Also, gay men were safe to be close with, and I trusted them in ways I couldn't imagine trusting straight guys. The last thing my BGFs (best gay friends) wanted was my body; all they cared about were my shoes!

As I sat at brunch with the boys in my new favorite city by the bay, I quickly ordered a mimosa and joined the fun.

"So, girl, how was your night?" Peter teased, already knowing the answer.

"Oh, you guys! We had so much fun!" I was still high on orgasms and lack of sleep. "After we left the club, he took me for a ride on his bike and then we came back to the hotel."

"Oh, I know, missy," Monroe interrupted, reminding me that he walked in on us at two a.m. to get to our room.

"Shit, that's right!" I shouted in shame, feeling terrible.

The boys and I snickered over egg whites and turkey sausage. "I'm sorry," I said sincerely and with a smile. Monroe blew me a kiss of forgiveness, and we raised our glasses.

"Cheers, honey! You got some!" Peter announced.

"Heeeeyyy!" a faceless comment chimed in from the crowd. "To PRIDE!"

"To PRIDE!" we all cheered, raising our glasses.

"So, you gonna see him again?" Monroe asked. "We don't leave until Tuesday night."

As a stripper, I was used to picking up one-night stands after work at The Wave, but meeting Michael was different. I was in an unfamiliar city, and he was beyond good-looking, almost too hot. He could easily pass for a younger Andy Garcia from *Black Rain*. I felt like I'd won the lottery, getting to take him home with me, so trying to roll the dice for a second time left me scared and unsure. But I was still breathing in the fumes of his kisses, and the taste of his patchouli and leather on my lips hadn't gone away yet. The thought of hanging out with him again made my clitoris throb. ("The question before us is, where's your clitoris!" —one of Monroe's hilarious lines whenever he visited me at the club while I was naked on stage).

"Oh God, that would be amazing, but how?" I wondered aloud.

I felt like we were in an alternative remake of the movie *Grease* where I was Sandy the Slut, and my boys were The Pink Ladies, offering pearls of casual sex wisdom.

"Girl, it's easy. Just do what we do. Call him up, tell him you had a great time last night and you'd like to see him again," Peter's boyfriend advised.

"Is it that easy?" I took a sip and looked up at the San Francisco skyline as the cool air kissed my cheeks. The speakers belted out Donna Summer's "I Feel Love," and the world around me was laughing, dancing, and letting its freak flag fly.

Monroe knew how my insecurities with my skin held me back and offered reassurance.

"Sweetie, he already knows you—how fabulous you are. You're beautiful. Now go get you some."

"Okay, I'm gonna do it!" I announced to cheers and walked off to find a payphone. (Remember those?)

My second night with Michael was even better than the first. He picked me up on his bike, and we checked out a local poetry reading at a dive bar in Haight Ashbury. We got drunk on cheap wine and shared artistic dreams: his desire to be a musician and me, a writer.

I'd just finished reading *Riders on the Storm: My Life with Jim Morrison and the Doors* by John Densmore, the drummer for the

Doors, and was excited to share my thoughts. I was elaborating on one of the stories from the book when he stopped to kiss me mid-sentence.

"Wow. You really are a writer," Michael said. His hands cradled my face, and I tightened up in my seat. Other than doctors, no one had ever touched my face, and they certainly didn't do so without needles and dry ice.

I thought about Monroe and his words: He knows how fabulous you are. You're beautiful. I took a breath while relaxing in my chair and kissed Michael back. We left the bar and headed back to my hotel room to enjoy my last night on the mainland together.

After sharing stories of our last night in the city, Monroe and I slept nearly the entire plane ride home to O'ahu. On the plane, I woke up to the sound of my cassette tape ending. I popped open my Walkman, flipped the tape over, pressed PLAY, and closed my eyes. "Not Enough Time" by INXS began, and my heart melted into the melody and lyrics.

"And I was lost for words in your arms…Not enough time for all that I want for you…."

I thought about Michael, knowing I'd never see him again. But I couldn't help but smile. I let someone touch my face and kiss me.

It was fabulous. And I was beautiful.

A couple of years later, in Waikiki, Monroe surprised me by walking into a club I was working at while I was naked on stage. He seemed nervous and frazzled and asked me to sit with him after my set so we could talk. Nestled in a booth in the back of the club, Monroe told me he was moving back to San Francisco the following day.

"What? Why?" I was stunned and felt a lump in my throat the size of a watermelon.

"It's just time," he said while holding my hand.

"But I don't...," I continued. I couldn't imagine my life without him. "Are you okay?" I prodded, still crazed at this shocking news.

"I promise, we'll talk every day," he assured. I was crushed and pissed off at the same time. Why the fuck was I just learning of his leaving now, ONE day before his flight?

Monroe gave me a huge squeeze, and we both shared tears and laughs as we threw out random memories from our short time together as inseparable friends.

The next day I received a phone call from Gary, Monroe's partner, the flight attendant. I assumed he called to explain their leaving was due to a transfer from his airline, but the news was much worse, and I wasn't ready for another gut punch.

"He didn't want you to worry and knows your heart, but I'm calling because you deserve to know." Gary's voice was serious, and I couldn't breathe.

"What?" I demanded, paralyzed with fear.

"Monroe is in the hospital in San Francisco, and his family is with him. He has a brain tumor and is scheduled for surgery tomorrow." I gasped and immediately started crying.

"What?" That was all I could say.

"I know, sweetie, but please don't be mad at him." Gary continued. "It's not the AIDS that's killing him; it's this fucking tumor." More silence. AIDS? What the fuck? This was the first time I learned Monroe was even sick.

"Oh my God," I cried out.

"Shh, shh, shh, I know." Gary whispered.

"Why didn't he say anything?" My words were drowning in an ocean of tears soaking my skin.

"Oh, darlin,' I know," Gary appeased. "He just knew how upset you'd be and wanted to protect you from the truth for as long as possible."

"I know, but…," I argued. It was unfair to make this moment about me and my feelings when the only thing that mattered was Monroe's health. But I was young and still lost in the vortex of my self-obsession.

A couple of days later, I received a call from the hospital. "Hi, honey," Monroe said on the line, his voice sounding groggy but jovial.

"How'd it go?" I asked about his surgery to remove the tumor. Before he could answer, I continued. "By the way, I wish I knew, you son of a bitch, so I could've helped you," I spat. I knew there was nothing I could do to help other than shower him with love, but I was still pissed off he didn't tell me he was sick.

"I know, girl," Monroe replied. "But you're already a basket case," he laughed. "This would've sent you over the edge." He wasn't wrong. Still, I felt cheated of the opportunity to be there for him even though I understood and loved him even more for protecting my heart.

Gary called a few days later and shared that Monroe had a massive seizure but could still talk. He suggested I reach out to him before it was too late. I called his hospital room immediately.

"Oh, honey, it was just a little Seizure Salad," Monroe quipped. We both laughed as I tried to hide my fear and that I was quietly sobbing, drool falling from my lips. I knew he was dying, and unlike Ki's passing, I was able to say goodbye this time. I loved that he was cracking jokes in the face of his demise to make me feel better, but I'd never felt more helpless.

"Oh, hang on, baby, I'm getting another call," he said, clicking on the two-way landline. The time I was on hold felt like an eternity, and I froze with my feelings, wrestling with the fact that this was happening.

"Sorry, girl," Monroe was back. "Everyone's calling to see what they're gonna get when I die," he joked again. I chuckled, and we shared precious time, sharing how much we loved each other. We eventually hung up, and I knew that would be our last conversation.

That afternoon, I received an unexpected envelope in the mail, a photograph of Monroe in the hospital wearing his cotton tie-back hospital gown, sitting in a wheelchair. He was bald with an 'x' tattoo above his forehead. I assumed this was for his surgeon to pinpoint the tumor. His legs were crossed, and he was holding a martini glass filled with water and beaming, wearing a pink stick-on Christmas bow on his bald head and his Tony the Tiger bedroom slippers on his feet. I laughed through sobs and shook my head. This is so Monroe. Later that night, I got the call from Gary. I knew instantly that Monroe was gone. I don't remember much from that phone call but felt oddly at peace that he was no longer in pain and having seizures, although I still struggled to believe it was real, just as I did after learning the news of Ki's death.

Gary provided me with Monroe's funeral information, and I thanked him, assuring him I'd be there. But I was completely freaked out. How could I possibly fly there to witness my thirty-two-year-old bestie being buried or whatever they do at funerals? I had zero experience in this area, and the idea of gathering with his friends and loved ones on the mainland who I didn't know to cry over our dead friend was too much for me to handle. I struggled for days and, in the end, decided not to go.

Harboring the guilt of my choice was debilitating, and the only thing that helped was numbing my pain with more of my faithful concoction of booze, blow and pills.

Years later, in my forties, I made an appointment with a well-known psychic medium who lived and worked in Costa Mesa near my neighborhood after learning of his gifts from my hairdresser, Robert.

"He's the real deal," Robert assured. "You should check him out if you're curious." I was. And the only person I wanted to come through from the other side was Monroe.

The day before my appointment with Bill, I dug through some old boxes in the garage and found the photo of Monroe in his hospital gown and Tony the Tiger slippers. I clung to the picture and fell asleep holding it, dreaming of talking with him just one more time.

Not only did Monroe come through, validating his presence through Bill reciting word-for-word things only he and I would know, but he also allowed me to forgive myself for not attending his service.

"He wants you to stop beating yourself up," Bill said. "Let it go," he's saying. Bill continued. "It's fine that you didn't go to his funeral. He knows how much you love him," he assured. "He knows you were there in spirit." I leveled into my chair, letting out a sigh, decades in the making.

"Thank you," I replied, wiping grateful tears.

Since Monroe's passing, I've seen Bill once a year, and in all my visits, Monroe always makes an appearance. He also visits me sometimes in my dreams, and I still laugh at the memories of our time together on this earth.

CHAPTER THIRTY

# A NEW LIFE

After Monroe's death, I left my waitressing job at the OCC. There were too many memories of us, and I needed a change of scenery. Approaching my late twenties, I was still trying to work my way out of the stripping world, so I landed a new gig at California Pizza Kitchen (CPK) in Kahala Mall, just down the road from mom's house where I had moved back to save up enough money to leave the island. I waited tables during the week while dancing at Club Rock-Za on the weekends. Within a couple of years, I'd saved up enough money to make the big move. I sold my beat-up Tercel, my secondhand furniture, and the rest of my belongings and headed to the mainland—with two suitcases and a dream! I had no idea what my dreams were other than to create a normal life for myself. A life without cigarette smoke blown in my moneymaker, with no offers of heroin at work, or my body being constantly naked, thinking my worth was attached to whether or not I received a dollar. I landed in Northern California at age twenty-eight in October of '96.

It took a minute for me to adjust.

When I finally told Kimmy I was ready to make the move, her usual encouraging words of how smart I was and how I could do anything I set my mind to were heartwarming. She also went into action mode, going to the CPK in Walnut Creek where she lived with her husband and new baby to see if I could transfer there. My transfer was immediately approved because I'd received so many customer compliments in the Kahala store. Kimmy offered up her living room floor for me to crash until I got settled. I stayed with Kimmy for a few weeks until I found a room for rent a couple of miles up the road from her place. As I started looking for jobs outside of waiting tables, I knew I had the sales chops, so I used my charm and moxie to get ahead, only this time, my clothes would need to remain on.

Trying to get a life in California in the nineties wasn't nearly as fun as stripping in Waikiki to avoid one in the eighties. And since I didn't have a car when I first arrived in California, I walked everywhere, making it even less fun.

During my first year waiting tables, one of my customers offered me a job at their full-service salon across the street from the restaurant as their front desk receptionist. So, I started working at the restaurant in the evenings and full-time at the salon during the day. Once I'd gotten into my groove at the salon, my affable disposition with a sales recruiter of IKON Office Solutions, who was checking out after getting her hair done, helped land me a normal sales job in the city of San Francisco, a short BART ride from Walnut Creek.

After three years of living in the East Bay, the cold winters became too much for this Hawaiian-raised gal. I relocated with IKON to Southern California at the suggestion of Tony, my first BGF on the mainland I'd met waiting tables at CPK in Walnut Creek. Tony, originally from SoCal, was moving back to the warmer L.A. climate after graduating from Berkeley. I decided to visit him after he'd made a move to check it out before making my decision. After cruising down Pacific Coast Highway (PCH), hugging the coastline at sunset from Newport Beach to Laguna, I was sold.

I moved in with Tony and his childhood friend, Eric, my BGFs to this day. Although I raked in good money at IKON, I couldn't stomach my new boss after learning he was cheating on his pregnant wife, so I left and sought new opportunities. With nothing but an embellished resume and my usual charm, I was hired as an Advertising Executive for a small firm in Irvine, just a few miles from our place in Laguna Niguel. I loved feeling so grown up, and I enjoyed the new sales pitches and account management game until I was let go due to downsizing. I was in my early thirties and scared shitless, having to file for unemployment. So, to assure I could pay the rent, I signed up with a temp agency who placed me in a medical device company in Irvine. My career as an Executive Assistant was born. (Thanks, Kimmy, for teaching me valuable computer skills!) Being an assistant was the perfect job for me, as I wanted to keep a low profile on my past life, and it afforded me that, especially since Google was becoming a thing. I was now thirty-three.

# CHAPTER THIRTY-ONE

# XANAPALOOZA

It'd been a stressful week at the office. My boss was particularly intense, and I suffered my first major panic attack that landed me in the hospital. I have experienced them in the past, but this was some next-level shit.

At the recommendation of the ER nurse, I made an appointment with a psychiatrist to help with my anxiety. My brain had an instant hard-on. Drugs! I get to have Drugs!

The room was dim and decorated with the usual credentials. I helped myself to one of the two faded brown leather chairs in front of an oversized mahogany desk. The wallpaper was just as dark and covered in plaid stripes, cracked at the seams. The gargantuan desk was so obnoxious, I was left with no other choice: I subconsciously began picturing how small his penis must have been. Not a great start when meeting a new doctor.

I mentally shook my head like an Etch-A-Sketch as soon I heard the door open and saw him walk into the room. There was an antique lamp on his desk next to a large medical dictionary with earmarked pages next to a land-line telephone. The lamp's green and brass colors provided much-needed ambiance to the otherwise banal space. It felt like Carol Kester, the plucky redheaded receptionist from *The Bob Newhart Show*, would walk in and interrupt our session because Bob's wife Emily (played by Suzanne Pleshette) was holding on line two.

"So, how can I help you?" he asked.

His eyes were peeled to his spiral-bound appointment book and not on my chart that I had just spent twenty minutes completing in the waiting room. It was instantly clear that the amount of shit this doc gave about me was directly proportional to how much I cared about his penis. It was also clear that his office smelled like mothballs and doubled as a set for a dark-comedy television show from the seventies.

"Hi, well, I had a panic attack last week and ended up in the ER," I said, fidgeting in my seat and explaining, surprised the words I was speaking were true. My tone was innocent and deceptive by habit. I was playing a character who wanted something she knew wasn't healthy for her. I mastered this version of myself during my teenage years whenever I spoke to mom about curfews and groundings.

It wasn't my first, but that last panic attack was particularly scary as it involved an IV drip and benzodiazepines, of which I was a big fan. I never felt an emergency room visit (because I couldn't catch my breath and was covered in flop sweat) was warranted in the past. But this episode was different. This one scared the shit out of me. If there were a spectrum or sliding scale to measure the severity of sheer terror brought on by anxiety, this one was off the charts. It invaded my body like water rising outside the Titanic, and all I could do was anticipate my drowning. I was at work, and my boss was releasing frustration over a minor error I made by screaming and throwing things in his office.

Even though I knew all would be fine, I felt like a five-year-old who'd disappointed her parent. Was my boss high-strung? Absolutely. And coupled with my anxiety and depression, his blow-ups didn't make for a healthy dynamic. But I was in my early thirties and new to the straight game of office work in the early 2000s.

This was my first job that felt like an actual career. I was finally "adulting." What I didn't realize was that having a career didn't automatically equate to surviving periods of tension so high that it impacted my health. My brain was already holding my mind hostage with depression, and now this.

"Those can be pretty scary," he qualified. After he spoke, I knew I was golden but still played along.

"It was," I confirmed, aware of his apathy. Can we get to the point, Doc?

"So, what is it that you do for a living?" he asked while scribbling something onto a sheet of paper. Finally, I was seen.

"I'm an executive assistant for a large financial firm." You know, a bullshitting, calendar-keeping, ego-stroking, corporate ass-wiper!

"So, under a bit of stress then?" Okay, now he was just taunting me. No shit, can I have the pills now? It was time.

"I took Xanax years ago, and it helped," I said casually. If there was one thing I learned while selling table dances in my youth, it was to assume the sale. This wasn't any different aside from the fact that my clothes were on, and instead of dancing for money to buy drugs, I now wanted a prescription. "Yeah, Xanax, I think that's what it was," I continued, impressed by my own performance of naïveté.

"Well, then, why don't we get you some?" the doc said matter-of-factly with a sly grin so eerie that if he weren't my new drug dealer, I'd have flipped out right there in front of him. But I was too excited. He could've been Jack the Ripper as long as he came home with my pills after rinsing off his knives.

My stomach was flipping like it did when Kenny kissed me for the first time in eighth grade, except I wasn't turned on sexually. What I was feeling was an all-over-body celebration. I would soon be high again, and the best part of this new drug deal was that it was one hundred percent legal.

After sashaying my way to the car with prescription in hand, I decided to stop at the grocery store for some wine. Mentally preparing myself for a marathon binge of the HBO series *Sex and the City*, I was looking forward to a fabulous weekend of flying alone in my studio apartment, which I had just moved into after my time with Tony and Eric.

When it comes to drugs, I'm an arrogant broad. A former party girl from the eighties (fine, and most of the nineties), my dance card was always filled with pot, blow, ecstasy, booze, and the occasional windowpane (acid, my innocent darlings) thrown in for good measure. Add to that a grueling stripper schedule of pole-swinging and bed-hopping, and it was enough to burn a gal out—which is exactly what happened.

At twenty-eight, when I'd fled the island toting two suitcases and a dream of living a normal life, I flung my proverbial beret in the sky, and Mary Tyler Moore'd my way around the culture shock of it all. The vast differences between growing up in Honolulu and living in Northern California were enough to entertain the friends I was making there. How I was petrified the first time I saw my breath in the cold air. How I hauled my umbrella everywhere for months (thinking the smog in the distance was the mountain rain heading to town), and how I called my mom, confused the first time I saw a squirrel, believing it to be a mongoose, which don't live in California.

I was embracing my new digs in Laguna Beach, secretly bragging to myself how I didn't need rehab to leave my old life behind. There were the occasional drug cravings, so I dabbled now and then, (normal, right)? Also, I kept the cocktails flowing because the worst was behind me. I was in my thirties. I had my shit together. Besides, me? A drug addict?

Fast forward a decade, and my recreational druggy-dance card was just as full as when I was stripping. I was back on the party dance floor, alone in my apartment, under the proverbial spinning disco ball of denial, not digesting the irony that I'd never really left. The scenery was different, but I could still shake my ass—even without the stripper pole.

And hey! New music! Damn, if those orange plastic pill bottles didn't make for perfect maracas. A lovely addition to the soundtrack of my dysfunctional existence.

After a few short weeks of abusing my new Xanax supply, I was in familiar territory, back at the candy store with my new dealer, my apathetic doctor with the big desk and tiny penis.

"Are you taking it daily, as prescribed?" Doc asked after I explained that .025 milligrams weren't doing anything for me.

"Yeah, but I don't think it's helping," I whined.

"Your tolerance is building," he observed. "Let's just up you to one (milligram). And feel free to take two, one when you wake up and the other before bed, as needed." I was so happy to hear this, I wanted to offer him a private dance right there on the spot.

"Okay, thanks," I replied, keeping my excitement under wraps.

As soon as I picked up my new, heavier bottle of pills, I scoffed at the cautionary words typed on the label: "as needed." Those two little words pack a punch. To non-addicts, they serve as a guideline, a written code of rules and responsibility, never to be taken lightly. These are people who had Vicodin in their medicine cabinet from getting their wisdom teeth pulled three years ago.

For us, pill-popping party animals, "As needed," is really code for, "Take as much you need to fly off your ass." Funny thing about double-dosing. The bottles get empty a helluva lot quicker. But addicts are nothing if not resourceful. I found a way around this little conundrum, doctor-shopping my ass around town like a clueless patient, having no concept that you could go to jail, dumbass.

Shady behavior aside, I knew I was back in party mode, but I didn't care. Ask anyone in the throes of using if they give two shits about the downside. We're feeling too good to be concerned, which is the whole point of drugs (duh).

So, party I did.

For the better part of a year, it was Xanapalooza. The disco ball was spinning out of control, and there were hundreds of little square-shaped mirrors shining brightly in my 400-square foot personal nightclub (apartment). All were begging me to look at myself and see clearly.

Work at the office was getting rough. When I wasn't rubbing elbows with the suits trying to keep my balance, I was isolating in my chick cave as soon as I got home. Months passed, and the aroma of depression began seeping through the cracks of my foundation. With every pill, I fought hard, pretending I wasn't close to going down in flames. There were hours spent online in random chatrooms, dancing naked in my living room, binge-watching television, and having deep conversations with Missy, my rescue cat, which I'm sure was entertained by how insane her human was.

I was living the dream.

That dream morphed into a nightmare the day I learned I might have a slight problem. One of my supplies was cut off, and suddenly I found myself with an empty bottle and no replacement pills for weeks. My arrogance wrestled with reason. I can do this.

The next few hours without Xanax in my system after a year of nine milligrams a day were spent trying to convince myself I was fine, that if I could walk away from blow and Ecstasy all those years ago, this would be a cakewalk. My heart thumped inside my sweat-soaked chest, and I fought hard to hang on.

By nightfall, I was climbing the wall of panic. Thanks to a dear friend and colleague whose mother-in-law is a psychiatrist and would likely know what to do, I reached out to her in tears. Soon, I was being wheeled into a ward on a gurney after being admitted to the hospital's ER. I felt like I was going to die.

"You need to be monitored at the hospital by a doctor in detox to help wean you from these pills," a drug counselor at the hospital said. I shared how I was able to walk away from blow in my twenties. "It's not like cocaine; these are Benzos (Benzodiazepines) in your system, and you can die trying to get off them cold-turkey without medical assistance."

I swallowed her words reluctantly but knew she wasn't sugarcoating my situation for a reason. So, the next day, I checked myself into the hospital's detox ward.

Life of Fuckery, The Sequel.

Attempting to describe the horror of detoxing from Xanax wouldn't do it sufficient justice. Even when Googling "Benzo withdrawal" or "Xanax withdrawal," I'm still not satisfied. Trust me when I say it's misery on steroids. Also, you could die, so there's that. I'd be a liar if I said there weren't times when I wished I had, just to kill the pain.

After detoxing for three days, being in a medicated slumber for most of it, I peeled myself out of my hospital bed and walked into the cafeteria. For the first time, I met and chatted with fellow patients. There was John, the fireman, who became addicted to opioids after back surgery before his stitches were removed. And Peter, the retired college professor suffering from crippling anxiety who was prescribed Xanax after his wife was killed in a car accident. I also met Mary, a housewife, who was in for Benzo withdrawal due to her doctor prescribing them like candy for her migraines. The more I looked around the dining tables, I realized a pattern. This was not your 80s Detox Show. These people were hard-working, law-abiding citizens who got clamped into the grips of addiction due to their doctor's instructions. Only two of our posse were traditional addicts from the streets, trying to get clean from meth and heroin. By dinnertime, I had more energy and was beginning to feel more like myself. A new patient joined us who looked lost and alone, so I stood up from my seat and pulled out a chair for him.

"Hi, I'm Christine-Xanax," I said, extending my hand. "This is John-opioids, Peter-Xanax and Cindy-Xanax. How are you? Well, don't answer that. I can imagine how you're doing. What are you in for?" The people in the room exhaled with a collective chuckle, and I was happy to let the air out of the room, if only for a moment.

"Methadone, and I'm Mike," he mumbled. His long hair was unwashed and covered most of his wrinkled and overly tanned face. He looked like a kid, but his face made us believe he was in his sixties.

"Methadone-Mike! Welcome!" I replied. "Do you want some water?" I asked as I refilled my paper cup from the pitcher on the counter.

"I'm good, thanks," was his answer.

"I remember my first day here, dude. If you need to stay in your room, we can bring you a food tray if you want," I assured. Methadone Mike nodded and shuffled away to his room.

The next day was Day 4 for me, and I was in morning mandatory group therapy with my new resort buddies at Club Detox. There were three meetings a day to attend, and I was starting to get a clue. It was during these meetings that I realized a few things. My past stripper-party-girl life and the one I was trying to live now were one and the same. I was a drug snob, telling stories of how I didn't need rehab the first time I got clean after leaving the island and how shocked I was that I was even there, in group.

"Holy shit! Every night, for how long?" a fellow user in the room asked me, in shock after I shared how many pills of MDMA I used to take back in my old life.

"About five years. Yeah, about six pills a night, for five years," I mumbled under my breath, which tasted of shame and shock (I was still alive). "But I started using blow when I was sixteen," I continued as if this information somehow watered down the danger of my excessive pill-taking. "My tolerance is pretty high."

"How are you not dead?" another group member asked, her arms in the air like a Baptist preacher from the South. "Shit, girl, that's a fuck-load of Estacy!"

"Right." I agreed, shaking my head nervously. I felt like I was winning some sort of drug addict contest of Most Fucked Up and Most Surprising to Still Be Breathing.

"You a cat," David chimed in. He earned his hall pass into Club Detox by way of heroin and methadone. A dude in his late twenties, looking like something you'd find stuck to the bottom of your shoe. I was surprised he could talk, let alone follow the conversation.

"I guess I am a cat!" I agreed, laughing off his comment while trying not to make eye contact. "How many lives do I have left, right?"

David scared me, and I judged his choices, a convenient way to take the focus off me.

After our daily therapy session ended, I dialed up my mother on the payphone from the hospital lobby.

"I can't believe it," I wailed, sobbing. "All this time, I thought I was just a party girl, when really, Mom, I'm a drug addict," I whispered, wiping away the steady stream of tears. It was my first and only time in detox, and I never went to a full-blown rehab facility, but that didn't matter. I was an addict and was ready to stay clean.

"Oh honey," Mom assured underneath nervous laughter. "No, you aren't you just have an addictive personality." She laughed. I chimed in and laughed at her naiveté (or denial about a daughter calling from the hospital detox ward).

Perhaps mom was projecting her own misuse of vices from her days in the sun, undermining the severity of her behaviors to help her feel less guilty. Either way, I wasn't in the mood for her passive-aggressive charm and hung up the phone after pretending I was being called into the cafeteria for dinner.

I suppose I picked the right profession when I was stripping. Nothing screams Employee of the Month like a stripper with drug connections. But now, years later, I was an Ann Taylor Card-owning member of the pearl-clutching community that is Corporate America. And I was shacked up for a week in Club Detox, still coming to terms that I was, indeed, also a hole-punch card-carrying member of the addiction community.

Sometimes full circle means having to relive our self-sabotage to finally get our head out of our ass. It took nearly a year to unhook the claws of Benzodiazepine addiction from my insides. Thanks to the excess cocaine and MDMA use from my stripping days and now, this Xanapalooza reunion tour, my brain may never fully recover. But maybe that's okay.

Recovering addicts are a beautiful brew. There's a certain type of vulnerability and compassion in the flavor of our hearts; we've tasted the poison of our decay and somehow managed to survive. With every fabric of our tattered souls, we are acutely aware our being alive is a kaleidoscope tapestry of luck and purpose.

My daily routine now consists of taking healthy doses of multivitamins and an antidepressant. Not so subtle reminders of how lucky I am to be alive and to never believe I can outsmart the disease of addiction again.

# CHAPTER THIRTY-TWO

# LIVING WITH DEPRESSION

I'd stopped dancing on stage years ago and cut down on my alcohol intake but trying to kick drugs was not so easy. Every time I was out with friends, and we would go dancing or to a bar, I felt the urge to do a line of cocaine. This went on for years until it didn't. As the triggers ran through me, I kept reminding myself that catching up with cocaine hangovers and blackout nights wasn't fun. Eventually, the cravings for blow faded.

After Club Detox, it was suggested that I join a sober living facility, but I declined. I wanted to get back to my regular life quickly without the daily reminders from others that I needed help. I knew I was a hot mess and sought therapy again as soon as possible. I had gone to NA and AA meetings a few times but just couldn't find my tribe and felt like a fraud because I didn't stop drinking alcohol completely. In my early thirties, I had wondered if I was an alcoholic, so I put the booze on the proverbial shelf for a year and fared well. I had some minor cravings but mostly missed the occasional glass of wine with dinner. So, I started enjoying a bottle on the weekends now and then. I was in control of my vices.

But my mental health was not doing well.

With less distraction, I found myself spiraling into a new place…a dark place. Living with depression is like battling cancer. I've been through both, and they suck. Equally.

Slipping through four-wheeled strangers crawling in a sea of asphalt, my drive from the office was grueling.

Hold on. Just one more block.

Turning left on my street, I unbuckled the seatbelt across my chest. I allowed a sigh within the walls of my lungs. My breath clung tightly to the fear. It was a welcome relief to let it out.

When I arrived home, the rubble of my life served up equal parts comfort and disgust. Piles of dirty laundry covered the floor, and stacks of papers blanketed my coffee table. The kitchen countertops were a nesting place for empty wine bottles, dirty dishes, and unopened mail.

There was a slight odor weaving its way up to my nostrils, and I couldn't tell if it was coming from my skin, my scalp, or the basic parameter of the area. Ashamed, I didn't have the strength (or desire) to investigate further. I undressed and climbed into my unmade bed. If only I knew what it was, what I could do. If I only took a shower, did laundry, washed the dishes, went for a walk, or had a piece of chicken (that last one's from mom). If only.

Through the darkness of my room, outside my bedroom window, I saw sunlight playing hide and seek with palm leaves in the breeze. Children playing on the street competed with the crashing waves echoing. That is what life feels like.

I didn't have the energy to cry. The guilt of feeling depressed was depressing. I wanted to evaporate.

"So, tell me." Her voice was soft. "Why are you calling?"

"I've never been suicidal, but I am having fantasies of not wanting to live."

I met Mary the next afternoon and hugged her as soon as she opened the door. She sat and listened to my story without judgment or pity.

In less than an hour, I bullet-pointed my life for her. Raped at thirteen, drugs by sixteen, a skin deformity by fifteen, promiscuity to feel beautiful, left home at seventeen...and on and on. Absentee father, abusive stepfather, and a mother who drank. The perfect sister everyone loved. And then there was me. The Stripper. The Fuck Up.

So, stripping was my thing. I drank. I snorted. I pill-popped. I bent over and counted my money one dollar at a time. I worked the pole, slept around, and pushed the envelope of reason. I rock-starred my ass in my one-woman show. And now, the music was over. The crowd was long gone, but I was still here.

"I'm trapped in darkness, and so much of what I see is light. How do I get there?" This time the tears managed to come.

"You will find your way. And I am going to help you."

It is not lost on me that I'm lucky. I'm a 2x cancer survivor, so aging is a privilege! And like everything else in my life it just happened. I was making routine doctor appointments like grownups do and sticking to them. I used to tell myself that I was a decade or so behind with these types of things because my maturity-evolution was sidetracked. Making and keeping appointments may seem small to some but for me, every meeting I didn't flake on and bill that was paid on time were personal victories.

Feeling proud to cross another annual checkup off my list, I was walking out of my OBGYN's examining room when something made me stop in my tracks.

"Oh, hey! I do have one question," I said to my doctor while standing in the doorway next to the reception area.

"Yes?" He replied.

"My monthly cycle seems way heavier than usual. Is that anything to worry about?" I asked.

After more Q&A with Doctor Lady Parts, a pelvic ultrasound was ordered and added to my chart.

"We'll just take a look and see what's going on. Probably just a polyp we can remove," he continued. His voice was paternal, and I had grown over the years to see Dr. LP as the trusted and kindly father-figure I never had.

"Cool, thanks," I smiled and made my way to the reception desk to get my parking ticket validated and confirm my local pharmacy's fax number.

A week or so after the ultrasound, at my desk after lunch with my office friends, I hopped online to check my personal email before tackling my To Do list for the afternoon. The landline telephone rang next to me, and my boss gave me a look through the glass walls framing his office. He had a thing with employees making personal calls on company time.

"This is Christine," I answered while minimizing my search engine on the computer screen and glancing at the Caller-ID on the base of the phone. I wondered why my doc's office was calling me at work. Did I lose an earring in the waiting room? Was there something wrong with my medical insurance?

"Hi, Ms. Macdonald, this is Emily from…," she said.

"Oh, Hi Emily," I interrupted; my nerves rudely cutting her off mid-sentence.

"We have your test results," she continued with a monotoned voice. Shit. The ultrasound. I had completely forgot about it.

"Uh huh…," I mumbled, hoping my lunch would stay down. Typically, after routine tests, I'd receive an all-clear letter in the snail mail and that would be it. This personal-call-at-work business was new and caused instant panic and nausea. I hadn't even heard the results yet and already, I was turning my pop the hood, check the oil appointment into Armageddon. It never entered my mind there would be something wrong. The darkness was behind me, and I did my time. I survived the cards I was dealt in my past and fought my way out with bloody knuckles. I was done. Look! I'm a grownup now who pays her bills on time! No. Just, Fuck No.

"We're referring you to a urologist," she explained at a higher volume due to my sharp breaths taking center stage through the mouthpiece.

"Okay…," I replied in the form of a question. *Jeopardy*, The Health Scare Edition!

Later that week after filling out forms and a quick hospital gown wardrobe change, I was escorted to a room where I enjoyed the privilege of having a tiny camera at the edge of a wire-like device inserted up my urethra. As painful as that Cystoscopy was, it saved my life. Technically, I saved my life. Had I not mentioned something not feeling right in my body, my OBGYN wouldn't have ordered the pelvic ultrasound, which is how my Stage I Bladder Cancer was found. An unexpected and purely accidental discovery, but still. Because of my inquiry the cancer was found early, which when you think about it, is a good thing; as my surgeon said: "Stage 1 is The Cadillac of Cancers."

And by the way, who gets bladder cancer at age thirty-six? A retired stripper who worked in nightclubs with second-hand smoke, a major contributor, and partied for over a decade, that's who. After lifting my jaw from the floor, I made the surgery appointment to cut the sucker out.

Fast forward ten years of remission and I'm feeling great, chatting with my dermatologist about everything from our southern California drought to which Bravo's *Housewife* series was our favorite. After agreeing to watch *New York*, I relaxed on his examination table for my annual full body mole-patrol.

"This one," I say while pulling my bra strap to one side and pointing. "It seems darker to me." I continued.

"Yup, I see it," my adorable freckled-faced, coppertop doctor agreed.

Doctor Coppertop and I met a couple of years back after I got to play Health Insurance Doctor Search Roulette, and as luck would have her way, we connected, and I adore him. He knows all about my skin story. I even gave him printouts of my surgery pics from high school, and shared about my past career as a stripper. This wasn't necessarily unusual. It's a safe bet that if you know about my previous life in Waikiki and we're connected in my current professional life in California, you're cool. I'll tell just about anyone after a couple glasses of wine in personal circles, but in grown-up land. I'm hush-hush until I know three things about you: 1. You're trustworthy. 2. You're non-judgmental. 3. You're fun. Doc Coppertop checked all the boxes so yea, he had security clearance.

"There're a couple here," he continued as his assistant marked my skin with a fine point sharpie and snapped photos on her digital camera.

"Ok." I agreed, closing my eyes, and breathing through the routine.

"Let's biopsy these three and take it from there," he said calmly. "Any questions? You good?" he asked.

"All good." I replied with a smile. And I was off. This wasn't my first or even tenth time getting my moles biopsied. Seventies and eighties Hawai'i is the birthplace of skin that could pass for an alligator bag years later. SPF wasn't mainstream back then. It was common for us teens to have tan line contests, using baby or pure coconut oil as marinade before the cooking show. As strippers, the contrast on our bodies were so dark with our white skin glowing under the black lights. It was a sight to behold. We went from Neon Barbie lookalikes in Day-Glow lingerie to Nude Glow in the Buff Babes strutting in spiked shoes and a smile. Entertainment perks aside, if you spend enough time in the tanning game, it's a safe bet the consequences will catch up with you. If you're lucky you get away with premature wrinkles and aging spots. Some of us didn't fare so well. I've lost count how many times I've had my moles surgically removed. All of them cancerous. Having both Irish and Scottish DNA means booking extra time for my regular visits with the doc to survey my skin properly. And usually, a biopsy or two was involved.

A week after my latest appointment I heard from Doctor Coppertop's office. The lab results from the newest moles in question were back and we needed to schedule another extraction surgery. For some reason, I wasn't as petrified with these skin cancer removal procedures as I was with the TURBT in my thirties. Maybe it was because I'd been through it already, or that I was middle-aged now and more at peace with things that were out of my control. Either way, I was ready. After the three clusters were removed, one Melanoma, two Basil-Cell Carcinomas, I chalked it up to another brick in my cancer wall, each one having a story. Through most of my forties I've had skin cancer removed and mostly from my back. But the most memorable procedure was the melanoma taken from my ass, specifically my ass-crack.

As the procedure began, I couldn't help myself and had to break the tension from holding in our laughter.

"If this isn't a sign, I was a stripper wearing G-strings in the eighties, I don't know what is." I joked. The three of us shared a laugh and the room felt instantly lighter.

"I wondered how you could catch sun in this spot." The surgeon quipped. "I forgot about G-strings in the eighties!" More giggles and before I knew it, we were done.

Whether bladder or skin, the cancers I've had removed from my body through the years have served me well as valuable lessons. Whenever I feel a sense of survivor's guilt, I pull myself out of those dark thoughts by remembering life has its own plan for all of us and whatever it is, there's only so much we can control. But being an ambassador for my health, paying attention and listening to what looks or feels off are things I can control. Which, in contrast to my old life on the stripper stage, is something I could get used to.

Though I always look for the upside, as someone living with clinical depression, I understand that pulling myself out of bed, brushing my teeth, and bathing is a huge deal. Those who don't suffer from the disease may never fully grasp the weight of those words: getting out of bed, brushing my teeth, bathing. Really. Big. Deal.

It's not that when I'm in the thick of a depressive state (which can last days, weeks or even months), I'm lazy or enjoy being a disgusting mess. The wiring in my brain simply short-circuits, and my ability to care for myself, for life, just disappears.

Each time I sink into the darkness, I want to evaporate, dissolve into a million finite pieces and duck into a envelope of shame and guilt. Every sigh pushes the envelope out the window, onto the street, and into the gutter. I feel safe there. And yet I still wish a street sweeper would roll by and put me out of my misery.

It sounds dramatic because it is. Depression is a slow-moving echo of numbness, reverberating waves of self-defeat with each passing hour. When I'm spiraling into depression, it feels like I'm headed to solitary confinement in prison, with one big difference. I'm always free to open the door but never do.

It's been a long road, but I'm finally at peace with the neurotransmitters in my brain. Maybe they were altered by using substances so early and now can't function without them. Maybe I was born this way. My shame and guilt have morphed into acceptance and education through a long process of self-awareness and letting go of attachment to judgment.

I've surrendered to the fact that my depression is not a choice I've made but rather a serious medical condition. I now manage my mental health through several avenues and own my ailments.

Part of releasing my shame is embracing that my specific case is treatable with therapy and medication. It took me years to allow myself permission to let go of the stigma that if I were to be medicated, I was crazy.

Each morning before I'm fully awake, I stand in the bathroom. My fingers deliver a little white pill to my tongue, and I lift a glass of water. I close my eyes as the magic slides down my throat. I'm reminded of a basic fact: I am mentally ill.

I smile, knowing I'm okay with this. Upon swallowing, I open my eyes and check myself in the mirror. Before long, I'm ready for the day. My feet step outside without thought, and my breath is uncompromised. I am filled with peace and featherweight optimism that I can navigate the world feeling normal—maybe even happy.

Embracing the warmth of the sun and exchanging smiles with strangers after a serious depressive episode is a victory. Once out from the darkness, my sanity is resurrected, and I finally begin to feel human again.

However, like cancer, even in remission from depression, painful fragments remain. They are stray pieces of thread from the tapestry of my happiness. I can never break them free. But I am managing these moments better than I ever have, and a huge reason for this is because I've stopped pretending I needed to be perfect.

So, I live with this naturally flawed way of learning to love who I am and remind myself of the now. Learning to be more present and not worrying about how I will feel tomorrow or what my day was like yesterday is a process. I practice gratitude in the little things. Getting out of bed. Brushing my teeth. Bathing. I try to be more patient with myself and others who don't quite understand. Mental illness isn't my fault, just as lack of comprehension isn't theirs.

There were so many moments in my life that nearly ended because of my depression. The romance of my suicidal fantasies was palpable. When in the thick of a serious bout, I had a love affair with sleeping forever and was obsessed with the idea of letting go. I never thought of inflicting insurmountable anguish on my loved ones after I was gone; I simply wanted my torment to end. There's nothing in life that prepares you for being a statistic. You can't rehearse feeling used. To truly know the role of the victim is to become one.

Yet, even as victims, we need not be marginalized by circumstance. We are not the sum of our horror stories but rather the embodiment of having survived them. The delicate balance of strength and suffering is difficult to comprehend.

So, we share our experiences, seeking only compassion and understanding, hoping others will find the strength to push through their darkness.

It's been over twenty years since receiving Shayla's cellulite-free comment, but far less time has passed since I truly appreciated it. In the blink of an eye, my rock star lifestyle of the rich and famous disappeared, morphing into middle-aged responsibilities of the tired and gracious.

Gone are the days of peeling off my Day-Glo lingerie for dollar bills and using my body as an entertainment sales tool. I can barely remember being cellulite-free, and while my fleshy stomach these days is lovely, it could give Buddha a run for his Rupee. But I'm happy. I feel beautiful.

Nobody with depression is lost forever, no matter how desperately we don't want to be found. Better days seem like someone else's story, and we don't feel deserving of the happiness up ahead. But we are. We just need to keep turning the pages and breathe through the words.

The first step is remembering that we aren't alone.

# CHAPTER THIRTY-THREE

# POETRY IN EMOTION

Spring was long gone. I was in my early forties and had just moved into my new apartment, where I was starting my new single life away from Darryl (more about him later). It was starting to feel like home, although there will still a few boxes left to organize. They were hanging out in every corner of my place, begging for my organizational attention. Some were filled with books I needed to place on shelves I had yet to buy. Other held CDs, DVDs, handwritten letters, and various office collectibles, like tangled mystery cords I couldn't bring myself to toss. If not filled with books, letters, or office junk, they were packed with photos. I'm talking hundreds, if not thousands, of misty water-colored memories piled to the gills, in no particular order. They represent the Kodachrome medley of my life's experiences. The boxes took me down memory lane. Whenever I'd sit down to organize them, I'd get lost in a maze of snapshots, listening to Billy Joel, frozen in time.

Some of my most cherished moments have been spent in solitude, free-falling into nostalgic memories. Remembrances wrapped in surprises are especially fun. I'd come across something extraordinary during one of my intimate archaeological photo dives. It was mixed in with my photos, just waiting to be read: a tattered cocktail napkin from Dan, a waiter from my stripping days.

I sat wondering why can't we see what others see when it comes to knowing ourselves? There were some people who saw right through me even when I was opaque to myself. People who might have bet on me at the Preakness as a favorite to win even when I felt crippled. Unconsciously, their faith bolstered that little kernel of hold back I possessed—the little voice that prevented me from walking over the precipice. I am grateful to them for holding a space I couldn't see, for offering me a sliver of hope. Darryl was one of them. Dan and Duke...were two.

Dan was older than me and one of the sweetest dudes I knew, which is saying a lot because my take on men wasn't great back then. Strippers are typically surrounded by one of the big three: Mr. Married, who wants to sleep with you, Starving Student, who tries to see you naked for free; or Mr. Scumbag, who's dating your stripper-friend but tries to get into your G-string every chance he gets.

Dan wasn't any of those. Dan had a plan for his life. He'd moved to Hawai'i from Minneapolis, earning his law degree by day at UH and supporting himself by serving cocktails each night at the club. Dan took a break from walking the floor and found a booth in the back to watch me dance whenever I was on stage. But he did more than check me out. He truly enjoyed my performances, appreciating my Bob Fosse obsession and Ann Reinking channeling. He saw my childhood Broadway dream in each sway of my hip, point of my toe, and nude pirouette. Dan probably felt I could have been more than I thought. After every one of my solo performances, four-song-sets on the main stage,

Dan would spring to his feet, applauding and whistling through his fingers, getting the crowd pumped. I knew he liked me, but it wasn't until finding this napkin that I realized how much:

I see the smile, it's halfway there

I wonder if

It really care

So many faces

So many times

I guess the smile

Comes from the rhyme

...it's still an ass-kicking smile

D

I remember the night Dan wrote this as he watched me on stage. After emerging from the dressing room, I saw him standing nervously by the bar. I read it aloud in front of him and was instantly embarrassed. What did he see in me? The faith echo of what I knew all along, hidden behind my youthful bravado, didn't fool Dan. Yet, the poem was a compliment I struggled to believe. Even in the thick of my self-doubt and insecurity, there was something inside of me he saw, and that something made me hold on to this piece of paper for more than a quarter-century. Whatever he saw was probably the same flicker that helped me break away from Darryl, knowing that I wasn't living in my truth and the same force that kept me believing I was worth more than the sum of my fears. It is hard to come face-to-face with fear. It took enormous courage, especially for a little girl who had no one's direction or guidance in their most fragile puberty period. Thanks to people like Dan, who helped me get to this point in my life. This personal history I held in my hand reminded me how far I've come, even knowing there was still a distance to go. If I knew Dan's last name, I'd look him up to thank him for being such an integral part of my journey to self-worth.

"And I wouldn't feel so used."

– "Linger" (The Cranberries)

As I was tripping down memory lane, I heard the echo of Duke's words, yet another anchor for my future.

Duke was a twenty-something delicious, tall drink of London with dirty blonde hair, emerald and gold flickering eyes, and sun-kissed abs. I usually dug the Mario's ("It's 'ma-dee-oh,' a lover once corrected me in bed) and Antonio's of the world. But with Duke, I made an exception. He was the precursor to David Beckham, only without the Spice wife, four kids, and bankroll. I'm not even sure he played soccer, football, whatever. But that accent. And the cocky attitude. Dead ringer. As soon as he said my name, I was all in. As if his royal dreaminess wasn't enough, he was the hottest new waiter at the club. Had he not been shagging my friend Madison; he would've been perfect for me. Hot guys. Always gay or taken, I grumped.

If possible, and it was, Maddie was even more stunning than her English prince. A dancer, she'd chosen "Madison" as her stage name to honor her Wisconsin roots. It was fascinating to watch two beautiful creations of nature meet for the first time. They knew they were born with winning lottery genes but could only appreciate it when locking eyes with their fellow ticket holder. So annoying. I wanted my aesthetically gifted friends to be assholes so that I could hate them. But they were cool and down to earth despite their good looks, and I adored them.

Duke and Maddie shacked up just days after they'd met. As much as I lusted after Duke's piping hot, witty, heavily accented, bounce-a-quarter-able ass, I never wanted to break the Stripper Sisterhood code of "Thou Shall Not Covet Thy Fellow Pole Dancer's Penis." We became fast friends. I looked up to Maddie, a couple of years older than me and decades wiser (Midwestern upbringing). And heartthrob Duke quickly morphed into the eccentric older brother I never had, serving as a kick-ass wingman.

After a particularly grueling shift, Maddie was wiped-out and decided to head home for the night. After shelling out watered-down draft beers to belligerent customers, Duke hit me up for a drink and sat listening to us girls complain about how men suck. Hanging in our usual "VIP" digs upstairs at The Wave, Duke witnessed yet another one of my glorious mini meltdowns fueled by too much blow and too little self-esteem. The drama was always the same: my dude du jour was ignoring me. Sure, he was banging half the club, but why the fuck was he ghosting me? Was I too fat? Too thin? Not tall, short, funny, pretty, happy, sad, ugly, scary, quiet enough? What was wrong with meeeee? In typical form, after my fifth vodka cranberry, I went all Glenn Close/*Fatal Attraction* on his ass. I will not be IGNORED, Dan. Nothing says, "Come take me" like a desperate coke whore going off. This was always followed by copious tears (and more blow) in the bathroom, pulling my hot-messy-self together and heading back to my seat to make my next move—find a new "Dan-from-*Fatal-Attraction*."

Duke was always front and center watching my wretched meltdown.

This revolving door of "Come be my no-strings, good-time fella." That had to be fun to see just before the part where I sat wide-eyed and in disbelief as I could never understand why these guys didn't fall head over stripper shoes in love with me. I guess a fucked-up exotic dancer with a coke problem, low self-esteem, and abandonment issues wasn't their thing.

Assholes.

"Stephanie, love, can I be honest?"

I always hated when people started sentences this way and was even more so when it came from Duke, as I knew he'd cut to the brutal chase. "Can I be honest?" is never followed by a compliment or something inherently positive.

"Yeah?" I smiled while bracing for his words.

"You're a jellyfish, doll." He yelled over the music like an Italian opera singer with his hands in the air.

"A what?" My question was sincere. I had no idea what he was talking about.

"A bloody jellyfish. You've got no bloody spine!" Duke replied with a laugh, sipping on his gin and tonic.

Inside, I knew just how right he was, and I hated it. "Fuck you." I raised my glass, letting him know I understood. We shared a laugh and polished off our drinks. As Duke flagged down our waitress, we both heard it. By some cosmic force with a wicked sense of humor, the song "Linger" by the Cranberries began to play through the speakers. Perfect.

"Do you hear this song, doll? These blokes you party with, they've got you wrapped around their fingers—or cocks, love. You've GOT to get a bloody clue!"

My empathetic English wingman. Always trying to help was not helping right now. But I couldn't get a clue. It would take years to wrap my head around just how much I needed one.

# CHAPTER THIRTY-FOUR

# FASCINATION STREET:
# A DREAM JOURNAL ENTRY

It was no longer 1993. It's now 2013.

It's been decades since I've pulled any Fatal Attraction scenes, but the memory of my self-induced drama still leaves a mark. I can now see how every choice I made was textbook behavior of a gal who just needed to believe in herself and not look for validation in men. By five or six years old, they say a child has already donned their mask to face the world. They perceive it's true, and it will take a hell of a lot of support to get that melded mask to come off without scars.

I lost touch with Maddie and Duke after they broke things off and split town. I heard Maddie headed back home to get her master's degree, and I have no idea what became of Duke. He's probably a retired English supermodel living on the French Riviera, endorsing a skincare line for men. Or maybe he's a crispy, balding beach bum with a hairy back, decked out in Speedos in Mykonos. Either way, I wonder if Duke ever thinks of the Jellyfish sister he once knew. He'd tried so hard to help. If only he knew how my spine has grown and is helping me write about just how far I've come from my Fatal Attraction days. This is a rhetorical question. Don't answer. Why are things we need to learn most right in front of our eyes, but it takes so much pain to see them? I'd had many dreams throughout my journey to recovery. One in particular helped me to clearly see this truth.

My boyfriend at the time was a guy named Darryl.

Dream Journal Entry:

We were parked parallel to a cliff on what seemed like an empty piece of land in the Hollywood hills. We were in separate cars. I was parked directly behind him. The scene below was bustling with the typical energy of big-city afternoons lacing up for the night. Street lamps and storefront signs began their evening routine while the sunburned horizon melted into its haze. The air around us was still. Darryl and I spoke to one another while sitting in our driver's seats, the windows rolled down. We each had our wallets in our laps and were counting out aloud the money we'd saved. We were excited and happy.

I saw her spring for Darryl first. An excruciatingly obvious drug-induced, amped-up twenty-something gal armed with a long black cane, complete with a metal tip. The cane looked more like a prop than a weapon, but we knew why she was using it. She slammed her cane on the roof of Darryl's car and peered at him through the open window. Neither of us screamed, but we were surprised enough to jump a little in our seats. From the front window of my car, I watched every move she made. She leaned in over Darryl, peered into his car, then noticed me.

Suddenly, I was the one who was nose-to-nose with this maniac.

Remaining calm, I looked deep into her eyes and noticed a pair of thick, black false lashes caked on like they had been glued to her eyelids for a week. Her dark hair was wild and long, and her bangs covered most of her face. "You are really pretty," I said to the mystery woman with truth and confidence. I wanted her to know that I could see through her mask of heavy make-up. I held onto my wallet, expecting her to try to pull it from my grasp, but our little friend didn't take our money for some reason, though she did wave her cane in our personal space, long enough to remind us that she could have. After she walked away, Darryl and I heard a voice say, "She's just looking for a place to sleep tonight." The voice assured us we were out of harm's way. He didn't speak again, and we never got a look at his face. There but for the grace of....

Darryl and I remained in our cars but shared a conversation through our smiles. We let the other know we were okay. We still had our wallets and took comfort in knowing we did have a place to sleep—to call home. That night, after closing our bedroom curtains and getting ready for bed, the ground began to rumble. It instantly morphed into a shake, and almost as soon as it began, we saw coverage of the small earthquake on the nightly news. Another jolt quickly followed. Having lived in California for years, I was used to these tremors, but they still made me crazy. I looked at Darryl, now sitting on the bed watching the television, and could see he was unruffled.

Darryl soon fell asleep.

I lay next to him. Not long after, I found myself venturing outside, walking down the hill into the night. I was dressed in an old stripping costume, and under the lights, I made my way through the crowd, looking for the club. The tiny hot dog stand was still across the street, and the old Vietnamese man who owned it remembered me. The tropical air mixed with his musky cologne carried me back to a place that was hauntingly familiar and way too comfortable. I found the club and stepped inside.

The view in the dressing room reminded me of what any college dorm room would look like, but with much more sequins and lip gloss. I caught a glimpse of myself in the smudged-up mirror behind the door and noticed I was wearing purple Velcro rollers in my hair. The other girls stared at me, but I didn't give a shit.

I'm retired.

I vaguely remembered songs I wanted to dance to, so I quickly made my way to the DJ booth before they escaped me. The booth perched above the stage like a treehouse meant I needed to step up a ladder to meet the man in charge of the music.

A stout Black dude with a shaved head and dazzling smile greeted me. He wore a Navy-blue t-shirt, flip-flops, and khaki knee-length shorts. He was smoking a cigarette, sitting on a tattered mahogany bar stool with hundreds of CDs surrounding him. I didn't want to disturb his chaos but wanted at least one song to call my own on stage with the other dancers, so I extended my hand to introduce myself.

After telling him my name, I placed my request.

"Do you have 'Fascination Street' by The Cure?" I asked.

It suddenly occurred to me that I was older. Fuck. He may not even know The Cure.

After a little mind search behind his eyes, the DJ nodded and spoke. "Oh yeah, yeah, yeah, yeeeeaaah, I got that one!" He seemed cool enough to show his appreciation for my taste in old-school alternatives.

Before I walked on stage, I noticed a step-through carousel blocking the entry steps.

"Oh!" My voice turned up a notch in surprise. "This is . . . new," I spoke to anyone who was listening and could explain this metal contraption to me. It reminded me of the turnstile you walk through when entering a subway platform.

"Here, we have a new way to track how many girls we have working per night." I heard a voice within the thick wall of smoke under the DJ booth at the heels of the stage. He was a crispy, deeply tanned bearded man who looked like a cross between David Caruso and Dog the Bounty Hunter.

"Let me take care of this for you," he flirted.

He placed two quarters in the machine and guided me through the carousel. My hips felt the clicking of the stripper counter. It was like walking through a time machine. I took comfort in knowing Caruso Dog liked what he saw, hair curlers and all. It felt good to think I still had it after all these years.

Assuring him that my special performance was just a one-time thing ("I'm retired, you see . . ."), I looked back over my shoulder. "Thanks. I won't be here every night."

He nodded, took a drag from his cigarette, and walked away.

Then I heard it—the groovy introduction to "Fascination Street." The bass guitar pulsed through my veins like an old lover coming back for more. I forgot how much I loved this song. The electric guitar soon welcomed the bass, and before I knew it, I was off, soaring through a cloud of melody and movement.

Standing four feet above the crowd on stage, beads of sweat responding to the neon lights, my body was along for the ride. My head swayed in unison with my hips, and with my eyes closed, I breathed in each pulse of the notes without distraction. I could sense the crowd watching me. I was almost sure it had nothing to do with my hair's jumbo purple Velcro curlers.

Apathetic to the money or my competition on stage, I floated down Fascination Street. A fucking awesome place to ride.

Hearing the DJ's voice shifted my presence some. I expected to hear the familiar rumble of a baritone voice mixed with radio-type exuberance, so I didn't stop dancing completely. What I didn't expect was what he called me.

Ladies and gentlemen, give it up for…Christineeeeeeee.

Christine? CHRISTINE? How does he know my real name?

My mind traveled out of myself and right into the DJ booth. Suddenly, I realized I'd introduced myself as Christine. I was so used to having people say, "Give it up for Stephanieeeeeeee," not "Christineeeeeeeee." I felt completely off my game. Frozen in shock, I looked out into the audience, then onto the stage, instantly forgetting how to move.

There were two other girls with me. One wore a white leather bikini with shiny rhinestone studs (handmade by the incomparable Ki), and the other was in head-to-toe black leather. The girl in black had heavy bangs and crusty-looking false eyelashes. As soon as I passed her on the runway in the center of the stage, I knew she was the same girl who'd tried to scare Darryl and me up on the hill earlier that day.

I stayed out of her way.

"She's just lookin' for a place to sleep tonight."

My plan to steer clear backfired because when she noticed I didn't pay her any attention, she immediately pounced on me. We were standing next to the pole, the song ending but still loud enough to fill the silence between us.

She spoke first.

"It's you…." She was trying not to laugh at the sight of my purple Velcro curlers.

"I think you're really pretty," I said assuredly. She didn't thank me but was happy to hear the compliment again. I knew she didn't believe me.

The next song on stage was En Vogue's "Giving Him Something He Can Feel." An excellent, strut-worthy tune.

Still feeling out of place after hearing "Christine" over the loudspeaker, I decided I was ready to leave.

Before the song was over, I took off my shoes and walked barefooted down the side steps next to the back bar. I stood for a moment anticipating the familiar throb of pain that usually rushed from the balls of my feet through to my heels. I then took another moment for myself to observe the crowd. No one noticed I had gotten offstage.

The bar was the same aside from the new girls and customers. The room was still dark, filled with cigarette smoke and the smell of stale beer. The music was still played way too loudly, and the dancers could've all used a meal.

Carrying my stilettos over my shoulders, I continued to walk barefoot on the dirty carpet. I couldn't wait to leave. I looked down at my right thigh to see how much money I had collected. Only a couple of dollar bills lay flat under my garter, but I didn't care. I was going home.

*    *    *

I awoke with clarity. It was time to move on from everything, including Darryl.

It's been a few years since I'd moved away from Darryl and the perfectly safe life we'd shared. Darryl was an amazing person I met online. He was one of the few loyal readers of a blog I started when I began my journey of chronicling my story. Complimentary comments turned into flirty exchanges, which then morphed into internet chats. After a few months of our exchanges, we grew enamored. We knew that meeting in person was the only way to know if our romantic chemistry would translate into an actual 3D relationship. What I DID NOT KNOW at the time was that Darryl was born female and was hiding behind a fake profile pic of being a male.

After it was clear we'd started developing romantic feelings for one another, Darryl disappeared. He felt so guilty catfishing me. I was devastated he no longer answered my emails or calls. This was a lesson in my journey of coming face-to-face with my mental health. I had no idea I was suffering from BPD (borderline personality disorder), a very slight case later diagnosed. Because of my trauma and neglect, my main issue with BPD was the extreme fear of abandonment. So, this triggered me beyond anything I had ever experienced, and I needed to go back to therapy. I felt Darryl's disappearance was because of something I'd done. Keep in mind that we had only talked on the phone, but I already felt we were an item because of my attachment issues.

After no word, I heard from Darryl six months later, and he confessed about his transition. I was livid at first but then felt extreme empathy and gratitude for him coming clean with his secret and for trusting me. I bought books to educate myself because I didn't know the difference between a drag queen, a trans man, a transvestite, etc. I learned that the number one demographic for suicide victims is the trans community. For someone to feel trapped in their own body, the body assigned to them at birth when their BRAINS were assigned to the other sex was fascinating to me and heartbreaking. I told Darryl we could be friends. I forgave him. With his permission, I asked questions. I became his biggest ally and cheerleader. After about ten months, Darryl and I admitted we still had feelings for each other. He lived in another state at the time, Idaho, and we decided the only way we could find out if we would make it as a true couple was to visit each other. I flew to see him, and we had a great weekend together.

I never felt it was romantic love, but I knew Darryl loved me with his whole and beautiful heart. So, I forced myself to be his romantic partner. I had just turned forty and was afraid to be alone for the rest of my life and had never experienced being treated so well.

Darryl moved in with me in less than a year. We moved to Irvine, a couple of towns over from where we lived in Laguna Beach. He treated me like a queen, and for the first time in my life, I felt truly loved for who I was as a person and not my body. Darryl was a great boyfriend, but we had nothing in common besides our big hearts and love of just and fair social issues.

We lived together for 2 years. I tried to make it work. But I was never IN LOVE. When Darryl purchased a diamond ring, I had a panic attack. I knew it was unfair to be with him because he deserved to be with someone who was in love with him. I was paralyzed with guilt. I had never broken anyone's heart. I asked my therapist to help me figure out how to break up with him.

When I finally had the courage to end our relationship, it was awful. I walked in on Darryl after he'd taken an entire bottle of pills. He was passed out, swimming in body fluids. I called 911. The cops came. I had to file a report. Darryl confessed he'd tried to take his life. He was hospitalized for seventy-two-hour surveillance. I was a wreck because I felt responsible. My therapist kept me sane and continued to help me leave him, which was even harder now.

As scary as it was leaving him, especially having just turned the Big-4-0, it was even scarier living a life with someone I knew wasn't meant for me. Staying with someone I wasn't romantically in love with would have been selfish to both of us. So, I did the hardest thing I've ever done where romance was concerned. I broke it off with him. It was the first and only time I would be on the giving end of heartbreak. And I felt like shit.

Fast forward a decade and Darryl is happily married and we are dear friends.

It's been years since I worked as a stripper. I remember many dreams since my days were over, from snorting blow and tasting the drip down my throat to feeling the sting of a boyfriend's fist as it clocked me on the cheek. This was the first time I'd woken up from a dream feeling enlightened.

I love that I wore curlers on stage, and my real name was announced. I'm empowered, knowing that I wasn't afraid of the scary girl anymore. The fact that I complimented her twice through her mask of pain made me realize that I am coming full circle.

I was the girl on the hill with the cane and the crusty false eyelashes. I needed to tell her that no matter what, she was beautiful. I woke up this morning knowing that it was true.

# CHAPTER THIRTY-FIVE

# 'YOUR SKIN IS LIKE AN ORANGE'

I sat upright on the examining table, the thin paper rustling under the backs of my knees. I tapped my heels against the sides like a restless child waiting for her lollipop. I wondered: at what age in child development did doctors stopped shelling out candy? And how cool would it be to have a martini bar in the waiting room?

My lungs were full. I pushed every ounce of air out from under my belly, through my chest. The room was suddenly filled with the heavy wind of my breath, penetrating the sterility of the space. The faint ticking of the second hand on the wall inside its circle of time reminded me how slowly it dripped in these moments (but when I hit snooze—lightning speed).

It's been decades since my first surgical consultation for my skin when I was in high school in 1984, but the scene was all too familiar. Butterflies still fluttered inside me. I knew that soon, I would lie on that same thin sheet of paper covering the table, my face centered under an oversized microscope and my eyes closed, protected from a lightbulb that would feel unnecessarily bright and way too close to the skin on my face.

The heat would remind me of the sun. It would carry me outside myself. I would fantasize about lying on an empty beach back in Waikiki. Anything but being under another doctor's lamp and an oversized magnifying glass. I'd rather live in my fantasy, far away from white robes and the smell of rubbing alcohol. In my mind, I was a swimsuit model with perfect skin, lounging on a golden stretch of pristine sand glistening under the afternoon glow of make-believe.

Shirtless Greek gods donning cocoa-buttered, six-pack abs and solid forearms would deliver a frosty Mai Tai in an unusually skinny but tall tiki-style mug. It would have two narrow straws and one tiny pink umbrella wedged on the edge of the mug beside a slice of fresh pineapple. Palm trees playing hide-and-seek with my perfect silhouette and the waves kissing the shoreline would provide a lovely accompaniment to my afternoon of bliss.

But then, fingers. The touch from a faceless doctor in a white coat professionally equipped to provide me with promises of . . . better snapped me out of my paradise reverie.

"Right now, your skin is like an orange," he tells me, using an unfortunate fruit analogy. "We can make it look like an apple." I heard the light switch click, felt the heat from the bulb disappear, and then opened my eyes.

The doctor gently pushed the glass microscope away from the table, and I was already missing my imaginary Mai Tai. He extended his hand to help me sit up as if I were a wounded gazelle, shot down with the sharpshooting penetration of his words. Your skin is like an orange.

There was another doctor in the room. I recognized the head-nod-grin combo of promises and pity when our eyes connected. My illusions of being bikini-model pretty, quickly dissolved. Reality. After nine surgeries—from sandblasting in the late eighties to the more recent cutting and laser burning—I was still Freddy Krueger, the scar-faced monster from the 1984 slasher movie, *A Nightmare on Elm Street.*

Freddy's face was disfigured and burned, and although his character wasn't real, I felt a kindred connection with the man behind the mask. I understood his pain and wondered if Wes Craven, the director behind Freddy's creation, had a history of skin afflictions himself.

I'd carried Freddy with me for decades like a soul sibling. When everybody wanted their MTV and Madonna was Like a Virgin, he'd been there alongside me, a moniker I couldn't seem to shake. Although I no longer woke up to blood-stained pillows or had to endure weekly cortisone shots for golf-ball-sized cysts on my face, my struggle with Freddy remained, even thirty years later.

"Really? As smooth as an apple?" I called out the doc's sales pitch, already knowing his answer. I learned the hard way that most plastic surgeons are used car salesmen in white robes and nicer shoes. I was too old and had been through too many surgeries to share his optimism, though well-meaning it was intended to be.

"Well, as close as we can get," he qualified. "Nothing is perfect."

He was right. No matter how many doctors I allowed to pierce my invisible facial force field, I would never be completely free of scarring from the severe acne I'd endured since I was a child.

After discussing my financing options and mentally circling my work calendar with the weeks off I would require to recover, I thanked the doctors for their time, accepted their glossy brochure, and slung my purse over my shoulder.

The commute home was a blur. Navigating through tears and self-assurances that there was nothing wrong with me, that I just wanted to look and feel normal, I tried not to compare myself to anyone. I searched for the answer that would never come to the same question I'd repeated and again through the years: why me?

I tried to remember I was still beautiful, but the word "still" is the dagger. "Still" is one of those words with a hidden agenda, a compliment with conditions. But it's a compliment, nonetheless. I'd take a "still" over none at all.

It didn't take much to temporarily erase years of working on personal self-improvement and esteem. When I recently read a tweet from a grown woman calling me Freddy Krueger (true story), I felt shitty again. Somehow, my worth and beauty were directly proportional to one cruel person's descriptor online.

Why is hate so much easier to feel for some of us than love? We struggle to believe that our inner voices of self-sabotage are so much louder than the kind and compassionate mantras we aspire to follow.

So many of us get tangled in a web of not enough, built from spinning our yarn of self-loathing. We dream about living a different reality; instead of understanding, we can tear down the cracked foundations of our past and create a new normal. Instead of being held back by our flaws, we can accept them. So. Hard. To. Do. But the good news? It's possible.

We are all unique, beautiful creatures of this world, and every struggle, each flaw shapes us…makes us who we are.

Having another surgical procedure on my skin is still a real possibility. However, accepting the reality of knowing nothing is perfect, and that my skin will always be scarred, is more important to me now.

Ironically, it took someone calling me Freddy K as an adult to remind me how far I'd come. No matter how much I struggled to find my inner peace and beauty, this person's ugly heart had been revealed, and her struggles were hers. Perhaps I should send my recent name-caller a thank you basket of fruit. I think apples and oranges would be a nice touch.

One of the hardest things to master is loving ourselves unconditionally, and thanks to people who try to hit us where it hurts, we are reminded that we do. What I knew was that even feeling fear, I was ready to embrace me.

# CHAPTER THIRTY-SIX

# VALENTINA

As we circled the block in search of street parking close to the restaurant in Hollywood, California, my eyes locked in on a fabulous sign that would dictate the course of our evening, unbeknownst to Todd. Todd is one of the people from a small crew of 'ohana in California who I met shortly after moving off the island in the late nineties. He was too busy looking for open pockets of asphalt to understand my laughing out loud after reading the words on the sign above the entrance:

"1000s of Beautiful Girls & 3 Ugly Ones."

Sold.

Putting aside my plan to kidnap Todd after dinner and take him to see female strippers, we enjoyed a long-overdue date. It's always a hoot to catch up with old friends, and when they're like family, even better. Time spent with them is entirely too rare.

We share the same trendy (at the time) tattoo of the symbol for friendship written in Kanji (Japanese) lettering on different patches of our skin, applied at different times in our lives. It's our wedding ring, a permanent symbol representing our vow to have undying and unconditional love, no matter where we are in our lives or how seldom we get to hang out.

Too corny? Fine, it's our gang sign.

We are diverse from different backgrounds, ages, ethnicities, and sexual orientations. Our common denominator is love. Isn't that really what it's all about? Todd also happens to be gay, which makes for fun entertainment on nights like this when I plan on surprising him after dinner with a visit to an all-nude strip bar across the street from our restaurant.

After a couple of toasts, some flirty gazes around the room, and a fun game of "Is He or Isn't He (gay)?" Todd and I were off to our next adventure after batting our lashes at our prospective targets.

"C'mon, let's go," I commanded after paying the bill.

"Okay, girl. Where we goin'?" he asked. He was tipsy from his beer and stoned from the joint he'd smoked in the car earlier.

"I told you!" (I hadn't.) Pointing to the hilarious sign across the street, I held Todd's hand, and we started walking.

"Um, uh-uh, honey...," Todd realized where I wanted to go.

I kept walking, pulling him behind me. Something was leading me to that club, and I couldn't turn back. We arrived just outside where there were two twenty-something gals, wearing skintight mini dresses, perched under the sign, smoking, and chatting it up with a couple of dudes on the sidewalk.

Todd leaned up against a street sign and lit up a cigarette himself.

"Hi, you work here?" My voice attempted hip but came out old-lady-desperate.

"Yup," one of the gals replied, uninterested in sharing words with some middle-aged broad who seemed too interested in her employment status.

"I was a stripper twenty years ago," I said proudly. I was still trying too hard to connect, but at least I won their amusement.

Todd watched from the wings, dragging on his cigarette, smiling at my fortitude.

"Oh, um, we're waitresses. We don't strip," the other woman said. Their judgment permeated the Hollywood air with each exhale of smoke.

"Cool," I retreated. Great. I now felt old and cheap. Any attempt at stripper-sisterhood banter fell by their twenty-two-inch waist size.

In certain circles, and in my day, there was a strip club hierarchy, an unwritten caste system among the girls. You were somehow deemed classier, less whoreish than a stripper if you were a strip-bar waitress. I wasn't too young to wrap my head around that thought back then, but now, I was old enough to appreciate the irony.

No sooner did I reply than the night sky flashed with blue and red police lights, followed by a deafening siren. Todd and I shot to attention, checking out the events across the street with concern and nervousness like we were somehow in trouble—for what, we didn't know.

It's funny. Even now, when I see or hear police sirens, part of me still feels busted. I wonder if that ever goes away.

"There they are, dude, same time, same block, like fucking clockwork," one guy standing nearby said.

"I know, right?" came the reply from the guy standing next to him.

It was hard not to overhear these guys hanging out in the doorway of the pawnshop next door.

"So, you guys work here and see this all the time?" I inquired.

"Pretty much. It's the same shit every night," he said, blowing smoke into the California sky. I offered a chuckle underneath my fortysomething armor of wherewithal and sensibility, but the conversation quickly fizzled. What did I have to share with these two young clerks on Hollywood Boulevard, and why was it so damned important (still) for me to fit in?

I promised a quick visit, taking a reluctant Todd into the club. We started up a dimly lit hallway with black carpeting and walls. The familiar purple hue of neon lights peeking from the quarter-inch space between the floor and the bottom of the tinted double doors was waving me inside.

"Just one drink," I promised.

The room was sparse, with just four customers sitting two rows back from the stage. They were nestled in the darkness far enough away from the "Dude I'm standing right in front of you, pull out a buck" seats but close enough to read the dancers' eyes, which were hoping you'd still come up and help a sister out.

I knew the place would be dead because of the hour. Having just finished dinner across the street, it wasn't even 9:30, so no surprises there. What did trip me up was the no-alcohol thing.

As soon as I noticed the gals on stage were wearing nothing but clear heels and a smile, I remembered: nude bars in California aren't allowed to sell booze. Come to think of it, I don't believe any nude strip bars in the United States are legally permitted to get your rocks and liver off under the same roof, which I never really understood.

I always found it ironic that at one time, back on the island, an eighteen-year-old could see a naked stripper, but the girls who showed their goods on stage had to be twenty-one.

When I started stripping in 1987, I wasn't naked; I was only nineteen. I shook my cocoa-buttered ass for lonely military boys in a neon G-string bikini. I may not have been taking off all my clothes at the beginning of my nine-year career, but I was still selling sex, or at least its fantasy.

By the time I was twenty-one, I was working up the street on Kapi'olani Avenue, dropping trou for serious cash. I'd played in the Big Girl's Club, just like the one Todd and I were visiting tonight.

After a quick trip to the bar (Diet Coke for Todd, water for me), I planted us in a booth at the far end of the stage. Todd looked so uncomfortable, I promised him once again that our visit would be brief.

"Is this what you expected?" I asked.

"I don't know," Todd admitted.

He surveyed the billowy cloud of dark nothingness as a couple of non-alcoholic waitresses tried to look busy, holding their empty trays.

"You've seen naked women before, haven't you?" I inquired, recalling a slap-and-tickle story of him and a girl in high school.

"Uh-huh."

I think he was trying to figure out why the hell we were there. I was beginning to wonder the same thing.

Then we got propositioned, at least in the strip club sense.

"Hi, there!" she said. She was as dark as the room, with a smile that lit up her face.

"Oh, hey!" Todd blurted, more startled than interested.

"Hi!" I added, casing her up and down, smiling, trying to peg her story.

"So, which one of you do I get to kidnap?" she asked playfully. A real sales gal, I thought, cutting to the chase.

After briefly introducing herself, she went on talking, but I stopped her politely.

"Oh, I'm sorry. He's gay, and I'm a retired stripper. We're just checking things out. Not tonight but thank you!"

We exchanged, "Hey girls!" and that beautiful smile carried her off.

I looked at Todd, realizing he didn't have a clue what just went down.

"She was trying to sell us a dance," I reassured him. I placed my hand on his knee, feeling maternal.

"Oh!" he laughed, sipping his soda. "Girl, I had no idea."

Now I was laughing. "I know. It's okay, honey, we can leave."

"Okay!" Todd beamed excitedly.

No fight from the homosexual peanut gallery.

No sooner did we agree to bail than a hot little brunette came up to greet us. She was a dead ringer for Mila Kunis.

"Hey, you two!" she began. She was tiny and bronze, wearing a gold sequined bikini. We couldn't just shine on this adorable, friendly kitten, so we sat for her pitch.

The conversation flowed after introductions and explanations of his gayness and my ex-stripper-ness. We learned that little Mila called herself Valentina. She announced her name proudly: "Valenteeena." Todd and I agreed it was the perfect stage name.

When I told Valentina that I was writing a memoir, her eyes lit up.

"No way! You're writing a book? That's so cool!"

"Yeah, it's taking longer than I thought," I explained, "because I'm having difficulty reliving some stuff. I was pretty high."

I peeked over at Todd who was totally into our connection.

"Oh, I used to party all the time back home in Chicago," Valentina said, "but that was before I started dancing."

What? No drugs now?

I was impressed.

"I think it's awesome that you're writing your story," she told me. "I always think I should be writing this shit down."

"Do it," I urged. "Trust me, write as much as you can because there's nothing like this world, and every stripper has her own story," I encouraged, feeling like her middle-aged auntie.

After the DJ belted out who was next on stage, Valentina and I stayed in our groove. I asked her a ton of questions about the business side of the stripping world now and offered up how things were run back in my day. I had to pick her jaw up off the floor when I told her we used to get paid for every set, averaging three or four sets a night in addition to earning tips on the smaller stages throughout the night.

"No way!" she said. She was shocked.

"I know! I hear you have to pay to work now," I said, "like you're expected to give management money just for being here?"

"Yeah, it's called a stage fee," Valentina confirmed. "It's fucking ridiculous. I have to stay at work some nights just to earn my fee."

It went on and on. I felt like her house mom and suddenly wanted to go to law school to help her fight The Man.

After a short while, a few more customers trickled in. I started feeling guilty about taking up her time and keeping her from earning cash. So, Todd and I excused ourselves and got up to leave. After we split, I realized how much more I wanted to share with my new friend. I wanted to tell her how sharp and real she was, that there's a life waiting for her beyond the pole. That I knew she had her head on straight and how excited I was for her future.

I wanted to talk about documentary filmmaker Hima B. and her quest to highlight the injustices of the biz. But it wasn't the right time. Just as something had pulled me into the club that night, a greater force had pushed me to leave. Besides, I could tell Todd had just about reached his vagina-viewing capacity.

A few days after our "interview," I wondered if Valentina had thought about our talk. Had she Googled me, checking out the hilarious old-school photos I promised were posted on my website?

I suppose our paths will cross again if we're meant to. But if we don't, and she's reading this now, I hope she knows she has a stripper-sorority sister in her corner who thinks she's pretty fucking rad.

# CHAPTER THIRTY-SEVEN

# A SAFE KIND OF HIGH

I'm standing behind this guy at Starbucks and swear he was one of my old customers from back in my stripping days. Unfortunately, it's too crowded for me to bend over and look at him upside-down through my legs to find out if it's him. But I digress. I've learned how to let these thoughts escape my mind as quickly as they entered. So, I return to the task at hand. Starbucks. Coffee. A large cup of joe was required if I intended to rally after a long workday at the office for a night out. I can't remember the last time I was out late on a school night, let alone going to a concert. But this was Depeche Mode! The dudes who'd provided soundtracks to countless wild nights (and mornings), whether I was on stage bending over for a buck or shaking my ass at The Wave to blow off steam. D.M. was my jam. There was no way I would miss the opportunity to see them live.

After fifteen years, you'd think my memories of rolling and free-falling would be strung together on a distant, blurry line. Addicts are a colorful brew. Our longing can percolate with anything that taps into sensory triggers: a passer-by leaving a trail of perfume, catching a scene from an old movie on television, inhaling a whiff of a crisp dollar bill (ask any cokehead about smelling money, it's pretty gross). Basically, anything our subconscious connected with when we were using can serve up as V.I.P. passes to The Dark Side.

Darkness for addicts is like sunflowers and rainbows to everyone else. There's an element of comfort and ease when we kick back in our own shadow. Our anguish is a warm blanket we reach for, which is hilarious when you consider our drug-taking was the very reason it got so cold in the first place. One of the most annoying things about drug addicts is that we have an inflated sense of entitlement and zero humility when it comes to getting high. We deserve to be higher, feel better, and be allowed in the V.I.P. room of doom. I can't begin to express my gratitude now that I finally get it; that flying high on the magic carpet of denial is just a short trip to the crash and burn that invariably follows. Then there's that whole dying thing that could happen.

I hadn't been high on MDMA (Ecstasy, Molly) in over a decade, so my cravings were long gone. There were indeed times when I allowed myself a memory or two of the mind-flashes wrapped in glittery and reckless abandon, all stitched together with youth and frivolity. Now I was older and wiser, living clear on the other side of that life for the most part, but DM was a definite trigger.

The harsh realization, thanks to my insane habit of taking multiple pills a day for years, is that my brain is permanently damaged and that always balances any warm and fuzzy emotions I get when I remember using. Now the docs and I have a good thing going with regular maintenance of Selective Serotonin Reuptake Inhibitor (SSRIs) therapy. There was no way I'd go backward, especially since it's a pain in the ass. Considering my Rockstar history, I got off easy. For one thing, I'm still here.

I knew going to this concert would stir up feelings. And you can bet your ass that when I got those floor seat tickets, I felt a flutter of anticipation. What I was not at all prepared for was the trigger floodgates blowing wide open when I started playing their music the night before the show. You know you're an addict when the idea of NOT getting high (to see one of your favorite bands you used to see when you were high) wrestles with any anticipation of seeing them play at all.

Back home, I texted Joey, my date for the festivities, another Kanji tribe member and BGF I shared how I really wished we could get high for tomorrow night's show. Then I sat at the foot of my bed, laughing alone like a crazy person at how ridiculous my brain was. I waited for the triggers to work through me and then turned up the volume on DM and began dancing in my bedroom.

This would be the first time I'd see Depeche Mode without rolling on Ecstasy, and so I began to appreciate what a gift it could be to be IN THE MOMENT with their live music, without drugs.

What? No drugs at a concert? Are you high? Thoughts are relentless.

Joey knows me well and returned my silly text by brushing it off. As long as I vocalize the little fuckers in my head, they'll quiet down in due time. Still, I was anxious about seeing one of my favorite bands without the sensation drugs provided me, carrying me places nobody else could go.

By the time we found our seats and chatted up fellow DM lovers (one flew in from Russia to Los Angeles just to see the show), I was solid. The triggers were gone, and now I was just pumped.

I couldn't help thinking about the lead singer of Depeche Mode, Dave Gahan, a recovering addict who has survived and thrived like the rock star he is. He's reportedly had a heroin overdose and a suicide attempt. His heart stopped for two whole minutes. This fucker is L.U.C.K.Y. After seeing his performance, there is no doubt he knows it. There's nothing quite like witnessing another human being savoring his passion.

I experienced tears and chills, screams, and stomps. Fifteen thousand of us were together on the ride of our lives. As grown-ups living in this big, bad world of responsibility, suffering and disappointment, to land back in the place of childhood freedom, giddy with excitement, screaming with joy, was an absolute revelation.

During the concert, there was a moment when Martin Gore sang "But Not Tonight" a cappella. Before letting out a note, he stepped back from the microphone and breathed in our energy. He was beaming with joy, taking us all in as we were with him. I still get chills when I see the clip online.

There was something about his lyrics that resonated with me.

"I haven't felt so alive in years."

Truer words have never been spoken.

I used to think I needed drugs to enjoy this kind of spiritual awakening. I've heard Depeche Mode many times in previous concerts, but this experience was by far the most beautiful. And it was wrapped inside one of the biggest lessons I've learned since being clean: you don't need drugs to feel high.

CHAPTER THIRTY-EIGHT

# FALLING UP

"So, you moved to California, and how did you end up here?" asked an old colleague of mine over Cobb salads and lemon water at Pier 39 in San Francisco. She was more than a co-worker; she had become a new friend. And as my friend, I translated her question immediately to mean, "How the fuck did you end up as a sales executive after being a stripper?" A fair question.

"Bullshit," I answered with a crooked grin. As my impostor syndrome kicked in, I suddenly felt like a con artist, working as I did in corporate America with barely a high school diploma from a public school on a tiny island in the middle of the Pacific. But then I remembered: I earned my way in the game as much as any of my co-workers have. I was adept at selling! The only difference was how we got there. She, selling copiers, me, selling my Fosse dance!

"What's bullshit?" Eileen asked while crumbs of blue cheese fell from her fork.

"No, I mean, that's how I got here," I admitted nervously. "By bullshitting my way."

Eileen pointed her face down, allowing her aviator sunglasses to slide over the tip of her nose. She batted her eyelashes and sat up in her chair. We locked eyes, and she spoke.

"Oh no, honey, you're gonna need to give me more," she said matter-of-factly.

I giggled and followed orders. "Think about it," I said. "Stripping is a sales job, right?"

I folded my napkin and placed it on top of my salad bowl. I found our server and mouthed, "May I have the check" while air-signing my initials with my left hand. I was officially a grown-up asshole.

"Uh-huh," Eileen replied, her voice pitched higher as she leaned in, preparing to receive the stripper equivalent of the U.S. Commander in Chief's nuclear launch codes.

"So, that's what I did," I noted. "I bullshitted my way into every interview and worked my charm, and now I'm selling copiers with you here!" It sounded like a boast, but it wasn't.

"Well, shit, girl, you're a natural!" Eileen marveled, glancing at her faux Rolex. "What's my half of the check?" she asked, reaching for her purse.

"No biggie, get me next time," I assured her while placing my debit card on the table. I couldn't even afford her fake watch and secretly prayed my card wouldn't be declined.

Eileen drove a new BMW and had highlighting foils in her hair every month. I needed to learn as much as I could from my fellow salesgirl and new bestie, so of course, I was buying.

And learn I did. Eileen was just one of the countless people I'd meet and whose behavior I'd emulate in my new life after hanging up my garter. As soon as I arrived on the mainland, I was back in school. But this time, the campus was huge. Soon my lack of funds would be solved if no one Googled me for a background check, and I wasn't ousted as a fraud.

As far as I was concerned now, The Good Old Days should just be called The Old Days and left at that. My past, sketched in my mental rear view mirror is forever memorialized within these pages. At the age of fifty-three, as of the writing of this book, I can truthfully tell you I'm cool with focusing on what's ahead of me from now on. I'm fine with not knowing the exact details of my last hurrah because my life is just so different now. It's taken me more than half my life to make sense of my why. There's no need to dissect the where, what and when more than I already have. Even recovering narcissists get tired of ourselves.

Mentally I have taken many steps forward. Other ways, notsomuch. I still wrestle with money. Learning to manage it, save it, and stretch it to the point I'm not living beyond my means is directly proportional to the years I spent taking it for granted and pissing it away. I hate that I struggle with my finances even now in my fifties, but I'm admitting that I'm still a work-in-progress.

"Whattayagonnado?" This is the answer whenever I ask myself the ridiculous question. "Why didn't you save any of your money, girl?" Whattayagonnado? What I didn't learn back in my youth in terms of saving my stripping cash for early retirement, I've made up from self-education in the real world and being creative in other ways. Net Net, I am falling up.

My history book is filled with pages of heartache and suffering but also packed with gems that lifted me up beyond comprehension and tickled my funny bone until I peed. No longer am I searching for who I am. Once I learned that feelings are fluid and that taking responsibility for my choices was the answer to finding the self-esteem it takes to change them, I did.

Pain and sorrow, I've learned, are to be expected in life. But if we hang on and try to use those moments as mental light posts instead of landmines to guide us through the darkness, the joy will always follow.

So far, it's working.

# CHAPTER THIRTY-NINE

# EYES WIDE OPEN

We found a spot near the base of a cliff close to the water. The sea wall was decorated with kaleidoscopic wildflowers as vibrant and crisp as the mid-morning sky. I slid out of my shoes and welcomed the tickle as the sand greeted my toes.

Mark, another attempt at love doomed from the start, was thrilled. We'd finally made it to Pirate's Cove, a secluded clothing-optional beach nestled among the Central California Coast. It's a darling place rumored to mirror the infamous *From Here to Eternity* location where Burt Lancaster and Deborah Kerr rolled around, locking lips on the sand, passionately oblivious to the crashing waves. Ironically, that scene was filmed on Oʻahu.

Mark's birthday weekend was off to an adventurous start. He was the first to fully disrobe, kicking his swim trunks in the air like a schoolboy on the first day of summer. I followed his lead, stepping out of my bathing suit. But unlike my boyfriend, I was not as jazzed. My trepidation answered his exuberance with adorable irony.

It was a delicious juxtaposition. The fact that I, now a middle-aged retired nude dancer, was anxious about being nude in public. Well, that floored me, but as soon as I joined Mark, standing on the beach together in all our glory, we shared a smile and settled on our towels.

I had no issues with my body in front of Mark. We'd been together for several years. I knew Mark loved my curves, so the hang-ups were organically mine. I was in my forties now, older, and out of shape compared to my stage years. I had not been naked in public for decades, and even then, not without six-inch heels, a nose full of blow, and zero body fat. So, what? Who cares? This was my man's birthday, and I wasn't about to let my body issues ruin the fun. But it wasn't easy.

There's a specific type of body issue that I, along with most of my stripper sisters, seem to have called body dysmorphic disorder. It's the same issues that people with eating disorders have when they look in the mirror; they see themselves as overweight when some are so malnourished they're close to death. It fucks with your psyche. I may as well have been 400 pounds, the way I felt.

The sky was cloudless, and Mark was in heaven. In the distance up the stretch of sand, we noticed others; people with dogs playing fetch; two couples standing waist-deep in the ocean laughing and splashing; an older man cultivating his tan while reading a paperback with yellow pages. Everyone was nude, and not a single person cared about what we looked like or checked us out. Still, I was uneasy. Mark picked up on it immediately.

"Stop!" he demanded, shaking his head, and smiling.

I hate it when the people we love know us well.

"You're more beautiful now." He was referring to the younger me. He hadn't known me then but had seen photos.

I loved his embellished white lies, especially when they stroked my ego. We were both past our hotness prime, and I'll just say neither of us was a fitness model.

"And thank you for this day," he added.

"You're so very welcome, birthday boy!" I said, kissing my fingers and then stroking his cheek before walking toward the water.

Mark sat back on his towel, watching me.

A step away from touching the water, I stopped, closed my eyes, and inhaled the day. Standing naked under the sun gave me something unexpected: I became a one-woman healing fest from every deep-seated insecurity I ever had. Right then, I chose to see myself through a healthier lens. And who I saw and what I felt—well, it was amazing.

This body of mine has beaten cancer twice. It'd managed mental illness (clinical depression, anxiety, P.T.S.D., cyclothymia). It shocks me that I'm still here. Could this beautiful, valiant physique stand to lose twenty or so pounds? Sure, but that didn't stop me. I immersed myself in the ocean. Mark met me shortly after, and we swam together, just like he wanted to do for his birthday.

I didn't expect to receive a gift as well. I was breaking open. Standing naked before myself. There was no darkroom or DJ announcing my stage name to strangers. No blasting hair-band music. No dressing rooms. No cocaine. No cigarette-filled air. Just a picturesque day with an actual pulse of which I was thrilled to be a part. The breeze talked to me in a language that could only be spoken by the shore. And that moment of clarity ushered in new moments and new growth.

I broke up with Mark a short while later. It wasn't easy because we loved each other but our relationship was toxic. To be fair, Mark himself wasn't toxic, but our pairing was anything but healthy. Just as two like-minded people who have their shit together create flourishing unions, the same can be said for damaged couples. Our childhood trauma history was similar, and we needed to work on healing without the distraction of my codependence and histrionics and his narcissistic tendencies and insecurities veiled as charm (sound familiar)? There was never a question about our love for one another; we just had no healthy template of what healthy romantic love was. Just as my friendship with Angela was riddled with addiction and temptation (the Hot Mess leading the Hot Mess), Mark and I were a similar pair. He used to say we were so much alike we should be wrapped in Caution Tape. It's funny 'cause it's true. Years later, we both laugh about it now, but it took a while to get here.

"If you cut off the heads of each past relationship, you'd have the same person," a therapist once said to me. I smiled at the thought of countless decapitated lovers wandering aimlessly through the halls of her building but understood the analogy.

"I know, right?" I agreed.

"So, what's the one thing in common here?" She prodded. I knew where she was going and felt the shame-colored flushing of my face and chest. After a long pause to process my truth, I smiled.

"Holy shit!" I perked up in my seat. "I don't need to keep picking these men!" I continued. "I'd rather be alone than allow myself to be disrespected, lied to, cheated on, used or manipulated again." The words fell out of my mouth as if set free from a lifetime of self-induced seclusion from reality. Learning to love myself took a while, but once I did it blew my eyes wide open and soon, Mark moved out.

After texting him, I immediately turned off my phone to hide from his reply. We'd been doing the same back-and-forth exchange, and he'd remind me I was the one who'd ended things with him for good (and I'm certain he was not heartbroken like Darryl). Even though the breakup was my doing, it felt like I'd been punched in the gut, and the agony tortured me for weeks. This juxtaposition of conflicting time-speed (my ending it and the hurt that followed) would've been far more amusing if it weren't so painful. Life as I knew it—for the last five years of my forties—was indeed over. The fear, what the fuck did I just do? came rushing in. I didn't know how to feel about amputating my love affair (over a text, I know, but we were newly miles apart). Also, I didn't trust my fleeting strength even over the phone with Mark's charm. I just knew I was ready to end it. Mark who would caress my face because he had always accepted my face as-is, scars and all. Shit. Would I ever find another person who'd accept this face?

This is good for you, I reasoned aloud. You did the right thing. The reality, it was me and my thoughts, alone in my apartment, staring down the barrel of Single and Fifty. (I wasn't turning the big 5-0 for eleven months, but who's counting?) I was officially heartbroken, but this time something felt different. Compared to countless other codependent love casualties, I felt safe and self-assured this time around. My coffee-stained Colgate-scented terrycloth bathrobe served as a fine makeshift blanket as I sobbed myself into fully accepting the breakup using toilet paper as tissue, tossing the soaked pieces, into the air. I was going to be okay by myself.

My new inner voice was loud, and I welcomed her babbling: You did the right thing. This is good for you. Old voice: Umm, don't you mean, don't fuck this up! You need to be better than all of his other women!

Being in my late forties and pulling from the well of therapy tools I've learned to use through the years, I decided to allow a new frequency to play in the channel of my mind, a station that's been waiting patiently for me to listen. When the tears finally stopped, I exhaled, smiling self-assuredly while picking up pieces of my feelings from the floor. I began to rinse my hands in the bathroom sink, peered into the reds of my gorgeous puffy eyes, and had an epiphany: This agony—like every heartache in my life since I was a teenager—was completely avoidable. If only I'd followed the signs instead of running from them. I used to think red flags were the same, and the bulls were more an exciting adventure than the dangerous creatures they are.

The next morning, I walked to the kitchen for a water glass and noticed the dewy shadows through the blinds above the filthy, dish-filled sink waving for my attention. Great. A new day (whether I wanted one or not). But instead of ignoring the forks and salad bowls mocking my apathy or collapsing back into the sofa with promises of Netflix and detachment as per my usual M.O., I surprised myself. I stood in the mess, allowing the sunrise to breathe by opening the windows and started cleaning. And not in the I have company coming over tonight tidying up. The way I was scrubbing the baseboards after tackling the kitchen sink, you'd think I was preparing for a visit from mom. (Fun fact: she prefers hotels when visiting, and both of us are cool with that.) After a few hours, I sat and appreciated my hard work and sparkling home. I felt proud and holy shit dare I allow myself to feel—happy. My heart felt different. Sparkling too. It was beating steadily without a trace of anxiety. At that exact moment, I knew I had turned a corner.

Finally.

Like so many people I've met along the way, Mark and I remained dear friends. I have come to understand better that my mother was doing the best she could given her circumstances. I've come to understand that my sister chose the path best suited for her to move forward. I have come to understand me. The one thing I know for sure is if I finally meet the perfect-for-me-partner, the love of my life, before I leave this earth, I'm at a point where I'm truly happy if I do and even if I don't. The caveat with my story is as much as I would love to find my soul mate, I'm prepared to be alone and happy.

I've come a long way in my fifty-three years. Through deep diving into my past choices, I've learned valuable truths; the most crucial lesson is that my joy isn't predicated on a boxed checked Single or Married, whether I cover my gray hair or have scars on my face or carry an extra twenty pounds on my body. My joy and happiness depend on me and are one hundred percent my responsibility. Wouldn't it be amazing if someone could invent a way to capture our joyous moments and somehow make it possible to inject this magic potion into our ass cheeks as they did with B12 shots in the sixties (and on *Mad Men*)? Until then, we can use our precious happy memories as life rafts, and when we sink into the darkness, these nuggets of joy can save us until the storm passes.

It's so easy for me to see now, but it took being alone to understand my patterns. Each partner I chose to attach myself to was damaged in some way, and I gravitated to them because it felt comfortable. It's a chemistry thing with trauma survivors; we sniff each other like animals and create a bond through our love affair with self-sabotage and shame. Once I owned my shit and understood that I was in control of my happiness, the joy came flooding in. Do I still have moments of loneliness and sorrow? Of course. The big difference is that I know they will pass and don't need another person to make me happy.

This is what it's about. Letting go of what you can't control. It was never yours to begin with. Honor yourself. And don't for one minute believe your worth is based on anything but who you are. (And you, my dear, are amazing.)

It's cool what we can accomplish once we push through our hang-ups and truly understand what's real. None of what anyone thinks about us—if they think of us at all—matters. As someone once said, what other people think of us is none of our business. Lather, rinse, repeat.

Life is short. Take your clothes off and swim. Or don't. But whatever you do, never hold back because your fears hold you hostage. YOU are the prize. Obliterate negative self-talk via positive mantras: I am loved. I am worthy. Just as I am. After five years, Mark and I separated, and though once devastated, I am now happier than ever—and still here.

# SECTION FIVE

# LET'S TRY THIS AGAIN

CHAPTER FORTY

# HEALING

Every party has an expiration date, and my last call came just after my twenty-eighth birthday. Too many hangovers and one missing drug-dealer boyfriend (rumored to have been murdered for stealing four kilos of cocaine) later, I had walked away from the only life I knew, having been a stripper since nineteen. I was nearing my thirties and started to freak about being a senior citizen on the pole, wondering when people would start giving me money for keeping my clothes on.

At the advice of my then-new therapist Dr. G. in Waikiki, I got myself a real job with a real paycheck. Through the years, and even after moving to the mainland to work in San Francisco as a sales rep, I learned the hard way (thanks to countless bounced checks) that money was not to be taken for granted. Neither was my heart.

Dr. G was one of many therapists I spent time with, and although it didn't come easy, the lessons I learned about my self-worth came in spurts.

"I just want to feel like I did in my twenties when I used to walk into a room and was convinced that I owned it," I whined to a therapist at age 34.

"Honey, you were high," she deadpanned, a retort so delicious we both burst out laughing.

"Fuck," I spat with a chuckle. My reply was unexpected, falling out of my mouth as if I were tasting the truth for the first time.

"Well, my coke-whore days are long over, so…," I said with a shrug.

Why does honesty always reveal itself in the most shocking of ways?

"God, I miss those days when a bender and total delusion could do the trick," I said earnestly. I giggled nervously, knowing I would need to find my confidence and self-worth the hard way: reliving the trauma and owning my survival instead of living as a victim.

It was so much easier to let the drugs navigate my brain. As I grow older, I realize I'm not invincible, which was the slogan of my twentysomething years: "Don't Even Try: I'm Invincible, Bitches!"

"Confidence, knowing who you are, loving everything about you—good, bad, ugly. This is what will bring back some of those feelings of owning the room like you felt when you were high," my hippie therapist assured. She truly believed her words. Her kind, pale blue eyes were framed perfectly by her thick mane of silver. She felt maternal, and I fell into her safety net with ease.

"I hope you're right," I replied. "Of course, you're right. I'm paying you to be right." I joked to ease my tension per usual.

God, I hoped she was right.

As I began to share more about my traumatic childhood in each therapy session, I learned that there's nothing wrong with me. I'm simply a product of circumstance and the cards I was dealt. I didn't even know the game, let alone how to play or what to do with the deck. So, I went all-in with everything: drugs, booze, sex, even my stripping performances were extreme, irritating the average stripper-sister on the stages we shared, I'm sure.

When my house of cards started to fall because of my choices, even years after The Pole, I started to understand through therapy that I had more power than I realized. Why was I still at the poker table? I could just toss the deck and walk away, start over and take the lessons I'd learned (always the hard way) with me.

There were so many signs from the universe, but until I was ready, I couldn't see them even if they were flashing neon. So many wake-up calls that I used to swipe left and ignore. Through therapy and sharing my stories, from Connie's friendship ultimatum that day in Denny's in Waikiki, and Club Detox in SoCal, to countless heartbreaks (pick a year, any year) because of my going after unavailable partners, I started to see the patterns of my open self-destruction. The design I was creating wasn't pretty. The good news, I was learning, was that patterns aren't permanent, and the cinderblocks pulling me under didn't need to keep being filled with the cement I was pouring.

I had more control than I thought and learned that I didn't need to keep living as a victim. My life started to change. Nearing the age of fifty, I broke things off with Mark, my latest trauma-bonded partner, and tested the waters with what it would feel like to wake up without a hangover for a change.

I used to resent my weeklong stint in Club Detox, but now I see that experience as one of my biggest lessons: my life is only as good as I choose it to be, and if I want, I can keep making it harder on myself. Or I can practice self-care by continuing therapy, taking my medications, and only putting healthy things into my body instead of the toxins that made me feel so fucking good.

But it was all an illusion.

Yes, the highs were amazing, but they were always tied to harrowing pain. So, when you think about it, the highs weren't that much fun because they were just precursors to pain. And I was done with unnecessary pain. Having to survive is exhausting, and life is hard enough without contributing to the pain it gives us.

Back in my cocaine-diet days (which began in high school at sixteen), I was addicted to more than just drugs; I was obsessed with my looks and knew that if I could keep my body fit, at least I had that going for me because my face was a lost cause. Those days are long gone. I'm choosing to hang on to the part of me that wanted to be fit, but this time, fitness would come by way of a healthier attitude towards my body instead of polluting it. The same goes for my mind.

I also learned to relax and be in the moment instead of worrying about the past and present. And to stop looking outward for happiness. I know now that this is an organic feeling that comes from within by way of helping others, giving back, laughing with loved ones (or alone), and creating magic with words, dance moves (I dance alone in my house often), or just making my bed daily.

Making my bed daily is a present to myself. (Thanks for the reminder, Chelle!)

The little things in life are really the big things; a smile exchanged with a stranger as I walk my dog after work. A career in assistance with a fantastic company with people I consider to be family. The fact that I'm still breathing after hearing "It's cancer" twice in my lifetime.

When I dream of a friend who passed on to the other side, fitting into my skinny jeans or buying the next size up seems asinine. It doesn't make a difference if I'm a little bigger if I'm healthy and happy. What matters is sharing a first kiss with someone worthy of my company. Learning about life by answering a child's innocent question and realizing I'm smarter than I thought. These are the little things that make up the big things: a passion for being a good person, finding gratitude daily, and forgiving myself and others. I hope I have contributed something worthwhile if I can help others by sharing my story.

I'm still a work in progress but man, have I come a long way to get here. If people take anything away from reading these pages, I hope it's the knowledge and belief that no matter what cards they were dealt in life, there's always the choice to toss the deck and start a new game with new patterns. Knowing I'm worthy of a meal instead of crumbs at the table feels better than any drug.

# CHAPTER FORTY-ONE

# DOES YOUR MOTHER KNOW?

My poor mother. She had no idea what she was getting when I popped out. It took years for me to confess my stripping life to mom. To tell her that I had enjoyed its power despite it all. What started as a bright-eyed nineteen-year-old contestant in a local wet t-shirt contest had morphed into an underground life because it filled me up with validation early on. Each dollar bill tucked into my garter was a wave of the magic beauty wand. The feeling I felt cheated of throughout high school.

However, my choices betrayed me somewhere along the nearly ten-year road of shaking my ass atop the thick, blinking Plexiglass and addiction. I realize now I was—am—a drug addict and a walking cliché. But I was just happy to be walking. So many of my old party friends weren't so lucky.

Mom would eventually learn all these things, but it would take me writing a book about my story for her to fully grasp the timeline of my demise. How her bubbly, buck-toothed drama queen who lived in roller skates and rainbow-colored leotards could morph into a sleazy, drugged-out shell of a person, snorting lines of blow and bending over naked for money. She learned the tragic tale of a twenty-eight-year-old burnout who had finally locked her lifeless eyes onto her reflection in the dressing room mirror one night and confessed aloud, "I think you're done."

I was.

To the outside world, I was unapologetic and brash. But underneath the audacious bravado resided a little girl still wanting to make her mama proud. Knowing my career choice didn't cater to this cause, I protected her from the truth for as long as I could.

For years, I kept my secret hidden. It's easy with people who don't want to see the truth. In her trusting naiveté, mom believed I worked the flower circuit. I was a delight in her eyes, selling roses to love-struck tourists dining in five-star restaurants in Waikiki. In reality, of course, I was working the deflower circuit.

When I finally confessed to the ruse, mom began to cry. She blamed herself, and part of me was glad. The other part quickly played defense, committed to protecting her from pain.

"Jeeez, Mom, it's not like I'm totally naked!" I insisted.

This was a lie. Waikiki strippers were fully nude, but I thought serving her a half-truth of "I'm just topless" would somehow cushion the blow in my twenty-five-year-old mind.

"Women in Europe are topless on the beach!" I declared as a lame justification. Even as I said the words, I knew my argument was ridiculous. I can't imagine any mother of a stripper not suffocating on, "Where did I go wrong?" but that's not my tale to share. My story is my own. The details of my mother's struggles and missteps aren't mine to unload or exploit.

It would have been easy to point my French-manicured acrylics at my mother all those years ago during my stripper confession. But blaming her for my self-destruction would've been like faulting the waiter for the jalapeno salsa that scorched my mouth. I may have had an idea of what I was getting into as I ordered, but the dish was just too tempting at the time. The only real difference is that the salsa never had to answer to its mother.

This part of my journey would not be complete if I didn't forgive Richard (Dick) as well, the only father I had ever known. It took me a long time for me to say to him the L-word. LOVE. In forty years, I never told him that I loved him. EVER. I was finally able to at the end of his life. Here's my goodbye letter of forgiveness to an abusive father which I never shared with him.

Dear Richard:

For close to forty years, you have been the only father figure in my life. Good, bad, ugly. You were the man I looked to when I needed one, even if you never could be. I have learned to forgive and even love you, but I never really liked you.

And now you are dying.

I am glad we spoke today. You welcomed my phone call like a surprise blindfold of tiny fingers from behind, a childhood father-daughter greeting that was never our style. But today was different. I could hear your smile on the line and felt your vulnerability. It was weathered but sincere—a new side of you that was refreshing.

You were surprised to hear from me from thousands of miles across the Pacific, but I could tell it made you happy. I was a bit unsettled (perhaps you were as well), but this call wasn't about me. I leaned into the discomfort and spoke.

"I know you'll be uncomfortable hearing this," I warned, "but I do love you."

Tears tickled my cheeks, knowing this was our last exchange. A feather-light silence filled the space on the line. I held my breath for what seemed like minutes, processing my very first "I love you" to you. I envisioned those words traveling through the phone line, wrapping around your damaged heart like the blanket of forgiveness you desperately needed to hear.

And then, you replied.

"Well, that's nice to hear, Chrissy."

Groggy but pleased and perhaps even teary-eyed, your voice was shaky. I did not expect, "I love you too, sweetheart," but I felt those words in your reply. Your language is borne from your abusive childhood. I know it well.

The cards you were dealt as a young lad with stoic parents (no birthday parties, no hugs, no love) shaped you into the man you are today. How can anyone know how to give or receive emotions when the very love template (of which they were raised) is empty?

I don't think of you as the enemy any longer. And although I understand the genesis of your projections—your verbal abuse and inability to love—I'm still navigating life, dismantling the negative self-talk landmines you planted. In a way, I'm grateful to you. The road of my adult life has gifted me strength through suffering and self-worth through the darkness.

Everyone's life is a process created from tools we were either given or not. As a father, you did the best you could; some men don't even manage that. Unlike my biological "Dad," you were there. As dysfunctional a life as you shared with mom and us girls, you stuck around.

What a ride.

Sleep well, Dad. I'll take care of mom, and we'll rejoice in knowing you're on the other side and finally released from your broken body. I have zero doubt you're in a place where you can now open your heart to love.

I know you have it in you.

# CHAPTER FORTY-TWO

# FAN MALE

Ever since I first built my website (www.poletosoul.com) in the 2000s, I've received random emails from readers from across the globe. They're usually people living with similar skin conditions, thanking me for shedding light on severe cystic acne problems, and specifically for what I had, Stage IV Acne Vulgaris and Acne Conglobata, which is quite severe but rare, with only a small percentage of people affected with disfiguring scars.

Meeting another person who shares the same DNA defect that impacts mental health was magical. It gave me a feeling of validation and commonality I'd been unable to duplicate. I am sure similar feelings exist with burn victims and others with deformed skin conditions.

Then there are those letters of thanks (for humanizing strippers) from fellow sorority sisters, some of whom have found and worked with me and others who are total strangers. These women choose to have no voice because they have families and children and never shared that part of their past. They live in fear of public judgment or worse, retaliation from their own mischievous teenagers.

However, I received one email that shocked me so much I had to share it with the world. It's easy to get wrapped up in the darker side of my story. PTSD from childhood trauma is like herpes. Even when it's dormant, it will forever be inside of you. So, when writing this book, I would sometimes forget about the fun stuff.

Enter a random email from a guy named Chuck.

The following is an actual email I received while simultaneously struggling with remembering a traumatic story:

Hi Christine.

I debated with myself on reaching out to you like this and finally decided that my need to express what's swimming around in my head exceeded the risk of your considering me maybe a little creepy.

I assure you that this isn't the opening gambit of an F.B. (Facebook) lurker looking to establish a relationship. It's just one person in the world finding something in someone else that resonates and expressing it to them.

So, here goes.

A little background:

I was a Navy Lieutenant stationed at Pearl Harbor from '83 to early '87. I lived at the Marco Polo on Kapi'olani and spent just about every off-duty minute either on the beach playing volleyball or out at the clubs. Or, really, two clubs in particular: The Wave and Pink Cadillac. Virtually all my friends were kids who circulated between the beach, Moose's after the beach, and those two clubs.

Now, if I'm you, I'm reading this maybe with a growing sense of "Where is this leading?"

Completely understandable.

I've learned enough from the Wave Waikiki Facebook group to know that you and I were Waikiki contemporaries during that time. But truly, this isn't about you specifically. It's just that the memories of my experiences living in and around Waikiki, and especially at The Wave, are so remarkably profound and alive in my head that I needed to reach out to someone who I know was there at the same time to express them.

I didn't know you. I don't think we ever met. But in seeing your photos from that time (on The Facebook group page), I think there's a strong chance that our paths probably converged—certainly at The Wave. I might even have been in the audience as you started your career in burlesque. (I went to the Lollipop once sometime in early 1987, but my friends and I were more often at the "peeler bars" on the Mauka side of Ala Moana Center.)

I'm thinking I probably saw you at the beach, likely at Fort DeRussey volleyball courts, or maybe in front of The Royal Hawaiian. I would occasionally hang out with some friends there and play drinking games. But 90% of the time, I was at DeRussey playing volleyball. Good times.

Anyway, the Wave F.B. page was the catalyst that led me to write you.

I loved The Wave. The feel and energy of the place and the people. Ethereal. Cool. Freaky. Sexy. Naughty. Wild. Sophisticated. Coarse. Crude. Randy. I think part of it was something in me that wanted to be all those things. Not just to watch but to be pulled in and absorbed by it. I couldn't, though. I think maybe the strait-laced military parts of me held me back. An aversion to commitment? I don't know.

All I know is that I couldn't stay away.

The best part was when the industry folks showed up after 2 a.m. Before that, it was interesting. After that, it was absolutely compelling.

You were part of that crowd. I envied you. Not you specifically, but the world you circulated in. Huddled in the upstairs lounge, piled on top of each other, super connected, super alive, and totally committed to each other and sharing experiences I could only guess at.

Which isn't to say that my experience was lacking in any way. I would not surrender those short few years for anything!

But you—all you—were So. Fucking. Cool.

The internet being what it is (and thanks to your prodigious skills of self-expression), I've come to understand that your story is a lot more complex than my impressions at that time allowed me to imagine. I'm sorry that you've endured what you have, but I exult in how you have built on your story. I admire that you've so openly shared your journey. It puts what I knew about that time in Waikiki in a much different light.

So, Christine, here's to you and what you have become.

Thanks for letting me get this out of my head. You came up at an amazing time, in an amazing place, as did all of us who were there. I couldn't help but express my thoughts to someone who I knew would understand. In that sense, you're an ambassador of the past.

All the best.

Mahalo.

Chuck

Good move, Universe. Thank you, Chuck, for validating how much fun we had and deciding to drop me a line. Your words helped me balance out my memories.

# CHAPTER FORTY-THREE

# IT GETS BETTER

Whenever we face adversity, it's a reminder of how fragile we are. We can take only so much until weighty challenges suffocate our spirit, and suddenly we're gasping for air. Happiness can be an impossible dream for bullied children. As an adult who spent her childhood being verbally abused at home and in school, I know all too well the feeling of wanting to end it all. Ending the pain of simply existing and the fear of never knowing a world where you feel normal. It doesn't matter if you're gay, straight, overweight, tall, short, or in my case, have a skin disease on your face. If you're different, it's all-consuming. But the darkness passed for me.

The upside is that with every storm, the sunshine does break through. Eventually. But how do you even begin to see the light when so much of your life is dim? My advice: trust the one-second, one minute, one moment at time voice that breaks through. It's a ray of light. Where does that type of blind faith come from? From the little voice inside those seconds, minutes and moments and knowing you're not alone is a start. Believing you'll get through the hard times in life is so dependent on hearing the stories of others, knowing the history of people who not only walked in your shoes but can share stories of how they were dragged knee-deep through the mud.

Thanks to organizations like the "Born This Way Foundation" and the "It Gets Better Project," countless people feel less alone.

In this book, I've shared how I weathered the storm of addiction and all that goes along with it to find my self-worth and learn the real meaning of beauty. I recently had the opportunity to be interviewed in Los Angeles on a local podcast about self-worth. It was another step in my evolving journey, and I knew I'd have a blast catching up with Sophie, the host.

What I didn't know was that she'd receive an email from my childhood friend who knew me when. As I read it, I fought back the tears of gratitude and took a moment to celebrate how far I'd come. I'll share it with you now.

> I met Christine when we were in fifth grade. I was in a new school and a new neighborhood, and she was my first new friend. She was nice and just like any other girl our age in the late seventies.
>
> We started high school in 1982. Christine was still just like any of us except that she had acne really bad! People called her all kinds of names, and I'm not talking about behind her back (although there were all kinds of rumors about her going around). Guys would yell from the second floor over the railing, 'Hey Pizza Face!' or 'Hey Moon Face!' or 'What's up, Crater Face?'
>
> They would yell things like this and, much worse, as loudly as they could at her. Then people would start laughing. Or if they would be walking behind her or

passing by her, people would make a comment about her or just say something mean.

At first, I didn't think about it, but after a while, I noticed this would happen pretty much all day, every day! Her sister didn't seem to care about what some of her friends were doing to her little sister. Kinda looked to me like she was mean to Christine, too. In the beginning, I would see her just trying to get through the day and go to class, but after a while, I didn't see her much and figured it all got to her—so she started cutting school. It wasn't until Facebook and reconnecting with my childhood friends that I heard what had become of Christine after high school. I would have never imagined that she would become a drug user and definitely not a stripper (of all things). She seemed to have hard times of a different degree in her twenties.

Now, when I see or hear the name Christine Macdonald, I see STRENGTH, and in my mind, I kinda feel like a kid in school saying, 'Nah, nah, nah, nah! You guys didn't beat her or keep her down!'

TO CHRISTINE, I SAY….

You must be so full of pride! You're doing what thousands only dream of, turning all the shit from the past into a positive here & now & into the future! WAY TO GO!! The 'buzz' about Christine doesn't have anything to do with rumors or drugs anymore, but the strength and talent of a beautiful lady!! ♥ it!

I couldn't stop reading it.

She was there. She'd noticed. It was real.

Like her story of encouragement, my story is a love letter to my childhood, and I happily share it with anyone struggling, suffering, or gasping for air with the weight of feeling less than suffocating their joy.

Finding my self-worth was a long journey, a war of hard-fought battles. I lost some but won many. Today, I am a survivor, standing full of love, firmly planted in my power. I wrote these last two letters to myself, the first one to that thirteen-year-old girl, confused and desperately searching for love in all the wrong places, and the second, to that young woman's body that never gave up on her despite her hatred and mistreatment of it.

> You're trying to fit in, I know. They're giving you attention, I know. You're feeling pretty. When you put your arm around their shoulders, they saw that as an invitation. When they asked you to take a walk away from the party, you felt special. I know.
>
> I know.
>
> Then he kissed you. Then the other one did, too. The ultimate validation. Your cloudy mind was spinning, believing you were wanted and adored. Seconds passed when you pushed yourself up, shaking off their grabbing hands.
>
> I know.
>
> "No, no, no. Just one." You felt in control by making one of the boys leave.
>
> And then there was one.

I know.

When you woke up to him leaving, you wondered how you got there, suddenly realizing that you were naked from the waist down.

Was that it? Did I…? Am I still…?

You lay there, searching for answers, but none would come.

On the ride home, you heard them making fun of you. You liked the attention, but I know you were confused deep down. Is he my boyfriend now?

Oh, sweet girl, I know.

Feeling pretty, like you belong, doesn't come with shame. Feeling special doesn't mean being made fun of. Those boys were using you. Trust me, I know. I wonder if somewhere inside, you know it, too.

If only I could wrap my arms around you. At thirteen, you're still a child. How could you have known? You couldn't have. But I know.

You were raped. And it's not your fault.

## A Love Letter to my Body

I can't believe I ever called you fat. I'm so sorry. For that and a million other reasons, I ask for your forgiveness and pledge to honor you until my last breath.

You are an estuary to my soul, and with all your bumps, stretch marks, and fat rolls, I'm more in love with you now than ever. No longer on the other side of our decades-long divide, I finally see, clear as sunshine, that you are my biggest cheerleader, warrior, and guardian angel.

Thank you for never giving up on me, even though I did everything in my power to destroy you.

You tried to warn me. My teenage baby-oiled freckles sizzled in agony, overexposed, and changing color from pale to petrified pink. Sometimes your efforts of escaping my torture were victorious: peeling yourself away from my chest and back, free-falling into oblivion.

I don't blame you for these melanoma cells floating through my veins today. In fact, I thank you for your patience while I finally got a clue and sought medical attention. Thanks to you, I will always look for and listen to your warning signs. I welcome more scars if needed, markings that share survival stories from the sun.

And it doesn't stop there. The toxins I inhaled, snorted, drank, and injected made valiant efforts to assure your demise, all while you were looking your most beautiful and with zero grace from me.

So young and clueless of just how striking you were, I continued releasing venom of hateful words and dangerous acts onto you. Instead of nurturing your cries, I muffled them with denial and insecurity. I exploited my breasts by forcing inanimate objects through my flesh and allowed unloving hands to touch you.

All the while, I thought this was a way out of my pain. I had no idea that I was the one causing it.

And now here we are. I stand before you, cloaked in humility, naked in honesty, hypnotized by my reflection. I'm not surprised but, instead, disappointed. My unwillingness to treat you better through the years has revealed itself in my middle age, and there is much work to be done.

I effortlessly smile and internalize the irony that I hated you while you were in your prime. Unable to escape time and punishment, you now long for rest and a peaceful existence.

I shouldn't be here continuing to breathe, but against all odds, I am. I wouldn't dance on spiked heels now, but I once did. I feel your joints crying out for relief. And I understand.

Did I mention I'm sorry?

Who knows why my Get Out of Life Free hole-punch card hasn't expired yet? But I am grateful. No matter how many times I prayed to sleep forever, you woke me with promises of elevation from my mental disease (depression), encouraging me to hang on when new darkness came.

You taught me that darkness always comes and have assured me that it passes. And you're right.

I vow today that I will no longer contribute to your pain. Instead, I salute your uncanny durability, awestruck by your strength while persevering through the unfortunate decisions I've made in the past.

Thank you for choosing me to be your person.

# FOR THE CURIOUS - WHY WE STRIP (IT'S NOT WHAT YOU THINK)

There are many misconceptions, ideas, fantasies, and judgments about strippers. And while I really can't speak for anyone but me, I wanted to shed some general light on five topics that always come up when I speak about my nine-year career on the pole.

### Strippers Don't Hate Men

Most men in a stripper's world are customers, and honestly, we don't feel much of anything about them. Like any business relationship, emotion is separated from the deal. Every customer is part of a business deal. Every tip is a sale.

Occasionally, some men cross the invisible friendship line, but that's rare. If a male friend came into the club to hang out with us and didn't have money, there wouldn't be much hanging out.

Seeing many wedding rings in the crowd did taint my view of men, but there was never any hate. A lot of therapy, but never hate.

So, fellas, you can knock the chip off your shoulders when it comes to strippers. We don't hate you. We just hate when you don't tip.

### It's (Literally) Dirtier Than You Think

Everyone knows porn is dirty, so the dirty I speak of is literal for the sake of argument. You germaphobes may want to bust out the hand sanitizer for this part. (Howie Mandel is slamming the book shut right about now.)

Think about money for a second. Think about how many fingers touch money and how many places a dollar bill has been. Now multiply that money into hundreds of bills stuffed in a garter on your thigh. Add a little sweat into the mix, and voila! You have a germ orgy. It's common for tiny red bumps (I called them Cash Rash) to appear on any thigh. It's not pretty, but it's real. Nothing a little soap and water won't get rid of in-between sets.

After painting a picture for you about how dirty money is, do I really need to get into the stage and pole? Stripping is dirty, people.

### We Are Not "Just Stripping to Pay for College"

This is a delicate subject because I don't mean to imply strippers aren't smart, educated or have professional goals outside of grabbing their ankles for a buck. I'm simply telling you that most of the ladies I worked with in the Nineties were as far away from a campus as James Bond was from an AA meeting.

College takes time, energy, and an enormous amount of focus. How could we engage in such a demanding world when we're up until four in the morning and sleeping until noon? In my years on the pole, I met only one woman who was in school. There're always exceptions to the rule. I marvel at those.

## We Have Issues

Surprised? Oh, come on.

Like any person who takes a different path than most do in life, strippers have their reasons. Those reasons can be hard to face, and some may never dig deep enough to hit the ocean floor, so they tread in a sea of sharks.

I pass no judgment in saying strippers have issues. I'm the first to say I had (and still have) a bucket load. One of the most beautiful things about life is realizing that we're human.

## We Are Not Prostitutes

Let's dispel that myth right here and right now. If you look up prostitution in the dictionary, you'll read: "Prostitution: The act or practice of engaging in promiscuous sexual relations, especially for the money."

I'm not debating the act of sexual entertainment. I danced naked for money, for fuck's sake. That said, I want to bring to your attention a line in the sand where this topic is concerned.

There are many types of strippers, so it's impossible to say there were none who crossed the line from performing on stage to doing a hand job under the table. But from my personal experience, I can say that most of us were just dancers who dropped trou for a buck.

# YOUR TOP FIVE STRIPPER QUESTIONS, ANSWERED

**Training**

Q: What sort of training do you get, or are you just told to go out there and start dancing?

A: Good old-fashioned self-taught, on-the-job training. In 1987, there was no such thing as a stripper class. Having natural timing and rhythm is not a stripping prerequisite, but it helps. Unlike Justin Timberlake (or, if you're my age, Denny Terrio), strippers tend to slow their moves down for their audience. Nothing says, "Don't tip me" like a G-string drive-by.

**Money**

Q: How much money did you make on a good night?

A: I would take home enough money to pay my monthly rent. Some corporate executives make a lot more for doing the same thing (selling dreams), and they get to keep their clothes on.

## Plastic Surgery

Q: Did you ever feel pressured to have plastic surgery?

A: I was never pressured but did get my breasts augmented early into my career. (I removed them in my 30s.) I'd love to start a line of boob-job bras for strippers and call them Cliché. Breast implants for strippers are what veneers are to actors: an occupational byproduct.

## Clientele

Q: What type of customers frequent strip clubs?

A: As many different types of people who swipe through Pornhub are what you will find in any given strip bar. The customer base is as diverse as the strippers themselves. I've danced for people of all ages and socio-economic backgrounds. It's an equal opportunity skin trade.

## Question for the Customer

Q: Are there any questions that you, as a dancer, have ever wanted to ask the men or women who frequent strip clubs?

A: "Do you plan on tipping me soon, or are you waiting for a rabbit to fly out of my ass?"

# GLOSSARY OF SONGS:
# THE SOUNDTRACK OF MY STORY

Stripper or not, the perks of being a professional dancer for me in the late eighties and most of the nineties had everything to do with music. I still stop and smile when hearing songs from *those days*. I'd be strolling through an outdoor mall or sharing a meal with friends in a restaurant when suddenly the echo of familiarity weaves its way through distant speakers and into my psyche. My lips can't help but curve as I hum along, *feeling it; remembering it all*—and then it passes.

But not without gratitude.

Music helped save my life. Her notes and melodies cradled me in times of darkness and lifted me beyond moments of elation from simply moving my body, feeling free and far away from my reality at the time. She's even kept me company while writing this book, sharing laughter through tears, and even igniting a solo dance routine or two in my living room.

My beautifully broken brain holds a near decade-long catalogue of tunes that serve as magic carpet rides to the stage, and I can still visualize what costume I wore and where exactly I danced (which club). Glam Rock hair bands and grunge were on the rise at the peak of my career, but I also enjoyed other genres like '90s Hip Hop and timeless legends like Rod Stewart, Elton John and of course, my eighties UK Alternative favorites from back in High School.

Since I consider music to be its own character in my story, I want to share a small taste of what tunes I performed to; and sang along to while crafting these pages so many years after walking away from The Pole. Here's a list of just some of the melodic herbs and spices that make up the recipe of my past:

*In no particular order*

| | |
|---|---|
| Walking in My Shoes | Depeche Mode |
| Hot Legs | Rod Stewart |
| Cream | Prince |
| Kiss Them for Me | Siouxsie and the Banshees |
| Blue Monday | New Order |
| Girls Girls Girls | Mötley Crüe |
| Sweet Emotion | Aerosmith |
| Wanted Dead or Alive | Jon Bon Jovi |
| Kashmir | Led Zeppelin |
| Tea in the Sahara | The Police |
| Epic | Faith No More |
| Not an Addict | K's Choice |
| So Alive | Love and Rockets |
| Welcome to the Jungle | Guns N' Roses |
| Talk Dirty to Me | Poison |
| Ku'u home o Kahalu'u | Olomana |

| | |
|---|---|
| Down In It | Nine Inch Nails |
| All Apologies | Nirvana |
| Down by the Water | PJ Harvey |
| Pleasure Victim | Berlin |
| Vogue | Madonna |
| Under Pressure | David Bowie/Queen |
| So Cruel | U2 |
| Fake Plastic Trees | Radiohead |
| Freedom! '90 | George Michael |
| Going the Distance | Cake |
| Wrapped Around Your Finger | The Police |
| Eyes Without a Face | Billy Idol |
| Linger | The Cranberries |
| Hotel California | The Eagles |
| Panic | The Smiths |
| Fascination Street | The Cure |
| Jane Says | Jane's Addiction |
| Dreaming | Blondie |
| But Not Tonight | Depeche Mode |
| Closer | Nine Inch Nails |
| Ghost Story | Sting |
| Lullaby | The Cure |
| California Love | 2pac Featuring Dr. Dre |
| Let Me Go | Heaven 17 |
| Stripped | Depeche Mode |
| Pour Some Sugar On Me | Def Leppard |
| Shook Me Al Night Long | AC/DC |
| Glory Box | Portishead |

# ACKNOWLEDGMENTS

I would not be around today without the support of my loves: Kimmy, Dany, Allyn, Layla, Carol Anne, Crystal, Becky, Angela, Margo, my Kanji Tattoo Tribe (you know who you are), Michelle, Nicole, Steve, Diane, Leslie, Tony, Hilary, George, Elena, Eric, Mark, and Adam. Without your support and encouragement, I don't know if this book would have been possible.

Stella, your heart is my heart, always. You've saved me from myself with every lick on my face and wag of your tail. You taught me what true love outside of myself is, and I am forever changed because of you.

My heart has a special place for every therapist in this world, particularly mine. They have been my guardian angels through the years, and I would be remiss if I didn't send a special Mahalo and Aloha kiss to Doctor Alia Harlan Kaneaiakala. Girl, you made it okay not to be okay. You also give the best hugs on the planet and laugh at my jokes. I love you.

For every person who has followed my very (very) long road to get here, whether it was donating to a writer's retreat in Guatemala via my crowdsourcing campaign, following me on social media, or reading my old blog posts from the very beginning, I am humbled and honored to be with you and thank you seems too weak a sentiment. Without you to read my words, I'd be alone with these pages and feel less connected to the world, so *mahalo*. I hope you feel my gratitude and love.

Finally, and most definitely not least, there's my publication team at Wordeee and independent editor-guru Ray Richmond. When taking me on Ray, you didn't know that you'd get a crash course in Hawaiian history and language, did you? Or that I was as mentally fragile as I am (this surprised me, too). We met over a decade ago, and you have survived my disappearing acts during bouts of depression and a global pandemic. You helped me learn that I was braver than I knew by pushing me to go to the most painful places because that's where the story was. And oh yeah, I know you had a lot going on, too. Marva and Patrice, when we met and spoke about possibly working together, I knew right away that my choice was made in Wordeee. From start to completion, this journey of bringing my book to life with you both in my corner has been a privilege and joy and I am so very pleased and honored to be a part of the Wordeee family.

And to my literary inspirations: your grace and generosity in offering your praise for my writing make me teary-eyed with gratitude. So, thank you again to Larry Smith, Piper Kerman, Kristen "Kjo" Johnston, Lily Burana, Betsy Murphy, Joyce Maynard, Jimmy Rice, Kirsty Spraggon, and Jeremy Toback.

I debated on whether to include my biological family in this section. I fear I'm still seen as The Problem Child. As of this printing, no one in my family speaks of my story (outside of mom, when I exhaust her with updates about this book; a dream of mine she nervously supports for which I am endlessly grateful) or about the fact that I've been published online and in print. But there's always hope. Hope that shame is lifted, and the spotlight can be on how far I've come, not how fucked-up I was.

Shit. I'm still cursing. Maybe some things never change. Regardless, if you ever read these words, I love you, Mom (your support is everything), Gail, Laurie, Sydney, and Kelsey.

To the stripper sisters with whom I worked. I dream of reconnecting with all of you, though I don't know your legal names. To the countless strangers who've worked the stage in strip clubs across the globe, I hope you know how incredibly unique and amazing you are. Your story is to be applauded and not judged, no matter what the world says.

There's a reason we chose our road, just as there is a reason we all make our choices. No one is better or worse. We're simply different and taught in varying ways about life. It kicks our asses and sometimes buckles our knees with grief. But we know we'll survive because we've come this far. And besides, everyone loves a good comeback story.

CPSIA information can be obtained
at www.ICGtesting.com
Printed in the USA
LVHW080107060323
740967LV00006B/27

9 781946 274915